# THE GOOD LIFE
# MONEY BOOK

A Complete Catalog

**Of Ways to Cash In**

**On Today's Economic Conditions**

# The Good Life Money Book

## IMPORTANT NOTICE

Additional copies of this book may be purchased directly from the publisher. To order, please enclose $24.95, plus $3.00 shipping and han- dling (California residents include 8.5% sales tax) for each book ordered. Send orders to:

American Publishing Corporation

15196 Benito Street

Montclair, CA 91763

Printed in the United States of America

0 9 8 7 6 5 4 3 2 1

# THE GOOD LIFE MONEY BOOK
## — Master Index —

# CHAPTER 1
# LEMONS TO LIMOS
# —AN ALL-PURPOSE CAR GUIDE:

# CHAPTER 2
# HOUSING & REAL ESTATE GUIDE:

## CHAPTER 3
## MORTGAGE GUIDE
## —HOW TO BORROW BIG-TIME FOR LESS:

## CHAPTER 4
## DEALING WITH BANKS & S&Ls:

## CHAPTER 5
## KEYS TO CREDIT AND CREDIT CARDS:

## CHAPTER 6
## BEST DEALS ON INSURING LIFE & HEALTH:

## CHAPTER 7
## INVESTMENT & WEALTH-BUILDING GUIDE:

## CHAPTER 8

## A QUICK GUIDE TO ESTATE PLANNING:

## CHAPTER 9
## HAPPILY EVER-AFTER — RETIREMENT GUIDE:

## CHAPTER 10
## LEGAL SURVIVAL GUIDE:

## CHAPTER 11
## DOLLAR-WISE GUIDE TO HIGHER EDUCATION:

## CHAPTER 12
## MAKE THE MOST OF YOUR JOB:

## CHAPTER 13
## INCOME BOOSTERS:

## CHAPTER 14
## CONSUMER GUIDE: CHEAPIES & FREEBIES:

## CHAPTER 15
## TAX FACTS & SAVINGS GUIDE:

## CHAPTER 16
## PASSPORT TO TRAVEL SAVINGS:

## CHAPTER 17
## PLAYING TO WIN:

---

# INTRODUCTION

H ave you ever heard anyone say, "You can't beat the system."? Unfortunately, for many working people that statement appears to be all too true. The "system"— your employer, bank, credit card companies, the IRS, insurance companies, car dealers, etc.— is stacked against most working people. And when times are tough — as they are now—it's especially hard for the average working person to get ahead.

While the system does hold a pat hand, anyone who tells you that it can't be beaten is wrong. All you need is inside information and you can actually use the system to make more money... and to keep more money. You won't get this inside information from your banker, your insurance agent, car dealer, or other member of the system because it would cost them millions of dollars in lost profits.

The insider information provided in this book can help make the system work for you. You'll learn proven, effective money-making and money-managing strategies that can put an end to all of your money worries in just a matter of months. If used properly, the money and career strategies in this book can help you get out of debt; make more money; save more money; and achieve your financial

---

dreams. You'll also learn how to start and operate your own profitable home-based business and where to find your dream job.

Hundreds of people have used these strategies to beat the system and ensure their own and their families' financial security. The strategies are easy to learn and easy to use by people just like you.

Besides insider tips and money-making strategies, the following pages also provide the phone numbers and addresses of important contacts and sources of information. There are chapters devoted to tax savings through legitimate deductions; sources of "free" money; high-profit, low-risk business opportunities; money-saving shopping techniques including over 60 sources for wholesale savings; and over 120 sources of products and items you can get free.

Even if your debts— mortgage, credit cards, car loans, personal loans, etc.— have you in a deep financial hole, the information and techniques in this book can help you eliminate your money problems and get you started on the road to financial and personal success. You don't have to be a college graduate or a financial wizard to use these techniques either. Thousands of people just like you have already used successfully the insider strategies described in this book to take control of their financial and professional lives.

The money-saving strategies and techniques provided in this book offer proof that the system can indeed be beaten. There are numerous ways you can go about earning and saving more money. There also are opportunities that can lead to incomes of $100,000 a year or more. If you know what you want, the following pages can provide you with insider information that may enable you to get it.

## CHAPTER 1

## Lemons To Limos
## An All-Purpose Car Guide

## No-Sweat Car Shopping

Depending on your perspective, shopping for a new car can be either a pleasurable experience or an intimidating hassle. If you have a talent for negotiating, you're likely to enjoy haggling with a salesperson to get the best possible deal. However, if just the thought of dickering on the price of a car makes you break into a sweat, you may be better off enlisting the aid of a car pricing or a car buying service.

According to industry estimates, more than 10 percent of all new- and used-car buyers opt to pay a service rather than dealing directly with a car dealer. Generally, these people dislike haggling and prefer to avoid the process as much as possible. If you're looking to buy a car, but have an aversion to "dealing," you might consider joining the 10 percent and pay either a pricing or a buying service to deal for you.

For a fee, a car pricing service can tell you exactly how much a dealer pays the manufacturer for a new car. The price you are quoted, which includes manufacturer-to-dealer rebates and incentives, is often hundreds of dollars less than the "sticker" price (manufacturer's suggested retail price) found on the car window. Many pricing services also provide information on the "true cost" of optional equipment and tips for successful negotiating.

Obviously, such inside information can put you in a better negotiating position when it comes time to deal with a fast-talking salesperson. Since you're armed with the actual dealer costs you may be able to dicker several hundred dollars off the sticker price. At any rate, you can let the salesperson know that you're aware of the true costs for the car he/she is trying to sell you.

Generally, pricing services charge $10 or more per report. The final fee you pay depends on the service you use, whether you're interested in a report on a new or a used car, how many reports you order, handling fees (if any), and in some cases, the type of reports you request. Basic service includes pricing and additional information on the make(s) and model(s) you choose. The information is provided in telephone quotes, or you can receive it by fax, E-mail or by regular mail.

Car buying services are for those people who want to avoid the shopping and dickering process altogether. Some buying services obtain competitive bids on the type of car you want from several area dealers. Armed with these bids, you choose the deal that's right for you. Other services will, in effect, do the shopping and the negotiating for the best possible deal. All you do is visit the dealer and finalize the transaction. And some buying services will handle the entire transaction, including locating the car you want, negotiating the lowest possible price, and arranging for delivery.

Of course you have to pay for such service. And with fees that range from less than $100 to $600 or more, you could conceivably end up paying more for a car than you would dealing on your own. If, however, you aren't a skilled negotiator, a buying service could save you hundreds of dollars on a new car, as well as help you avoid the hassle of trying to negotiate a good deal yourself.

## * Car Pricing And Buying Services

You can locate car pricing and buying services through listings in the Yellow Pages and in business directories available at most public libraries. Some credit unions, motor clubs and discount retailers also offer such services.

Here are several of the leading car pricing and buying services available nationwide. Keep in mind that prices and services do change and may have done so by the time you read the following:

— **AutoAdvisor**, 3123 Fairview Avenue E., Seattle, WA 98102; (800) 326-1976. Price reports are $15 each. Buying service includes a fee of $599 for a one-week search to find the car you want, negotiate the price, and put you in the driver's seat. Other buying services (and price ranges) also are offered.

— **Automobile Consumer Services**, 6355 Corbly Road, Suite 33, Cincinnati, OH 45230; (800) 223-4882. Price reports are $29 each. Buying service fees range from $295 to $395, depending on the make and model car you want.

— **CarBargains**, 733 15th Street, N.W., Suite 820, Washington, DC 20005; (800) 475-7283. For a fee of $135, this service will contact several (5 to 7) local dealers and obtain competitive bids for your business.

— **Car Price Network**, (800) 227-3295. New car reports are $7 each and used car reports $4 each. There also is a $4 per order handling fee.

— **Car/Puter**, 1500 Cordova Road, Suite 309, Fort Lauderdale, FL 33316; (800) 221-4001. Pricing reports are $19 each. Additional reports are $16 each. Also offers a buying service, which is available to members of a participating auto club such as AAA, or gasoline credit card.

— **Consumer Reports New Car Price Service**, (800) 933-5555. Offers first pricing report for $12, additional reports $10 each. Reports include comparisons of sticker vs. dealer invoice prices.

— **Fighting Chance**, (800) 288-1134. The first price report is $19.95. Additional reports are $7 each. There is a handling fee of $3 per order.

— **Intellichoice**, (800) 227-2665. Price reports are $15.95 each. A comparison of any two equivalent cars is $19.95.

— **Nationwide Auto Brokers**, 17517 W. 10 Mile Road, Southfield, MI 48075; (800) 521-7257. Offers both a pricing and buying service complete with delivery from the manufacturer. Prices vary, depending on the type service you order.

## How To Beat The Dealer

New and used car dealers are in business to make as much money as possible. That means that as soon as you set foot in a showroom, you represent a potential profit. As a consumer, your goal should be to get the car you want at the lowest possible price. If you know what you're doing, you can accomplish that goal and beat the dealer by getting him/her to accept a smaller profit than usual.

Most car dealers know that they make 80 percent of their profits from 20 percent of their customers. And they make those profits in three different ways: the markup on the new car; the resale of your trade-in; and financing, insurance and extras. They try to combine these three profit-producing strategies as often as possible in such a way as to convince you that you're getting a super deal.

As soon as you show a dealer that you're a knowledgeable consumer, and that you know what you're doing, he/she is likely to forego his/her clever tactics, and settle for less profit. You're much more likely to get a better deal on a new car if you know beforehand exactly what you're looking for and how much you're willing to spend. If you know what you want and what you can afford, you're less likely to feel pressured into making a hasty or expensive decision.

Here are several ways you can "beat the dealer" and get the best possible deal on a new car:

* Evaluate your needs and financial situation. Before you visit a dealer, decide on the type of car—a luxury car or mid-size or compact economy model. Do you need a sporty vehicle or a more practical family vehicle? Once you determine your needs, choose a few makes and models you can afford.

* Find out the dealer's invoice price for the car and options. That's what the manufacturer charged the dealer for the car. You can get this information for a fee from a car pricing service or from consumer publications available at your local library.

* Find out if the manufacturer is offering rebates and incentives that will lower the cost of the car you want. Again, this information is available for a fee from car pricing and buying services. You also may find this information in weekly publications such as "Automotive News" available at most libraries.

* Get price quotes from several dealers. And be sure to find out if the amounts quoted are the prices before or after rebates and/or incentives are deducted. Tell each dealer you're shopping around and are prepared to buy from the dealer who offers the best deal.

* Keep your trade-in negotiations separate from the main deal. If you talk trade-in before you negotiate the price of the new car, the dealer is likely to add the trade-in amount to the new car's final price. Don't let that happen. The price you get for your trade-in should have nothing to do with the final price you pay for a new car. Make sure you know the value of your trade-in (consult price guides at your public library) and negotiate for that price after you have agreed on the price of the new car you're buying.

You'll probably be able to get more for your old car by selling it yourself rather than trading it in. In most cases, a dealer will offer you a trade-in price which is near whole-sale. However, if your car is still in good condition, you should be able to sell it yourself for close to its retail value.

* Inspect and test drive the vehicle you plan to buy. Make sure it's the car you want and that it handles properly. Don't take possession of the car until the entire deal, including financing, is finalized.

* Don't buy on impulse. And don't buy because the sales-person is pressuring you into making a decision.

* Read carefully and make sure you understand every document you are asked to sign. Pay special attention to the sales contract, including the fine print. If there's something you don't like or something missing from the contract, ask that it be changed to your satisfaction. And don't sign anything until you've made a final decision to buy.

\* Compare financing from different sources, for example, banks, credit unions and other dealers, before you sign the contract. Sometimes manufacturers will offer low-interest financing, usually on specific models or on short-term loans. If this type of financing is available, it may save you hundreds of dollars over the life of the loan compared to average bank rates. However, if such financing isn't available, check with several other sources before accepting the dealer's financing.

You can get additional information about buying a new car in the free FTC booklet, "New Car Buying Guide". Write: Public Reference, Federal Trade Commission, Washington, DC 20580.

## Three Expensive Extras— Car Buyers Beware

If you do decide to buy a new car, watch out for the "extras" many dealers like to add on to the purchase. In most cases, such extras are unnecessary. Here are three of the most common, most useless and most expensive new car extras you should avoid:

**1) Rustproofing.** Some dealers try to add charges for services such as rustproofing, after you have agreed on a price. Don't fall for this gimmick. Most cars don't need this expensive extra. In fact, new cars today come with all necessary underside coating. If the dealer suggests you need this extra, just say no.

**2) Paint and upholstery preservatives.** Paint sealant and fabric protection are two more unnecessary extras many car dealers will try to tack on to the final price. Avoid both.

**3) Service contracts.** Generally, these contracts cost from $300 to $1,000 and are an added expense you can safely avoid. You'll be better off to save the money you would have spent on such a contract and use it if your car needs a major repair.

## New Cars For Less

If you're not hung up on a specific brand name car, you may be able to save several thousand dollars by purchasing a twin or clone. While look-alike models often have different manufacturer names than their twins, they typically share the same design, chassis, and transmission, as well as other features. There also may be some differences in outer-body features, but in many cases twins roll off the same assembly line. What all this means is, that if you can't afford a new car priced over $20,000, you may be able to buy virtually the same car under another name for thousands of dollars less.

For example, you can compare the prices of the following popular twins: Geo Prizm/Toyoto Corolla; Dodge Stealth/Mitsubishi 3000; Ford Probe/Mazda MX-6; Ford Taurus/Mercury Sable; Isuzu Rodeo/Honda Passport; Eagle Talon/Mitsubishi Eclipse; Ford Explorer/ Mazda Navajo; Chrysler Cirrus/Dodge Stratus.

That's just a sample of the many twins now being manufactured. There are a large number you can choose from. Just keep in mind that direct comparisons sometimes can be misleading. Some cars may have options that are not available on their less expensive twins. For example, a less expensive twin may not feature options such as power windows and door locks, electronic cruise control, front-seat recliners, a larger engine, etc., found on its higher-priced counterpart. If that's the case, you'll need to decide whether or not you need those options and if so, how much they're worth to you.

However, if you can find a look-alike model with the same options as its more expensive twin, you'll likely be able to save $3,000 or more on the final price. If you're willing to settle for a different name and a slightly different outward appearance, you can get the new car you want for a lot less.

## Car Buyer's Dilemma— Financing

Unless you can afford to purchase a car outright, the method of financing requires careful consideration. First of all, you have the option of checking the dealer's rate against other lenders, such as banks, credit unions, savings and loans, and other loan companies. And since interest rates vary, you'll need to shop around for the best deal and compare the annual percentage rates (APR). All this can be quite confusing, and a dilemma for many car buyers who are trying to arrange the best financing deals possible.

Sometimes automakers and dealers offer below-market financing rate loans, which can save you a great deal of money compared with a typical bank loan. However, this type of low-rate financing often applies to specific cars or models, and the dealer may not be willing to negotiate the price of these cars. In addition, you may be required to make a large downpayment in order to qualify for these special dealer interest rates. With these conditions, dealer financing may not be your best option. You should check out banks, credit unions and other lenders for better terms on a typical car loan.

You also may want to consider financing your car purchase with a home equity loan. The average interest rate on a home equity loan is generally lower than rates on typical consumer loans. And unlike interest on car loans, interest payments using a home equity loan are generally tax deductible. While those factors may make financing a car purchase with a home equity loan cost-effective, you'll also be faced with an increased debt against your home. If you can't make the payments, you could lose not only your car, but your house as well.

The method of financing you choose may be the most important decision you'll have to make when purchasing a car. Whatever method you choose, make sure you get the best terms possible. Otherwise, you could end up paying hundreds or thousands of dollars more than you have to over the life of the loan.

The Federal Trade Commission offers a number of helpful car-buying brochures including, "Car Ads: Low Interest Loans and Other Offers," which can provide more information on financing and other factors involved with buying a new car. For a free copy write: Public Reference, Federal Trade Commission, Washington, DC 20580.

## Leasing Or Buying — Which Makes More Sense For You?

You've probably seen car-leasing ads inviting you to "drive away in a new car for only $1,500 down and $199 a month!" At first glance, it looks like an unbeatable deal. And it just might be, for some people.

More and more people are responding to such offers every year. In fact, industry experts predict that by the year 2000, nearly 50 percent of all cars sold will be leased. This surging popularity in leasing is because many more people are now finding that for them, leasing makes more sense than buying. For these people, the advantages of leasing, such as low down payments, low monthly payments, easy exchange for a new car, and a bigger tax-write off on cars used for business, outweigh the disadvantages of no equity buildup and little flexibility during the term of the lease. Generally, leasing makes driving a nicer automobile more affordable for people who don't mind "renting" one.

Whether or not it's better to lease than buy a car, depends on many factors. And ultimately, the decision is a matter of personal preference. To help you decide, consider the following questions:

* Do you have the ready cash for a downpayment? If you don't, leasing may be your best option. That's because you may have to come up with only $1,000 or $2,000 for fees and the first payment. On the other hand, if you buy a car and finance it, you could have to put up as much as 10 percent of the purchase price, as well as 6 to 8 percent sales tax.

* Do you want to drive a new car every three years or so? If you do, leasing will help you avoid the hassle of selling your car and allows you to get another new car while maintaining low monthly payments. On the other hand, if you like to buy a new car every year or if you plan on owning the same car for ten years or longer, buying might be your best option.

* How many miles do you drive per year? If you drive around 15,000 miles a year and maintain a car in good condition, leasing may be a sensible option. However, if you drive substantially less than 15,000 miles a year, you're probably better off buying. And if you drive a lot more than 15,000 miles a year and still want to lease, you should negotiate the cost of the additional mileage before you sign the leasing contract.

* Do you use your car for business purposes? If you do, the IRS allows you to deduct a larger portion of your car's depreciation from your taxes if you lease.

If you decide to lease, there are two types of contracts to choose from: the closed-end lease (sometimes called a "walk-away" lease) and the open-end lease (sometimes called a "finance" lease).

**Closed-end leases** are the most common type of lease and are less risky than open-end contracts. Under a closed-end lease, you return the car to the leasing company when the agreement expires and walk away from any further repsonsibility. However, you must return the car in good condition,which includes normal wear and tear, and not exceed the mileage specified in the lease. Since the leasing company takes on the risk as to what the value of the car will be when it's returned, monthly payments generally are higher than they would be with an open-end lease.

An **open-end lease** may have lower periodic payments, but you take the risk that, at the end of the lease, the car will be worth an amount specified in the lease documents. When the car is returned, the leasing company will either sell or appraise it and compare it with the residual value specified in the lease. If the car is worth less at the end, you will be responsible for the difference. However, if it's worth more, you could get a refund or could purchase the car for it's remaining amount, if stipulated in the contract.

Before you sign a lease, you should shop around for the best deal. And be sure to read lease promotions carefully. The attractive low monthly payment might be available only if you make a large down payment or a balloon payment at the end of the lease.

It might be helpful to use the following Federal Trade Commission checklist to compare the costs of leasing against the costs of purchasing through a conventional loan. In making such a comparison, you'll need to consider three categories of cost: initial, continuing and final. However, when deciding whether to lease or buy, you may not want to base your decision on total costs alone, but also may wish to consider when or if any large outlays of cash are required.

## — Leasing vs. Buying Checklist

### * Initial Costs

| —Leasing— | —Purchasing— |
|---|---|
| _____Security deposit | _____Downpayment |
| _____Capitalized cost reduction | |
| _____First periodic payment | |
| _____Last periodic payment | |
| _____Total amount of fees | _____Total amount of fees |
| _____Insurance | _____Insurance |
| _____Trade-in allowance | _____Trade-in allowance |
| $_____ | $_____ |

### * Continuing Costs

| —Leasing— | —Purchasing— |
|---|---|
| _____Periodic payment (expressed as monthly) | _____Monthly payment (including finance charge) |
| _____Insurance (expressed as monthly) | _____Insurance (expressed as monthly) |
| _____Estimated monthly maintenance and repair costs considering warranty coverage | _____Estimated monthly maintenance and repair costs cnsidering warranty coverage |
| $_____ | $_____ |

**\* Final Costs**

| —Leasing— | —Purchasing— |
|---|---|
| _____Maximum end-of-lease payment based on estimated residual value | _____Balloon payment (if applicable) |
| _____Excessive mileage/wear charges | |
| _____Disposition charge | |
| _____Total amount of fees | _____Total amount of fees (license, registration, taxes) |
| _____Trade-in allowance (if applicable | _____Trade-in allowance (if applicable) |
| $_____ | $_____ |

Keep in mind that if you are leasing and have a purchase option, you may wish to consider the amount of the option price in your final costs comparison.

You can get a free publication on car leasing, "A Consumer Guide To Vehicle Leasing," by contacting the Federal Trade Commission, Public Reference Section, 6th and Pennsylvania Avenue, N.W., Room 130, Washington, DC 20580.

## Skip Those Expensive Factory Options

Do you really need a sunroof or an eight-speaker stereo? A new car dealer will try to convince you that you do. And if you're not careful, you'll end up paying for a package of factory options that you can do without. For example, that sunroof the dealer says you can't live without can add over $1,000 to the cost of the car you're considering. Four-wheel drive or all wheel drive, while nice in the winter, can add from $900 to $2,500 to a car's cost. And that super stereo system could cost you over $1,000.

According to the dealer, these and other factory options serve to "sweeten" the deal. But figure it out for yourself. Why should you pay several thousand dollars more for a car just to get fancy factory options you don't need or want? Let the dealer know you're not interested in such options and that you're definitely not interested in paying for them.

## Shop Overseas And Save

If you're planning a vacation in Europe, you also might consider buying a new car while you're there. Insiders say you may be able to cut up to 10 percent off the cost of Volvos and other European models by shopping overseas and having the car shipped back to the United States. However, you'll need to make arrangements with a U.S. dealer before you go overseas to shop.

Besides Volvo, BMW, Mercedes and Saab also have "buy-abroad" plans which can cut the cost of a new car. But with each manufacturer, you'll have to initiate the purchase with a U.S. dealer before you head overseas. You should make arrangements with a dealer in the U.S. one to four months before you leave for Europe, because the model you want may not always be available.

Also make sure that the car you want conforms to U.S. safety standards and that the manufacturer participates in a program which allows foreign car makers to certify that their vehicles meet all U.S. safety and environmental tests before they're shipped. That way, when your car is shipped to the U.S. there will be no delays— you can pick it up and drive it home as soon as it arrives.

## Oldies But Goodies— Used Car Buying Guidelines

This year, nearly 20 million Americans will buy used cars. If that's what you're planning, you'll need to make several carefully considered decisions before you begin looking at used cars. First of all, you'll need to decide what car models and options you want and how much you're able or willing to spend.

When considering costs, remember the real cost of a car includes more than the purchase price. You'll also need to factor in loan terms, such as interest rates and the length of the loan. If you intend to finance the purchase, you'll need to determine how much money you can put down and how much you can afford in monthly payments.

* Check newspaper ads and used car guides at your local library so you'll know what's a fair price for the car you want. Guides such as the "Kelly Blue Book" and the "NADA (National Automobile Dealers' Association) Used Car Guide" provide both wholesale and retail value. These guides are updated frequently to reflect price changes, so make sure you consult the latest issues. And keep in mind that all prices are negotiable.

* Look up repair recalls for car models you might be considering. You can contact the Auto Safety Hotline at (800) 424-9393 to get this information. Authorized dealers of the make of vehicle you're considering must do recall work for free no matter how old the car is.

* Shop during daylight hours so that you can inspect the car thoroughly and take a test drive. Be sure to check all the lights, air conditioner, heater and other parts of the electrical system.

* Have the car you're considering inspected by an independent mechanic of your choice. If the seller won't agree to such an inspection, walk away from the deal.

* Ask questions about the previous owner and the mechanical history of the car. Contact the former owner and find out if the car was in an accident or had any other problems. Also ask the previous owner (or the vehicle's manufacturer) for a copy of the original manufacturer's warranty. The warranty might still be in effect and transferable to you.

* Read the "Buyer's Guide" sticker required to be displayed in the window of the car. The sticker gives information on warranties, if any are offered, and provides other information.

* Beware when buying from a private owner. Keep in mind that private sellers have less responsibility than dealers for defects or other problems. Private sellers generally are not covered by the Used Car Rule, which requires the use of a Buyers Guide providing information on warranties. Also, private sales probably will be on an "as is" basis.

* Don't sign anything you don't understand. Make sure you read all documents carefully. Negotiate with the seller any changes you want and get them written into the contract.

* Contact your state consumer protection office and find out your consumer rights. Some states have laws giving extra protection to used car buyers.

You can get additional information on buying a used car in a free publication offered by the Federal Trade Commission. Contact the FTC, Public Reference Section, 6th and Pennsylvania Avenue, N.W., Room 130, Washington, DC 20580; (202) 326-2222.

The Council of Better Business Bureaus, 4200 Wilson Blvd., Washington, DC 22203; 703-276-0100 also offers valuable information, including the brochure, "Tips On Buying A Used Car." This organization also can provide information regarding complaints about local car dealers.

## Buyer Beware— Some Additional Tips For Used-Car Buyers

It would be nice if you could trust everyone and not have to worry about being ripped-off by an unscrupulous dealer. Unfortunately, when buying a used car (or making any other consumer purchase) caveat emptor should be the guiding principle. If you plan on buying a used car, the following "let the buyer beware" insider tips can help you avoid making a bad deal:

* Investigate a dealer's reputation before you buy. Find out from experienced people whose opinions you respect which dealers in your area have good reputations for sales and service. You also may wish to check the complaint record of car dealers by contacting your state or local consumer protection agency or Better Business Bureau.

* If buying from a private individual, make sure the seller isn't actually a dealer posing as an individual. That could mean the dealer is trying to skirt the law and might indicate that there are problems with the car. Inspect the title and registration. Make sure the seller is the registered owner of the vehicle.

* Read the "Buyer's Guide" sticker which is required to be displayed in the window of the car. The guide gives information on warranties (if any are offered), and provides other information as well.

* Consider carefully buying a car being sold "as is." In most states, used cars can be sold "as is," meaning there is no warranty. If that's the case, you'll likely have to pay for any problems yourself unless the seller makes a written promise to repair the vehicle. The Buyer's Guide sticker should indicate whether or not a car is being sold "as is."

* If the "warranty" box is checked off on the Buyer's Guide sticker, ask for a copy of the warranty and review it before you agree to buy the car. You may be responsible for any problems that aren't covered by the warranty. Because the terms and conditions of written warranties can vary widely, you may find it useful to compare warranty terms on cars or negotiate warranty coverage.

* Check the car over carefully before you buy. Be on the lookout for two things many sellers try to hide: high mileage and repainting. By law, dealers must certify that the odometer reading is accurate. Ask to see any available service records for the vehicle. Such records can help confirm the accuracy of the mileage, as well as indicate how well the car has been maintained. Repainting may signal accident damage or rust— either being a serious problem which can lower the price of a late-model car by over $1,000. Look for paint on rubber seals, wires or weather stripping in a car's trunk or gas filler opening.

## Check Out The Auction Market

If you're considering buying a used car, you may be able to find a good deal at an auction. Cars that have been repossessed or abandoned by their owners are often sold at auction. Some of these cars are in very good condition and make excellent bargains. However, cars on the auction block are generally sold "as is" with no guarantees. In other words, it's "buyer beware."

Many government agencies also auction off vehicles, including sports cars and family sedans. Agencies, such as the U.S. Customs Service, the Bureau of Alcohol, Tobacco and Firearms, the Department of Agriculture, and the General Services Administration all have sales programs featuring excess and confiscated cars of all types. As with repossessed and abandoned cars, government vehicles are sold at auction in "as is" condition.

The "U.S. General Services Administration Guide To Federal Government Sales" can provide you with more information about government auctions. The guide, available through the U.S. Government Printing Office, is a low-cost publication which is listed in the free "Consumer Information Catalog." To get a free copy of the Catalog, write to Catalog, Consumer Information Center, P.O. Box 100, Pueblo, Co 81002.

The publications listed in the catalog also are available online. Use your modem or Internet connection to access the Consumer Information Center Catalog Electronically: Electronic BBS: 202-208-7679; Internet WWW:http://www.gsa.gov/staff/pa/cic/cic.htm.

## — Auction Tips

Before picking up a car at an auction, auction executives advise that you:

* Examine the car before you buy. Be sure to check oil, water and transmission-fluid levels. If fluid levels are up, it's a good sign that the car has had care and that there aren't any leaks. Avoid bidding on any cars whose interiors and engines you haven't been allowed to inspect thoroughly beforehand.

* Start the car. Check the brake pedal. If the pedal doesn't go down more than half way, the brakes are ok.

* Take at least $200 cash for a deposit. A winning bidder typically has a week to pay for a car or lose the deposit. You'll also need a temporary license tag from a deputy registrar to drive the car off the lot.

* Arrange financing before you buy. Since this is a large investment, it should be treated that way.

* Be aware that the bankers who hold the outstanding loan on a car have the final word on its sale. They can refuse a sale at a price they consider too low.

Keep in mind that when buying at an auction you'll find both gems and junkers. You'll be looking at cars loaded with options and cars that are missing vital parts, as well as cars with less than 2,000 miles and cars with more than 200,000. So make sure you know what you're getting before you buy.

## One Hotline That Is Worth The Money

The National Highway Traffic Safety Administration's Auto Safety Hotline can help you make a safe, money-saving decision when you're considering a new or used car. The Hotline distributes recall and safety information on used and new cars, trucks, vans, motorcycles and other motor vehicles. It also provides vehicle crash test information, tire quality grading reports and other information which can help you make an informed decision when purchasing your next new or used car. To get any of this information free of charge, call the Auto Safety Hotline at (800) 424-9393.

## Doubling Your Car's Life Expectancy

Properly maintained, your new car should be in good running condition for many years. In fact, automotive experts say that by following a schedule of preventive maintenance most motorists can double the life expectancy of their cars. That's especially good news for do-it-yourselfers and "shade-tree mechanics" who are adept at changing oil and other preventive maintenance services.

Even those car owners who don't know a dip-stick from a wiper blade can benefit by keeping well maintained vehicles. And it's not that difficult. The first step is to read your owner's manual and then follow the manufacturer's recommended service schedule. A car that receives regular routine maintenance is more enjoyable to drive, will last longer, and could command a higher resale price when it comes time to buy another car. Regular maintenance checks and simple service also can greatly reduce the cost of car ownership.

Whether or not you know your way under the hood and around your car, or you rely on a trusted and qualified mechanic, the following nine preventive measures can help keep your car running at peak performance for years to come.

**1)** Check oil every other fill up. To maintain peak performance, change oil and filter every 3000 miles— more often if your driving is mostly in-town or consists of frequent short trips. Also check other fluid levels— transmission, power steering, radiator and brakes— at every oil change.

**2)** Check the antifreeze/coolant level periodically. The cooling system should be flushed and refilled about every 24 months. A 50/50 mix of anti-freeze and water is usually recommended. (If you do it yourself, never remove the radiator cap when the engine is hot.)

**3)** Inspect belts and hoses periodically. Replace all worn, glazed or frayed belts and worn hoses.

**4)** Check the air filter every other month. Replace it when it's dirty or as part of a tune-up.

**5)** Keep tires inflated to their recommended pressure. Also examine your tires for remaining tread life, uneven wearing, cuts and bulging. Be sure to check the sidewalls for cuts and nicks. Rotate as recommended in your owner's manual.

**6)** Check your car's battery periodically. Scrape away corrosion from posts and cable connections; clean all surfaces and tighten all connections. If the battery caps are removable, check the fluid level every month. Be sure to avoid contact with corrosive deposits and battery acid when performing routine care. Wear eye protection and rubber gloves.

**7)** Have your car's exhaust system checked for leaks at least once a year. Look for loose or broken exhaust clamps and supports. Check for holes in the muffler or pipes. Replace any rusted or damaged parts. Also inspect the trunk and floor boards for small holes.

**8)** Check shock absorbers. Look for signs of seepage, and test shock action by bouncing your car up and down. Replace leaking and/or worn shocks in pairs.

**9)** Inspect your windshield wipers regularly. Check the wiper blades whenever you clean your windshield. Replace old blades before the rubber is worn or brittle. Blades should be replaced at least once a year.

## Avoiding Auto Repair Rip-Offs

Even with regular maintenance, most cars need some type of repair work sooner or later. And unless you already know a competent and trustworthy mechanic, you could wind up paying a lot more than you should to get your car repaired. Besides being overcharged for necessary work, you also could end up paying for unnecessary repairs. In fact, according to a report by the Department of Transportation, 40 percent or more of all car repairs performed are not necessary.

So, how do you know you're being ripped off, and how can you prevent it from happening? Here are several tips from the U.S. Office of Consumer Affairs that can help you answer both those questions:

* Look for a reliable repair shop before you need one. Get recommendations from family or friends or from an independent consumer rating organization. If possible, choose a shop where mechanics have ASE (Automotive Service Excellence) certification. While such certification isn't a guarantee of competent service, it is a good sign that the shop's mechanics know what they're doing.

* Check out the repair shop's complaint record with your state or local consumer protection office or Better Business Bureau.

* Speak directly with the mechanic who will work on your car. Describe (don't diagnose) the problem as best you can. Let the mechanic know that you plan to ask questions and may request a second opinion before you authorize any repairs.

* Get a written estimate before the work begins. Also make sure you get written assurance that no additional work will be done without your prior approval. Your estimate should

be itemized by diagnostic work, parts costs, and labor charges. Once you have an itemized estimate, visit several other repair shops and get their written estimates for the same work.

* Make it clear that no repair work can begin without your authorization. If the problem can't be diagnosed on the spot, make sure the shop contacts you to provide you with a written estimate and to get your authorization to begin work once the trouble is found.

* Before authorizing any repair work, ask the mechanic to save all the old parts for you. Once the work has been done, and the old parts discarded, it's really difficult to prove that the repair was unnecessary.

* Always test drive your car before you pay for expensive repairs. Once you've paid and drive away, you'll have a tough time proving the repair was not done right.

* Never sign a blank repair order. Make sure the repair order reflects what you want done before you sign it.

* Examine the repair bill carefully. The bill should include the repair warranty, stating how long the work and parts are guaranteed.

* Always pay for major repair work by credit card. That way, if you have a problem with the repair shop which can't be resolved, you can send a letter to your credit card company explaining that you are disputing the charge and why. You won't be required to pay the repair bill until the problem is resolved.

* Keep good records and copies of all paperwork.

## Insider's Tips On Slashing Car-Repair Costs

You pamper your car with regular checkups— oil, tires, battery, hoses and belts, muffler, shock absorber, lights, and so on. You practice safe driving techniques. You've found a reputable car repair shop with competent mechanics, just in case some sort of repair is needed. Such attention to detail allows you to be free from the worry of costly repairs, doesn't it? Well, not quite.

Certainly, your efforts will go a long way in reducing the necessity of costly repairs, or the chances of being gouged by a repair ripoff. But some things in this life, including major car repairs, are unavoidable. Regardless of the care you give your car or the skill and honesty of your mechanic, you still could end up on the wrong end of a hefty repair bill. It's just another one of the financial risks you take by owning a car.

To reduce that risk, and as a result, slash repair costs (and in some cases get your car fixed free or at minimal cost), consider the following insider tips:

* Follow your owner's manual schedule of routine maintenance. This is the best way to avoid costly repairs altogether. If you take good care of your vehicle, any problems that arise are likely to be minor and relatively inexpensive to correct.

* Avoid repair-shop rip-offs (see "Avoiding Auto Repair Rip-Offs elsewhere in this chapter). Find a reputable repair shop and be aware of underhanded tactics, such as "lowballing" (repair shops advertise amazingly low prices for certain repairs, then try to sell you on more expensive repairs to make up their profit); "phantom repairs" (shops charge you for repairs that were never made). You always should ask to see the old parts the mechanic has replaced, as well as the new parts he has installed; and "bill padding"

(you're charged a "flat-rate" for routine repairs even though the repairs were completed in much less time than was estimated).

* Don't pay for any work covered by warranty. Make sure you check your warranty before authorizing any work on your car. It doesn't matter where you bought the car, dealers are obligated to perform the warranty work for free. Contact the vehicle manufacturer's regional office or corporate headquarters if you have problems getting your warranty honored.

* Find out if there are any "secret warranties" issued for your car. A secret warranty is an unpublicized policy whereby manufacturers acknowledge "inherent" defects in certain vehicles. These vehicles are defective when they roll off the assembly line. The manufacturers are aware of the defects and acknowledge them by sending notices or service bulletins to dealers. The notices describe the defects and how to fix them. The manufacturers also are required, by federal law, to send service bulletins to the National Highway Traffic Safety Administration (NHTSA). They aren't, however, required to send such notices to car owners.

If your car is covered by a secret warranty (even if your new car warranty has expired), you may be entitled to have the necessary repairs done free of charge. The problem is finding out whether or not there is a secret warranty applicable to your car. Unless you live in one of the few states that have anti-secret warranty laws, the manufacturer won't tell you. The dealer won't tell you. You'll have to uncover the secret for yourself. One way to do that is by contacting the Technical Reference Division (TRD) of NHTSA. If there are any service bulletins applicable to your car, the TRD will send you copies of them at no cost.

Armed with proof that one or more secret warranties apply to your vehicle, you can contact your dealer about getting the necessary repairs done free of charge. If the dealer rejects your complaint, contact the vehicle manufacturer's customer service department (check your owner's manual for the address and phone number).

For information about secret warranties, write to the Technical Reference Division, National Highway Traffic Safety Administration, 400 7th Street, SW, Washington, DC 20590.

* Find out if you've missed a safety recall that applies to your car. The National Highway Traffic and Safety Administration oversees the federal government's safety recall program which provides for free repairs of safety-related manufacturing defects and design flaws in affected vehicles.

Under federal law, manufacturers are required to notify (by first class mail), owners of vehicles subject to safety recalls. However, according to the NHTSA, nearly 35 percent of the car owners notified of safety recalls fail to take advantage of the free repairs. Perhaps these owners simply ignored the recall notices, or perhaps they purchased previously owned vehicles and aren't aware of any recall notices. In any case, these people will likely end up paying for repairs that they are entitled to have done free of charge.

You can contact the dealership to find out whether or not you've missed a safety recall that applies to your vehicle. You also can call the NHTSA's hotline, (800) 424-9393 for recall information.

## Don't Get Stranded On A Deserted Roadway

Getting stranded is no fun— it's also dangerous. Obviously, the best way to avoid such a mishap is to reduce the chances of a breakdown by keeping your car in peak running performance. You also could try to avoid travelling on deserted roadways. But even the most careful and conscientious driver can be faced with an emergency situation. Your car could break down far from help, and if you're not prepared for such an eventuality, you could be stranded and in danger.

If your car should break down on a deserted stretch of highway, use your common sense and the following tips to protect yourself and to get help:

* Get off the roadway out of the path of any oncoming traffic, even if you have to drive on a flat tire. The tire is replaceable.

* Turn on your emergency flashers. If you have emergency roadway flares in your trunk, position them 10 and 300 feet to the rear of the car and 100 feet to the front.

* Raise the hood and tie a distress flag (or handkerchief) to the antenna or door handle.

* If a roadside telephone or call-box is nearby, use it to call for help. If not, stay in your locked car and wait for help.

* If a motorist stops to offer assistance, it's best to stay in the car and ask him/her to get help by calling the police, the highway patrol, or your auto club at the next phone box or tollbooth.

* Keep the following tools and supplies in your car to handle common emergencies:

— **General equipment**: flashlight and spare batteries; a light that plugs into a cigarette lighter or clips to the car battery; emergency flares and distress flag.

— **Supplies**: gallon plastic jug to hold water or gas; quart of engine oil; tire sealant-inflator; jumper cables; scrap electrical wire for lashing down a sprung trunk lid or hood or for tying up a dropped tail pipe; duct tape.

— **Tools**: adjustable wrench; insulated slip-joint, needle nose, and locking pliers; insulated screwdrivers—one phillips head, one standard; utility knife; jack; lug wrench.

Whenever possible, you should travel on well-lighted busy streets. You can spare those extra minutes it may take to avoid a deserted and potentially unsafe area. However, if you have to drive on lightly traveled roadways, make sure you'll be well-prepared in the event of a breakdown and reduce your chances of being stranded.

## Improve Your Fuel Efficiency And Save

Regardless of the type of car you drive—new or used, fuel efficient driving can save you a bundle of money. In fact, the following fuel-efficient driving practices, recommended by the U.S. Department of Transportation and the Department of Energy, can save you ten percent or more on fuel costs:

* Avoid high speed driving. According to the Department of Transportation, for every mile-per-hour over 55 mph, the average car or truck loses about 2 percent in gas mileage. That means that your vehicle uses almost 50 percent more gasoline at 80 mph than it does at 55 mph.

* Drive smoothly. Sudden starts and stops takes more fuel (and increases tire wear) than maintaining steady speeds. If you gain speed slowly following a full stop, you'll save as much as two miles per gallon. Sudden or "jackrabbit starts," on the other hand, use up to 50 percent more gas than smooth starts. Sudden braking also wastes gas. Even in stop-and-go traffic, ease up on the gas pedal and slow gently to a halt.

* Maintain proper tire pressure. You should check the pressure on all four tires every two weeks to ensure they're inflated to the recommended pressure. Under-inflation decreases gas mileage (a half-mile or more per gallon) and shortens the life of each tire.

* Minimize engine idling. An idling engine wastes gas, so don't start your car until you're ready to go. And turn off the motor if you're going to be idling for an extended period of time such as in stalled traffic.

* Use the correct fuel for your vehicle. According to a report released by the General Accounting Office, less than 10 percent of motor vehicles on the road today need high-octane or premium fuel. Unless you drive a turbo-charged or high-performance vehicle, use regular gas and save as much as 20 cents a gallon. And you can cut that price even more by pumping your own at self-service pumps.

* Reduce the load you carry in your car's trunk. The more weight you carry in your car's trunk, the more fuel your car consumes. So find another way to transport heavy items, whenever possible.

* Don't drive with the windows open. This creates drag and at highway speeds will increase fuel consumption. Also avoid using the air conditioner as much as possible because it can consume an extra three miles per gallon in city driving. Use air vents as often as possible.

* Make fewer trips. This doesn't mean you should become a hermit. However, if you can consolidate errands and visits into one trip whenever possible, you'll cut down on fuel consumption and save money.

## What If Your Car's Simply A Lemon

Virtually every state has a new car (and in some cases, used car) "lemon law" that allows owners to claim a refund or replacement when a new vehicle has a "substantial problem" (one that seriously impairs a vehicle's usefulness and value) that is not fixed within a reasonable number of attempts. Many state laws specify a refund or replacement when a substantial problem is not fixed in four repair attempts or the vehicle has been out of service for 30 days within the first 12,000 miles/12 months. A few states, including Connecticut, Hawaii, New Jersey and North Carolina, allow two years.

If you think that your car is a lemon, take the following actions recommended by the U.S. Office of Consumer Affairs:

* Contact your state or local consumer protection office (see below) for information on the laws in your state and the steps you must take to resolve the matter.

* Provide the dealer with a list of symptoms every time you bring your vehicle in for repairs, and keep copies for your records.

* Get copies of the repair orders showing the reported problems, the repairs performed and the dates that your vehicle was in the shop.

* Contact the manufacturer, as well as the dealer, to report the problem. In some states, consumers are required to do so in order to give the manufacturer a chance to fix the malfunction. Your owner's manual will list an address for the manufacturer.

If the problem isn't resolved, you might have the option of participating in an arbitration program offered by the vehicle's manufacturer or by your state. Under most such programs, an arbitrator's decision is binding on the manufacturer, but not on the consumer. If you aren't happy with the arbitrator's decision, you then can file suit against the manufacturer. Depending on the outcome of such a suit, the manufacturer can be ordered to provide you with a replacement vehicle or a refund of the amount you paid for the vehicle, minus a "reasonable" amount for the use you were able to get out of the vehicle.

For additional information about lemon laws, contact the Center for Auto Safety (CAS) and ask for a copy of "Lemon Law Summary." Write to CAS, 2001 S Street, N.W., Suite 410, Washington, DC 20009. Include a SASE (52 cents postage) with your request.

* State-By-State Contacts For Lemon Law Information

— **ALABAMA**:

Consumer Protection Division,
Office of Attorney General,
11 South Union Street, Montgomery, AL 36130;
(800) 392-5658.

— **ALASKA**:

Office of the Attorney General,
Anchorage, AL 99500;
(907) 562-0704.

## — ARIZONA:

Consumer Protection,
Office of the Attorney General,
1275 West Washington Street, Phoenix, AZ 85007;
(800) 352-8431.

## — ARKANSAS:

Consumer Protection Division,
Office of the Attorney General,
200 Tower Building, 323 Center Street,
Little Rock, AR 72201;
(800) 482-8982.

## — CALIFORNIA:

Department of Consumer Affairs,
400 R Street, Suite 1040, Sacramento, CA 95814;
(916) 322-3360.

## — COLORADO:

Consumer Protection Unit,
Office of the Attorney General,
110 16th Street, 10th Floor, Denver, CO 80202:
(303) 866-5189.

## — CONNECTICUT:

Department of Consumer Protection,
State Office Building,
165 Capitol Avenue, Hartford, CT 06106;
(800) 842-2649.

## — DELAWARE:

Division of Consumer Affairs,
Department of Community Affairs,
820 North French Street, 4th Floor,
Wilmington, DE 19801; (302) 577-3250.

— **DISTRICT OF COLUMBIA**:

Department of Consumer and Regulatory Affairs,
614 H Street, N.W., Washington, DC 20001;
(202) 727-7080.

— **FLORIDA**:

Department of Agriculture and Consumer Services,
Division of Consumer Services,
218 Mayo Building, Tallahassee, FL 32399;
(800) 435-7352.

— **GEORGIA**:

Governors Office of Consumer Affairs,
2 Martin Luther King, Jr. Drive, S.E.,
Atlanta, GA 30334;
(404) 656-3790.

— **HAWAII**:

Office of Consumer Protection,
Department of Commerce and Consumer Affairs,
828 Fort St. Mall, Suite 600B, P.O. Box 3767,
Honolulu, HI 96812-3767;
(808) 586-2636.

— **IDAHO**:

Office of the Attorney General,
Consumer Protection Unit,
Statehouse, Room 113A, Boise, ID 83720-1000;
(208) 334-2424.

— **ILLINOIS**:

Governors Office of Citizens Assistance,
222 South College, Springfield, IL 62706;
(800) 642-3112.

## — INDIANA:

Consumer Protection Division,
Office of the Attorney General,
219 State House, Indianapolis, IN 46204;
(800) 382-5516.

## — IOWA:

Consumer Protection Division,
Office of the Attorney General,
1300 East Walnut Street, 2nd Floor,
Des Moines, IA 50319; (515) 281-5926.

## — KANSAS:

Consumer Protection Division,
Office of the Attorney General,
301 West 10th, Kansas Judicial Center,
Topeka, KS 66612-1597; (800) 432-2310.

## — KENTUCKY:

Consumer Protection Division,
Office of the Attorney General,
209 Saint Clair Street, Frankfort, KY 40601-1875;
(502) 564-2200.

## — LOUISIANA:

Consumer Protection Section,
Office of the Attorney General,
State Capitol Building, P.O. Box 94005,
Baton Rouge, LA 70804-9005; (504) 342-9638.

## — MAINE:

Consumer and Antitrust Division,
Office of the Attorney General,
State House Station No. 6, Augusta, ME 04333;
(207) 626-8849.

— **MARYLAND**:

> Consumer Protection Division,
> Office of the Attorney General,
> 200 St. Paul Place, Baltimore, MD 21202-2021;
> (410) 528-8662.

— **MASSACHUSETTS**:

> Consumer Protection Division,
> Department of the Attorney General,
> 131 Tremont Street, Boston, MA 02111;
> (617) 727-8400.

— **MICHIGAN**:

> Consumer Protection Division,
> Office of the Attorney General,
> P.O. Box 30213, Lansing, MI 48909;
> (612) 348-4528.

— **MINNESOTA**:

> Office of Consumer Services,
> Office of the Attorney General,
> 117 University Avenue, St. Paul, MN 55155;
> (612) 296-3353.

— **MISSISSIPPI**:

> Office of Consumer Protection,
> P.O. Box 22947, Jackson, MS 39225-2947;
> (601) 354-6018.

— **MISSOURI**:

> Office of the Attorney General,
> Consumer Complaints for Problems,
> P.O. Box 899, Jefferson City, MO 65102:
> (800) 392-8222.

## — MONTANA:

Consumer Affairs Unit, Department of Commerce,
1424 Ninth Avenue, Helena, MT 59620:
(406) 444-2682.

## — NEBRASKA:

Consumer Protection Division, Department of Justice,
2115 State Capitol, P.O. Box 98920,
Lincoln, NE 68509;
(402) 471-2682.

## — NEVADA:

Commissioner of Consumer Affairs,
Department of Commerce,
State Mail Room Complex, Las Vegas, NV 89158;
(702) 688-1800.

## — NEW HAMPSHIRE:

Consumer Protection Antitrust Bureau,
Office of the Attorney General,
State House Annex, Concord, NH 03301;
(603) 271-3641.

## — NEW JERSEY:

Division of Consumer Affairs,
P.O. Box 45027, Newark, NJ 07101;
(201) 504-6534.

## — NEW MEXICO:

Consumer Protection Division,
Office of the Attorney General,
P.O. Drawer 1508, Santa Fe, NM 87504;
(505) 827-6060.

## — NEW YORK:

New York State Consumer Protection Board,
99 Washington Avenue,
Albany, NY 12210-2891;
(518) 474-5481.

## — NORTH CAROLINA:

Consumer Protection Section,
Office of the Attorney General,
Raney Building, P.O. Box 629, Raleigh, NC 27602;
(919) 733-7741.

## — NORTH DAKOTA:

Office of the Attorney General,
600 East Boulevard, Bismarck, ND 58505;
(800) 472-2600.

## — OHIO:

Office of the Attorney General,
30 East Broad Street, State Office Tower, 25th Floor,
Columbus, OH 43266-0401;
(800) 282-9448.

## — OKLAHOMA:

Office of the Attorney General,
420 West Main, Suite 550,
Oklahoma City, OK 73102;
(405) 521-4274.

## — OREGON:

Financial Fraud Section,
Department of Justice,
Justice Building , Salem, OR 97310;
(503) 378-4732.

# The Good Life Money Book

— **PENNSYLVANIA**:

Bureau of Consumer Protection,
Office of the Attorney General,
Strawberry Square, 14th Floor, Harrisburg, PA 17120;
(717) 787-9707.

— **RHODE ISLAND**:

Consumer Protection Division,
Office of the Attorney General,
72 Pine Street, Providence, RI 02903;
(401) 274-4400.

— **SOUTH CAROLINA**:

Office of the Attorney General,
P.O. Box 11549, Columbia, SC 29211;
(803) 734-3970.

— **SOUTH DAKOTA**:

Division of Consumer Affairs,
Office of Attorney General,
500 East Capitol, State Capitol Building,
Pierre, SD 57501-5070;
(605) 773-4400.

— **TENNESSEE**:

Antitrust and Consumer Protection Division,
Office of the Attorney General,
450 James Robertson Parkway,
Nashville, TN 37243-0485;
(615) 741-3491.

— **TEXAS**:

Consumer Protection Division,
Office of the Attorney General,
P.O. Box 12548, Austin, TX 78711; (214) 742-8944.

## — UTAH:

Division of Consumer Protection,
Department of Commerce,
160 East Third, South, P.O. Box 45802,
Salt Lake City, UT 84145-0802;
(801) 530-6001.

## — VERMONT:

Office of the Attorney General,
109 State Street, Montpelier, VT 05609-1001;
(808) 828-3171.

## — VIRGINIA:

Office of the Attorney General,
Supreme Court Building,
101 North Eighth Street, Richmond, VA 23219;
(804) 786-2116.

## — WASHINGTON:

Office of the Attorney General,
111 Olympia Avenue, NE, Olympia, WA 98501;
(206) 753-6210.

## — WEST VIRGINIA:

Consumer Protection Division,
Office of the Attorney General,
812 Quarrier Street, 6th Floor,
Charleston, WV 25301;
(800) 368-8808.

## — WISCONSIN:

Department of Agriculture,
Trade and Consumer Protection,
801 West Badger Road, P.O. Box 8911,
Madison, WI 53708; (608) 266-9836.

**— WYOMING**:

Office of the Attorney General,
123 State Capitol Building, Cheyenne, WY 82002;
(307) 777-7874.

## Consider Insurance Rates Before Buying

There's more to getting a good deal on a new or used car than getting a good price from the dealer. Your final decision also should be based on insurance costs. Vehicles that are expensive to repair, or that are favorites of car thieves (high-profile cars) have much higher insurance costs.

For Example, the Chevy Camaro, a popular sports car, also is a popular target for car thieves. Your insurance premiums for such a car will generally be much higher than for a more sedate sedan. Cars that are more easily damaged in accidents or expensive to repair also may cost as much as 15 percent more to insure. That's why industry insiders advise consumers to check out the insurance costs of the vehicles they want to buy before making a commitment. Your decision could mean a savings of several hundred dollars a year in total insurance costs.

## What Kind Of Car Insurance Do You Need?

The kind of auto insurance you need depends on several factors. First of all, you must meet state laws which require that you be financially responsible for your actions. You also need to protect your financial and legal liability in case you or your vehicle cause an injury accident. And of course, you need to protect your investment in the event your car is damaged or destroyed in an accident.

Without adequate coverage, a single automobile accident could result in extreme financial hardship for you and your family. Choosing a policy that provides the protection you need requires an understanding of the many different coverages and features available. The following types of automobile insurance provide coverage for a wide range of risks. Separate premiums are charged for each type of coverage with the cost of each coverage adding up to your total premium.

### * Bodily Injury And Property Damage Liability

This insurance covers claims made by pedestrians and by occupants of other cars for injury and property damage resulting from an accident caused by you, a member of your family or a person driving your car with your permission. Insurers generally use a three-part numerical designation to categorize a driver's liability coverage. For example, in a policy with the designation $25,000/ $50,000/ $10,000 (or 25/50/10), the first number indicates the maximum amount an insurer will pay for bodily injury per person; the second number gives the maximum dollar benefit per accident; and the third number indicates the maximum payment for property damage.

In most states, the minimum coverage required is very low, ranging from $10,000/ $20,000 to $25,000/ $50,000. Considering the liberal court awards for injured parties the minimum requirements may not provide enough coverage. That's why it's a good idea to insure for more than the minimum required by law. If you can afford it, coverage of at least $100,000 liability per person and $300,000 per accident is recommended. In addition, you may want to consider $50,000 to $100,000 for property damage.

### * Uninsured Motorist Coverage

This insurance protects you against bodily injury liability claims if you're injured by a hit-and-run driver or in an accident caused by an uninsured driver. If an uninsured motorist is at fault, this coverage will pay for injuries (including pain and suffering)you and any of your passengers sustain as a result of the accident.

### * Medical Payments Or Expense Coverage

This coverage pays for medical and funeral expenses for any person injured or killed in an accident involving the policyholder's vehicle, regardless of who is at fault. While such coverage is relatively inexpensive, it may not be necessary if you have adequate health insurance.

### * Collision Coverage

Collision coverage pays for repair or replacement of your vehicle regardless of who causes the collision. Premium rates depend on the amount of the deductible, the type of vehicle and the type of coverage. If you have an older car, with a book value of less than $1,000, you can cut your costs by dropping this coverage.

### * Comprehensive Coverage

As the name implies, comprehensive insurance covers a multitude of eventualities including fire, vandalism, theft, glass breakage, damage from falling objects, hail, earthquakes, water damage from floods, and many other risks. This is an optional coverage that may not be cost effective, especially if you drive an older car. Consider the risks, and then decide if you really need this coverage.

## A Better Idea For Liability Coverage

Depending on the value of your assets, you may want to consider additional liability coverage. Generally, for a reasonable cost (considering the large monetary awards frequently awarded by juries), you can extend the minimum coverage required by state law. If you have accumulated more than $100,000 in assets, you should consider raising your coverage to $100,000/$300,000 (plus $100,000 for property damage).

If, however, your assets are valued at more than $300,000, you may choose an umbrella liability coverage which extends liability protection to limits of $1 million or more. The additional premium for this maximum liability protection is relatively low in cost.

Many companies also now offer a "special package automobile policy" with a single limit that covers the total limit of liability for both bodily injury and property damage accidents. While such a policy may have more exclusions than a regular three-part policy, it also may cost 10% to 20% less.

## Raise Your Deductibles And Save

Deductibles represent the amount of money you pay before you make a claim or the amount you pay "out-of-pocket" for repairs. If you're willing (and able, if necessary) to pay a higher deductible, you can usually qualify for a lower premium. For example, by increasing your deductible from $200 to $500 you could reduce your annual rates by 15% to 30%.

Determine the amount you can pay out-of-pocket and then ask your insurance agent to adjust the deductibles on collision and comprehensive (fire and theft) coverage accordingly.

## Five Additional Ways To Save On Car Insurance

Besides increasing your deductibles, there are several other ways you can cut the cost of car insurance. Here are five proven cost-cutters:

**1)** Take advantage of discounts. Most companies offer a number of policy discounts. You may qualify for a discount if your car is equipped with automatic seat belts, airbags, anti-lock brakes, and anti-theft devices; if you're a non-smoker; if you have a good driving record; are fifty years of age or older; if you completed a driver's safety course; and if you participate in a car pool. Other discounts also are available. Ask about any discounts for which you might qualify.

**2)** Buy your auto and homeowner's policies from the same insurance agency. Most companies will give you lower rates for purchasing more than one policy. You also can reduce your premiums for each vehicle you have by insuring them all on the same policy. For example, most insurance companies offer a 15-percent discount to two-car families insuring both vehicles with the same company.

**3)** Take a driver safety course. Many insurers reward even experienced drivers who complete defensive driving courses with lower premiums. Depending upon your insurer, you may be able to reduce your premium by 5% to 10% by taking such a state-approved defensive driving course. However, before you enroll, check with your insurer. In some states, the discount for taking a defensive-driving course is available only to drivers 55 or older.

**4)** Join a carpool. Many insurance companies now offer lower rates to motorists who carpool on a regular basis. The reasoning being, that if you join a carpool, you'll be driving your own vehicle less thereby reducing your own personal risk.

**5)** Make sure your coverage reflects current driving habits. You should report any changes that might reduce your premium. For example, if you've reduced the number of miles you drive, you may be eligible for a lower rate. Say you used to commute 60 miles to work and you're now working at home. Report that change to your insurer, and you're likely to receive a reduction in your premium.

## Trim the Fat From Auto Policies

Study the details of your auto insurance policy carefully. There's a good chance you'll find areas of your coverage you can trim or cut out altogether, lowering your costs even further. For example, It generally isn't "cost effective" to maintain collision and comprehensive on cars that are worth less than $1,000. That's because any claim you make isn't likely to be much greater than annual costs and deductibles. Generally, it's advisable to drop collision coverage when the premium is at least 10% of your vehicle's market value. (If you're not certain of your car's market value, check the NADA price guide at your local public library). You may save as much as $100 a year by dropping such coverage on an older vehicle.

You also should avoid buying duplicate medical coverage. If you have adequate health insurance, you may be able to eliminate paying for duplicate medical coverage in your auto policy. In some states, dropping this coverage could reduce your personal injury protection (PIP) cost by 30% to 40%. Contact your state insurance department to find out whether or not such coverage is required in your state.

## Finding The Cheapest Car Insurance

The insurance rates you pay for your car(s) can vary by hundreds of dollars depending on the insurer, agent or broker you choose, the type of coverages you choose, and the kind of car(s) you drive. That's why it will pay you to shop around to find the best rates.

The first thing you'll need to do is get price quotes from several insurers. Ask your friends for recommendations, check the yellow pages or call your state insurance department and ask for a free guide ranking companies by price. You also can check consumer guides, insurance agents or companies to get an idea of price ranges and which companies or agents have the lowest prices. Select three or four companies and get their estimates. Tell each agent that you are comparison-shopping and ask them to give you their best rates. Also get a written summary of each offer.

Along with price, you also should consider service. While quality personal service may cost a bit more, it can make a good deal even better. Ask each agent what he/she would do to lower your costs. Try to get a feeling for the quality of service of each company you're considering.

Once you've narrowed the field to three or four insurers, ask for price quotes. Then, check with an insurance rating agency to find out whether or not the company you're considering is "financially sound." The major rating agencies include, A.M. Best, (908) 439-2200; Standard & Poor's, (212) 208-1527; Moodys, (212) 553-0377; Duff & Phelps, (312) 368-3157; and Weiss Research, (800) 289-9222. Some rating agency reports are available at public libraries, others are available free or for a nominal charge by telephone.

You also may want to check out "commission-free" insurers. These companies, also known as "direct writers," sell directly over the phone, eliminating commission charges. Direct writers, such as Geico (800) 841-3000, and Amica (800) 622-6422 can reduce your automobile insurance premium by 5% to 15%.

## What About Your Teenage Drivers?

There are actually several ways to cut the cost of insuring teenage drivers. First of all, you should contact several companies and compare rates and services. While most insurance companies offer slightly different features, the same type of coverage can vary in cost by 50 percent or more. Another insurer may be able to provide coverage for everyone in your family at a savings of hundreds or thousands of dollars.

You can add to those savings by taking advantage of discounts offered for young drivers. For example, if your teenager(s) is not a "principal" driver (drives the car less than half the time), he/she may qualify for an "occasional driver" discount. Discounts also are available for students who maintain good grades and college students who go to school more than 100 miles away from home without a car. Each of these discounts for young drivers can reduce your premiums by 10 percent or more. Some insurers also give new drivers discounts of 5 to 10 percent for completing professional or driver school training courses.

You can get more information about automobile (and other types) of insurance by contacting the National Insurance Consumer Helpline (NICH), (800) 942-4242 and/or the Insurance Information Institute, 110 William Street, New York, NY 10038; (800) 331-9146.

Your state insurance department also can provide you with information to help you make informed insurance buying decisions. Contact your state department at:

**ALABAMA:** (205) 269-3550

**ALASKA:** (907) 465-2515

**ARIZONA:** (602) 255-5400

**ARKANSAS:** (501) 686-2900

**CALIFORNIA:** (800) 927-4357

**COLORADO:** (303) 894-7499

**CONNECTICUT:** (203) 297-3800

**DELAWARE:** (800) 282-8611

**DISTRICT OF COLUMBIA:** (202) 727-8002

**FLORIDA:** (800) 342-2762

**GEORGIA:** (404) 656-2056

**HAWAII:** (800) 468-4644

**IDAHO:** (208) 334-2250

**ILLINOIS:** (217) 782-4515

**INDIANA:** (800) 622-4461

**IOWA:** (515) 281-57056

**KANSAS:** (800) 432-2484

**KENTUCKY:** (502) 564-3630

**LOUISIANA:** (504) 342-5900

**MAINE:** (207) 582-8707

**MARYLAND:** (800) 492-6116

**MASSACHUSETTS:** (617) 727-3357

**MICHIGAN:** (517) 373-9273

**MINNESOTA:** (800) 652-9747

**MISSISSIPPI:** (601) 359-3569

**MISSOURI:** (314) 751-2640

**MONTANA:** (800) 332-6148

**NEBRASKA:** (402) 471-2201

**NEVADA:** (800) 992-0900

**NEW HAMPSHIRE:** (800) 852-3416

**NEW JERSEY:** (609) 292-5363

**NEW MEXICO:** (505) 827-4500

**NEW YORK:** (212) 602-0203

**NORTH CAROLINA:** (800) 662-7777

**NORTH DAKOTA:** (800) 247-0560

**OHIO:** (800) 686-1526
**OKLAHOMA:** (405) 521-2828
**OREGON:** (503) 378-4271
**PENNSYLVANIA:** (717) 787-5173
**RHODE ISLAND:** (401) 277-2223
**SOUTH CAROLINA:** (803) 737-6117
**SOUTH DAKOTA:** (605) 773-3563
**TENNESSEE:** (800) 342-4029
**TEXAS:** (512) 463-6464
**UTAH:** (801) 530-6400
**VERMONT:** (802) 828-3301
**VIRGINIA:** (800) 552-7945
**WASHINGTON:** (800) 562-6900
**WEST VIRGINIA:** (800) 642-9004
**WISCONSIN:** (800) 236-8517
**WYOMING:** (307) 777-7401

## NOTES

_____

_____

_____

_____

_____

_____

---

| CHAPTER 2 |
| :---: |
| **Housing & Real Estate Guide:** |

## Smart Ways To Buy That First Home

The purchase of a home is, to most people part of the American dream. It's also likely to be the biggest single investment they'll ever make. The savings of years of hard work are invested in this one venture. It doesn't take a financial expert to realize that it's extremely important that a prospective buyer make the right decisions. With that in mind, here's a step-by-step home buying guide that offers several smart shopping tips for first-time buyers:

### * Determine How Much Home You Can Afford

You can save yourself a lot of time and frustration in your search for a house if you first figure out in just what price range you should be looking. It's important that you know exactly how much you can afford in a monthly mortgage payment. Lenders follow certain guidelines to decide whether or not to lend you the mortgage money you need to buy your home. Most lenders will want your monthly mortgage payment (and other housing expenses, including interest, taxes and insurance) to total between 28% and 30% of your total gross monthly income (see Chapter 3). These guidelines will vary somewhat from lender to lender, so you'll want to check with your mortgage lender for specific requirements.

Once you determine how much you can spend on your monthly mortgage payment, you're on your way to finding out how much home you can afford. The loan interest rate you pay also will make a big difference. For example, you'll be able to buy a higher-priced home if you pay 8% interest than if you pay 10% interest. Your real estate broker should be able to help you estimate your interest rate and then figure a realistic price range which should guide your home search.

When figuring how much home you can afford, don't forget to consider the down payment. Generally, you'll need to come up with 10% to 20% of the purchase price of the home to meet down payment requirements. However, depending on the lender, you may be able tobuy a home with a down payment of as little as 3%. You should shop around for the best terms.

## * Decide What Type Of Home Is Best For You

Deciding on the right home for your needs requires some time and thought. Is your dream home a traditional single-family house, a condominium, or a multifamily unit? You should make a list of your priorities for the home. Consider the length of time you plan to live in the home. Will you need more room to accommodate a growing family or less space as your children move away? Make a list of your priorities and needs, and then determine what type of home is right for you and your family.

## * Location, Location, Location!

According to the "real estate brokers' rule" the three most important factors in buying a home all involve location. While that's a tongue-in-cheek rule, location should be a major consideration. Is the house close to work, shopping, school, and recreation facilities? What's the crime rate? How good are the local schools? Are there any medical facilities nearby? These are just some of the questions you should ask about the location of any home you're considering.

The following home shopping checklist can help answer any concerns you may have about a home's location. Of course, you can add (or subtract) items to the checklist to address your particular concerns.

| — Neighborhood | Good | Average | Poor |
|---|---|---|---|
| Appearance/condition of nearby homes/businesses | ____ | ____ | ____ |
| Traffic | ____ | ____ | ____ |
| Safety/Security | ____ | ____ | ____ |
| Age mix of residents | ____ | ____ | ____ |
| Number of children | ____ | ____ | ____ |
| Parking | ____ | ____ | ____ |
| Fire Protection | ____ | ____ | ____ |
| Police | ____ | ____ | ____ |
| Zoning Regulation | ____ | ____ | ____ |

| — Near to: | | | |
|---|---|---|---|
| Schools | ____ | ____ | ____ |
| Work | ____ | ____ | ____ |
| Supermarket/Shopping | ____ | ____ | ____ |
| Hospitals/Doctor/Dentist | ____ | ____ | ____ |
| Parks/Recreation | ____ | ____ | ____ |
| Church/Synagogue | ____ | ____ | ____ |
| Major highways | ____ | ____ | ____ |

| — Schools | | | |
|---|---|---|---|
| Age/condition | ____ | ____ | ____ |
| Reputation | ____ | ____ | ____ |
| Quality of Teachers | ____ | ____ | ____ |
| Curriculum | ____ | ____ | ____ |
| Class Size | ____ | ____ | ____ |
| Busing distance | ____ | ____ | ____ |

## * Find A Good Real Estate Broker

Once you've decided to buy a home, you'll want to start searching for a broker. Talk to several, and choose someone you think understands your interests. Ask friends, relatives and co-workers for recommendations. You can find out which brokers specialize in the kind of home or the area you want by looking in the Yellow Pages or the classified real estate ads in your local newspaper. You also can drive through various neighborhoods and take note of the broker's names on "for sale" signs.

An experienced real estate broker will be able to tell you about the areas and types of homes in which you're interested. He/she also can help you locate a home within your price range and explain the advantages and disadvantages of different types of mortgages. Of course, you'll have to pay a broker's commission for such help, so make sure you're getting the best deal.

It may pay you to choose a "buyer's broker." These real estate professionals work exclusively for potential buyers, and will negotiate the purchase price of a home on the buyer's behalf (see "Dealing Successfully With Real Estate Brokers" later in this chapter).

## * Get A Professional Home Inspection

Before you commit to buying a home, you should be certain it's in good condition. That's why it's a good idea to get a professional inspection of any home you're considering— even before you make an offer. A home inspection will enable you to learn as much as you can about the condition of the property and the need for any major repairs before you buy. It can help you minimize unpleasant and costly surprises afterwards.

You can find a qualified home inspector by checking the Yellow Pages under headings such as, "Building Inspection Service" or "Home Inspection Service." Your real estate broker also should be able to provide you with a list of home inspectors in your area. (See "Some Caveats If You're Looking At A Newly Built Home" later in this chapter for other sources of information about professional home inspectors).

### * Shop Around For The Best Deal On Financing

You can finance your home with a loan from a bank, a savings and loan, credit union, private mortgage company, or various state and federal government lenders (see Chapter 3). Shopping for a home loan is like shopping for any other major purchase— you'll save money by looking around for the best deal. Different lenders can offer substantially different interest rates and loan fees, so you should talk with several lenders before you decide. That way you'll have an idea of competitive rates and terms in your area.Ask your real estate broker for the names of lenders you can contact for loan information.

## Your State Government Wants To Help You Buy

If you're a first-time buyer or you meet certain low-to-moderate income requirements, you may be eligible for below-market-rate financing from your state housing agency. While the federal government offers reduced rate financing to some homebuyers, many state programs also make it easier for qualified buyers to finance the purchase of a new home. In fact, there are hundreds of state housing programs offering low-rate loans, down payment assistance, help with closing costs and settlement expenses, construction assistance for self-help builders, repossessed properties at low cost and with deferred payment loans, and many other programs providing assistance to first-time homebuyers. Most of the loans and financial assistance available through such state programs are administered by financial institutions.

You can get information about housing programs in your state by contacting the appropriate state housing agency from the list at the end of this chapter. You also can look in the "Blue Pages" of your phone book for addresses and numbers of local and state housing agencies for additional information.

## Home Buying With Nothing Down

Traditionally, lenders have required a down payment equal to 20% of the price of a home to get a home loan or mortgage. For many people, a down payment of 20% is the biggest obstacle they face when buying a home.

The good news is that more and more lenders are now granting home loans to qualifying home buyers with little or no down payment required. In fact, home loans with down payments of less than 20% (some as low as 3%) are increasingly common. For example, the Federal National Mortgage Association (Fannie Mae), has been offering loans requiring a 3% down payment to low- and moderate-income borrowers since 1994 (you can get a free list of Fannie Mae lenders in your area by calling 800-732-6643). And borrowers who put down less than 10% accounted for 22% of all mortgages in 1995.

Some lenders have launched programs that allow borrowers to pledge bank certificates of deposit equal to at least 10% of the home price in lieu of traditional down payments. The CD, which can belong to the buyer or a relative, cannot, however, be used to cover loan fees and closing costs. The borrower is still required to come up with 3% of the home's purchase price, which can, in turn, be used to pay all fees and closing costs.

The following two popular government programs also offer low down payment loans and in some cases, if you qualify, no down payment is required.

* Veterans Administration (VA) Loans: If you're currently in the armed services or you're a military veteran, you may qualify for a VA loan that allows you to buy a home without making a down payment (you will, however, have to pay closing costs). To be eligible for a VA loan, you must be a qualified veteran, the unmarried widow of a veteran, or on active duty (check with the VA, 1-800-827-1000 to find out about eligibility requirements) and have a certificate of eligibility from the government. The maximum amount for a VA loan without a down payment is $184,000. If you or your spouse have been in the military, it'll pay you to check into a VA loan.

* Federal Housing Administration (FHA) Loan: This type of loan is a good choice for the first-time buyer who isn't eligible for a VA loan. Most FHA loans allow borrowers to finance some of their closing costs, and the down payment requirement is generally much less than that of most conventional loans.

The FHA loan program was set up so that Americans who can't afford the 10% to 20% down payment required by most lenders can still buy a home. An FHA loan will allow you to purchase a home with as little as 3% down. However, in some instances, no downpayment is required. The FHA will recognize "sweat equity"— your own labor— as all or part of the down payment on a house you are building. There are specific guidelines you must follow in order to qualify, but generally you may be able to use your own labor in building your home in lieu of a downpayment.

You also may be able to take advantage of sweat equity when applying for a conventional home loan. Many banks will recognize your personal efforts to reduce construction costs on a home you're building, translating your labor (sweat equity) into the required down payment. Not all lenders will accept sweat equity as down payment, so you should check with area financial institutions if you're interested in this aspect of financing a new home.

Another option for buying without a down payment is to find a partner. In this scenario, your partner, who could be a relative, friend or business associate, provides the down payment. In return, you agree to make the mortgage payments, maintain the property in good condition, and make improvements while you live in the house. Then, when (or if) you sell the house, you'll split any profit with your partner— or you can repay him/her at a higher rate of interest. Obviously this option isn't for everyone, but if you do bring in a partner, make sure you write up a legal contract to specify exactly how the partnership is to work.

You also might consider looking for a home on which the seller is behind two or three mortgage payments. In such a case, the seller is likely to be flexible in his/her terms, and you can negotiate a deal requiring little or no down payment.

While there are many programs that allow borrowers to buy without a down payment, most buyers still can't get a loan unless they pay at least 10% of a home's purchase in cash. The smart thing to do is shop around for a lender offering the best terms possible.

## Some Caveats If You're Looking At A Newly Built Home

For most people, the American dream includes owning a home that is uniquely theirs— a home no one else has occupied. Purchasing a newly-built home is one way to realize such a dream because it's new and it's yours. However, if you're not careful when buying a newly built home, your dream could end up being a nightmare.

The main thing to remember when considering a newly built home is that new doesn't necessarily mean quality. Even though the house has never been lived in, it still could be "falling apart" due to poor quality construction materials and incompetent workmanship. As a buyer, you must pay attention to detail and inspect the home and its builder thoroughly before you make a commitment. Otherwise, you could find yourself stuck with a seemingly never ending barrage of costly repair and maintenance bills.

With these caveats in mind, here are several things you should do before buying a newly built home:

## * Check out the builder and the quality of materials used.

Contact the Better Business Bureau in your area to find out whether or not the contractor has a history of complaints from dissatisfied customers. Also find out the brand names of materials and products used including the heating/cooling system, faucets, windows, bath fixtures and flooring. Keep in mind that a good price on a home can be negated by poor quality workmanship and cheap materials.

## * Have the home inspected

The best way to avoid getting stuck with a poorly built new home is to conduct a thorough home inspection before you buy. That way you'll be aware of any existing or potential problems and be better able to make an informed decision on whether or not to buy. A thorough inspection should include the home's heating/cooling system, plumbing and electrical systems, roof, attic and visible insulation, ceilings, walls, floors, windows, doors, foundation, basement, and the visible structure.

If you feel competent to do so, you can conduct such a home inspection yourself or you can hire a professional home inspector to check out the house for you. You can find a professional home inspector in your area by contacting one or more of the following sources:

— the American Society of Home Inspectors,
85 West Algonquin Road,
Arlington Heights, IL 60005; (708) 290-1919.

— the National Association of Property Inspectors,
303 W. Cypress, San Antonio, TX 78212-0528;
(800) 486-3676;

— American Real Property Inspection,
26133 U.S. 19th N. Suite 301, Clearwater, FL 34623;
(800) 947-2774.

### * Check out the warranty

It's important that a builder stands behind his/her work. Otherwise, if problems arise, you could end up being involved in a lengthy and expensive legal battle. Some builders may try to include clauses that place restrictions on "implied warranties" or on the builder's responsibility to compensate buyers if problems occur. You should demand a clear warranty that doesn't limit your rights as a consumer.

### * Make sure you know what you're paying for

If you're considering a newly built model home, make sure you find out what's standard and what's optional. In some cases, builders furnish the model with expensive furniture and extras that aren't clearly defined as such. As a result, you could end up paying extra for items you thought were included in the sales price.

### * Have the home tested for radon

Radon is a naturally occurring, odorless carcinogenic gas that could seep into your home and cause major health problems. In fact, contamination by radon is considered a potential health threat in all 50 states, affecting at least 10% of all American homes.

Any home— new or used—may have a radon problem. This includes well-sealed and drafty homes, and homes with or without basements. As a precautionary measure, you should consider having any home you're considering, including a newly built home, tested for radon. There are many kinds of inexpensive, do-it-yourself radon test kits you can get through the mail and in hardware stores and other retail outlets. Make sure you buy a test kit that has passed the EPA's testing program or is state-certified. These kits usually will display the phrase "Meets EPA Requirements." If you prefer, you can hire a trained contractor to do the testing for you. You can call 800-SOS RADON to locate your state radon office, which, in turn, can provide you with a list of qualified contractors in your area. You also may be able to have radon testing done as a contingency of the contract to buy.

While ownership of a new home can be a dream come true, it shouldn't be entered into on impulse or emotion alone. Caution is a consumer's best ally in making any transaction and buying a newly built home is no different. While the price, outward appearance and location all may be appealing, there could be a number of problems that could detract considerably from that appeal.

## Consider Building Instead Of Buying

The decision whether to buy a previously owned property or to build your own home depends on several factors. Cost obviously is a major consideration. If your funds are limited, a previously owned home may be your most affordable option. However, there are other considerations besides cost that should figure into your decision as well.

There are several advantages to building instead of buying a new home. When you build your own home, you're involved in the entire process— planning, financing, design, construction and closing. You can have the home built to your exact specifications, including the floor plan you want, number of rooms, landscaping and so on. And a well-designed and built home in a good neighborhood will appreciate in value rapidly.

Another big advantage to building is that a new home has a warranty. A one-year warranty is standard but many contractors now are offering 10-year warranties for additional protection. On the other hand, a previously owned home may have, at best, a limited warranty with great risks.

While an existing home may be your least expensive option, you may not be getting the home you really want. The best way to do that is to build it yourself. If you do decide to build rather than buy, you'll want to hire the best contractor to do the job.

## Surviving The Remodeling Jungle

If you plan on remodeling your home, you'd better be prepared. Growth in the home remodeling industry has led to an increase in fraud and shoddy work. According to industry insiders, "fly-by-night" remodeling contractors are very common. Whether you're spending money to remodel your kitchen, bath, family room, or an addition, you should shop around for a contractor, and by all means, verify that the remodeler you choose is bona fide.

Here are some insider guidelines to follow when entering the remodeling jungle:

* Plan ahead. Know what you want or need to have done before contacting a contractor.

* Get detailed estimates from reputable contractors. Keep in mind that a low bid isn't necessarily the best. "Low-ball" bids sometimes come from contractors who operate without insurance or skimp on work or materials to keep their prices down. Generally, three or four bids should be obtained on a major remodeling project.

* Contact your local or state consumer agency or Better Business Bureau (listed in the Blue Pages of your phone directory) for information on contractors' licensing or registration, complaint records and for brochures containing advice. Also ask any prospective remodeler to supply current references— preferably from jobs recently completed or underway.

* Check to see if contractors are members of recognized trade associations, such as the National Association of the Remodeling Industry (NARI) and the Remodelers Council of the National Association of Home Builders.

* Contact your local building inspection department to check for permit and inspection requirements.

* Call your insurance company to find out if you're covered for any injury or damage that might occur. Also find out whether or not your contractor has the required insurance (worker's compensation and liability) for his/her workers and subcontractors. You may even contact the contractor's insurance company to be sure the policy is in force.

* Insist on a complete written contract. Know exactly what work will be done, the quality of materials that the contractor will use, timetables, the names of subcontractors, the total price of the job and the schedule of payments.

\* Find out whether or not you have cancellation rights (typically, within three business days). Many home remodeling contracts include such rights, but you should find out for certain before you sign a contract. Check with your local or state consumer protection agency to find out if you have cancellation rights and, if so, how they apply.

\* Understand your payment schedule. You can get your own loan or the contractor might arrange financing. Either way, be sure you have a reasonable payment schedule at a fair interest rate.

\* Find out what lien rights apply where you live. In some states, lien rights might give the contractor or subcontractors the ability to "attach" your house for unpaid bills. Your local or state consumer agency can explain how lien rights apply where you live.

\* Be especially wary if a contractor:

— comes door-to-door or attempts to get your business by telephone solicitations;

— just happens to have material left over from a recent job:

— promises a lower price if you allow your remodeling job to be used as a "demonstration" or model to advertise his/her work;

— offers you discounts for finding him/her other customers;

— quotes a suspiciously low price for the work you want done;

— pressures you for an immediate decision;

— can be reached only by leaving messages with an answering service; or

— has a company name, address, and telephone number and other credentials that can't be verified.

The American Homeowners Foundation (6776 Little Falls Road, Arlington, VA 22213; 703-536-7776) offers a model contract that can help you avoid the pitfalls of a remodeling project. The contract includes tips on how to find a qualified contractor and provides for agreements on such important points as the payment and work completion schedules, changes in contract and the correction of deficiencies. You can get a copy of the six-page model contract by sending a check or money order for $6.95 to the American Homeowners Foundation.

The National Association of Home Builders also offers detailed information about remodeling on its Internet site, The Home Page. The site— http://www.nahb.com— will be updated frequently so that the latest information is available.

## Cash In On Home Improvements

Now that you've been forewarned about the risks of remodeling your house, consider the benefits. Obviously, the improvements made to your home— adding a deck, remodeling your kitchen, etc.-- provide immediate benefits in comfort, convenience, and appearance. Such improvements also offer long-term benefits, especially if you decide to sell your house. The costs of permanent home improvements, while nondeductible, are added to the basis (generally, the amount you paid for the property) of your property. The basis is your starting point for figuring a gain or a loss if you later sell your home.

To qualify as a permanent improvement, rather than a repair (which is considered a nondeductible personal expense), the work done must add to the value of your home or prolong its life. For example, permanent improvements might include putting a recreation room in your unfinished basement, adding another bedroom or bathroom, putting up a fence, putting in new plumbing, or paving your driveway (some other examples of IRS-accepted home improvements are listed below).

The amount you add to the basis of your home for permanent improvements is your actual cost, including any amount you borrowed. This includes all costs for material and labor (except your own labor), and all expenses related to the improvement. For example, if you have your property surveyed to put up a fence, the cost of the survey should be considered as a part of the cost of the fence.

In order to cash in on home improvements when you sell your home, you'll need to keep good records. Besides your home's purchase price and purchase expenses, your records also should include receipts and other proof of improvements that affect the basis of your home. It's important that your records include the date of any improvements as well as their actual cost.

## * Examples of IRS-accepted Home Improvements

Keep in mind that the IRS considers work you do—or have done— on your home that does not add much to the value or the life of your property, but rather maintains the property in good condition, a repair, not an improvement. To qualify as a permanent improvement, the work must add to the value of your house, prolong its life or adapt it to new uses.

— **Additions**: bedroom, bathroom, deck, garage, porch, patio.

— **Lawn & Gardens**: landscaping, driveway, walkway, fence, retaining wall, sprinkler system, swimming pool.

— **Heating & Air Conditioning**: heating system, central air conditioning, furnace, duct work, central humidifier, filtration system.

— **Plumbing**: septic system, water heater, soft water system, filtration system.

— **Interior improvements**: built-in appliances, kitchen modernization, flooring, wall-to-wall carpeting.

— **Insulation**: attic, walls, floor, pipes, duct work.

— **Miscellaneous**: storm windows and/or doors, new roof, central vacuum, wiring upgrades, satellite dish, security system.

## Dealing Successfully With Real Estate Brokers

If you're in the market to buy, a real estate broker can tell you what is or might soon be available and can give you an accurate picture of the current local mortgage lending activity. However, brokers are generally paid by the seller and therefore may not reveal every fault of a house. In fact, they may "exaggerate" the good qualities of the property in order to make a sale. While your goal is to buy the house you want for as low a price as possible, the broker's goal is to get you to spend as much as possible.

The thing to keep in mind when dealing with a seller's broker is that the more you are willing to pay for a home the bigger the broker's commission. That means that the broker has a keen incentive to get you to pay as high a price as possible. The best way to deal successfully in such an instance is to be prepared. Gather current information on the market and have a definite spending limit in mind. Be discreet with the broker, giving him/her a general price range without revealing how high you're willing to go. If you tell the broker how high you'll go in making an offer he/she will tell the seller and you may end up paying much more for the house than the seller would have been willing to accept.

If you do decide to use a real estate broker to help you buy a home, you may want to consider a "buyer's broker." As the name suggests, a buyer's broker works in the interest of the buyer and not the seller. If you hire a buyer's broker, he/she will be working for you and will be legally responsible for negotiating the best price, and identify any problems with the property or the neighborhood (other than those a seller is required to disclose).

To find a buyer's broker, check your local phone directory. You also may contact Buyer's Resource (800) 359-4092, a Denver-based company with 40 offices in 13 states that specialize in buyer's brokers. If you don't live in one of those states, Buyer's Resource also provides a referral service involving more than 500 buyer's brokers across the country. Buyer's Resource doesn't charge for a referral and will answer any questions you might have about the buyer's broker process. Another source for finding a qualified buyer's broker is the Buyer's Broker Registry, P.O. Box 23275, Ventura, CA 93002; (800) 729-5147. The Buyer's Registry also has posted its 700 to 800 agent list online at HTTP://WWW.U-BUILD.COM/WHOWHO/BBR.HTM .

You also may contact the American Homeowners Foundation(AHF), (800) 489-7776. The AHF, through a program called "Buyers Power!" offers free referrals to exclusive buyer's brokers.

If you're ready to sell your house the first thing you should do is decide whether or not to use a broker. While realtors (members of the National Association of Realtors) and other licensed brokers will bring in many prospective buyers, their fee is usually 5 to 7 percent of the selling price. If you can afford such a fee, a broker can provide many services and help you get top dollar for your home.

Typically, a broker appraises your property and estimates what price it might bring, arranges an open house, provides a listing fact sheet, takes care of advertising, shows the house, and helps close the sale. In other words, the broker is involved in the entire process from start to finish.

Once you choose a broker, he/she will list your property in one of several ways. Each type of listing has its advantages and disadvantages, and you should try to get the one that is most likely to work for you.

* With an "open listing" you list your home with several brokers, but only the selling broker gets a commission. Under this type of listing you can even sell the home yourself. If you sell the property yourself, you don't have to pay anyone commission. You may have a tough time getting a broker to agree to this type of listing arrangement, because he/she isn't guaranteed a commission.

* Under an "exclusive agency listing" you pick one broker and pay a commission only if he/she sells the home. However, if you find a buyer, you don't pay the commission. Since this type of agreement gives only one broker the right to earn a commission, he/she may be motivated to give an extra effort to selling your house.

* An "exclusive right to sell" listing means that the broker gets his/her commission regardless of who sells the home. Be wary of this type of arrangement, because you lose the right to sell the home yourself without paying the broker a commission.

* Under a "multiple listing" arrangement any broker you use may handle your home exclusively or share the listing with other brokers. This type of listing guarantees your broker some commission no matter who sells the home. The broker who actually sells the home splits his/her commission with the broker you hired. Depending on your agreement, you may have to pay the commission even if you locate a buyer yourself without the help of a broker.

Make sure you read any agreement carefully before you sign it, and have your lawyer negotiate for any changes you would like. Listing agreements may run anywhere from one to six months, and you'll still owe commission if the sale is made up to a certain amount of time after the expiration and if the buyer looked at the house while it was listed. However, both time periods are negotiable.

## A Comprehensive Guide To Selling Your Home Yourself

If you decide to avoid a real estate broker's fee, you can try to sell your home yourself. Saving the broker's fee gives you the option of lowering the price for a faster sale or keeping the proceeds. However, you'll have to finance your own advertising and promotion.

Here's a basic step-by-step guide for selling your home yourself:

* Decide on a price. You can get an idea of prices for comparable homes by looking at ads and listings for similar

homes in your area and by checking recent sales records with the local tax assessor. You also can get opinions from several real estate agents as to how much your home should bring. Or, if you don't mind the expense, you can have your home appraised by a professional. An independent appraisal by a professional appraiser will enable you to set a fair and reasonable price for your home. You can find a professional appraiser by contacting the National Association of Master Appraisers, P.O. Box 12617, 303 W. Cypress Street, San Antonio, TX 78212-0617; (800) 229-NAMA; or the Appraisal Institute, 875 N. Michigan Avenue, Suite 2400, Chicago, IL 60611-1980; (312) 335-4100.

* Market your home agressively. Begin by placing ads in area newspapers. Detail what makes your property unique and worth every penny of the asking price. Also state, at the end of the ad, that the home is for sale by the owner. That's an indication to potential buyers that they may get a lower price because there's no agent's commission to pay. You also can place a large "for sale by owner" sign in your front yard. The sign should include your name and phone number. You even may want to hold an open house on weekends in order to attract potential buyers.

* Get your home ready to show. Look at your house for faults as if you were a buyer, then fix it up to look its best. Paint, clean, cut the grass, trim the shrubbery and remove excess furniture and clutter from the rooms. You also might prepare a one-page description of your home's features, and include a photo and floor plan to further entice prospective buyers. Your description should include the age of the house, lot size, room sizes, taxes, and costs for utilities and water. Also specify what comes with the house, such as carpets and appliances. Have plenty of copies of your description sheet on hand and make sure you're available whenever a potential buyer wants to drop by and inspect your home.

*   Disclose all of your home's problems in writing to prospective buyers. Your disclosure document should include any problems related to the home's structure, utilities, and municipal status (building permits, zoning restrictions, property tax rates, etc). In many states, such disclosure is required. Even if it isn't required by law in your state, furnishing such a document is still a good idea. A buyer's signature on such a sales disclosure document serves as proof that he/she was informed of the home's problems and absolves you of further responsibility for any of the problems listed on the document.

* Have a real estate lawyer draw up a sales contract and make sure all the closing details are handled correctly. A sales contract, also known as a contract to purchase, should include a description of the property and all the terms of the sale, including the price and the method of payment. Also make sure that the contract specifically mentions everything that will stay or go, and keep insurance in force until after the official closing of the sale.

## Remodeling Can Cut Your Taxes When You Sell

Remodeling or restoration improvements, such as building a garage; adding a room; bathroom remodeling and landscaping, while costly and nondeductible, can pay off handsomely if you decide to sell. The cost of such remodeling is added to the basis of your home increasing its value thus reducing your taxable gain on a profitable sale.

For example, remodeling improvements which generally will add the most immediate profitable resale value to your home include bathroom and kitchen remodeling, adding a second bath or another bedroom, new carpeting, wallpaper and decorating. With the increased value due to such remodeling, you're likely to realize a significant gain when you sell the home. And the IRS allows you to post-pone the tax on the gain on the sale of your home if you meet certain qualifications (see the following section, "Other Items You Can Use to Eliminate Taxes When You Sell").

It's important that you be aware of the distinction between what the IRS considers remodeling improvements and repairs. That's because repairs, such as fixing your gutters or floors, repairing leaks or plastering, and replacing broken window panes, while maintaining your home in good condition, do not "add to its value or prolong its life" and you can't add their cost to the basis of your property. However, the cost of remodeling work which enhances your home and adds to its value, such as replacing an entire roof, paving your driveway, installing central air conditioning, and rewiring your home, can be added to the basis of your property when you sell.

## Other Items You Can Use To Eliminate Taxes When You Sell

There are several ways you can save on taxes when you sell your home. One of, the most commonly overlooked tax write-offs involves increases to the tax basis of property sold. Many people overlook this tax break because there is no immediate deduction at the time expenses such as the costs of remodeling or permanent home improvements are incurred. As noted earlier in this chapter, such expenditures can be added to the basis of your property when you sell. But in order to take advantage of this deduction, you must keep accurate records of all expenditures that enhance the value of your home.

Every qualified expenditure will increase your basis and will, in turn, reduce your taxable gain on a profitable sale. There are many items that can increase your basis including obvious capital improvements that increase the value of your property and lengthen its life, the cost of extending utility lines to the property, and legal fees, such as the cost of defending and perfecting a title. It's a good idea to check with your tax preparer for a list of what qualifies as a capital expenditure to increase your basis. If you prepare your own taxes, the IRS can provide you with information about current allowable expenditures.

Remember, in order to take advantage of this tax write-off, you must keep accurate records. Without documented proof of capital expenditures, you'll have no way of convincing the IRS that you qualify for this deduction when you sell your home.

Other ways to save taxes when you sell include the following:

## * Postponing or Deferring Gain

This IRS-approved tax break allows you to postpone or defer tax on gain from the sale of your main residence. Generally, you can defer taxes on gain if you sell your main home and purchase a new primary residence of equal or greater value within the replacement period of two years either before or after the sale of your home. You also can defer tax on gain if you buy a home of lesser value and use the difference in price to renovate the new home within two years.

In order to qualify for this tax deferment, you must meet the following test:

— The home you sell and the one you buy to replace it must both qualify as your main home. Generally, the home you live in most of the time is considered your main home.

— You must buy and occupy a new house within two years before or after the date of the sale.

— You must build or buy a new main home at a cost at least equal to the amount you received from the sale of your old primary residence.

### * Exclusion of $125,000 Capital Gain

You can choose to exclude from income $125,000 of gain on the sale of your main home ($62,500 if you're married on the date of the sale and file separate returns) if you meet the following IRS age, ownership, and use tests:

**1)** You were 55 or older on the date of the sale.

**2)** You must have owned and lived in your primary residence for at least 3 of the past five years before the sale.

You can use this $125,000 exclusion on the profit from the sale of your main residence only once. If you're 55 or older and planning to marry someone who's already used the exclusion, you might want to consider selling your house and taking the exclusion before you marry. Once you're married, the IRS will not allow you to claim this exclusion if your spouse has already used it on the sale of a previous home.

Adding to your basis to reduce taxable gain, deferring gain, and the $125,000 exclusion are, like other tax matters, complicated. If you are considering using any of these items to cut your taxes, you should first consider consulting your tax preparer or a tax attorney to determine whether or not you qualify. You also can get more information about these and other tax matters involved in the selling of your home by contacting the IRS at (800) 829-3676 and ordering Publication 523, "Selling Your Home." There's no charge for the publication.

## Don't Overpay Your Homeowners Insurance

One of the major concerns of every homeowner is insurance. In fact, Americans spend over $17 billion a year on insurance policies to protect their property from theft, burglary, fire, windstorms, floods, and other perils. It's a part of home ownership that requires careful consideration because being underinsured can be disastrous in the event of a loss. However, in your zeal to get the most comprehensive coverage possible, you also may be "overinsured." In that case you'll end up paying more than you should. Here are several ways you can avoid "overpaying" your homeowners insurance:

**\* Shop Around For The Best Policy At A Fair Price**

Comparison shopping is the best way to get the coverage you need at the most reasonable price. You'll need to do some research and contact several insurers but the results could be a savings of hundreds of dollars. Ask your friends and colleagues, check the Yellow Pages or contact your state insurance department for a list of potential insurers. You also can check consumer guides at your local library, insurance agents and companies to get an idea of prices and services offered. Get price quotes from three to five insurers before you make a decision. Go with the company that offers the type of coverage and service you need at the best price.

**\* Raise Your Deductible**

Deductibles are the amount of money you have to pay "out-of-pocket" toward a claim before your insurance company starts to pay according to the terms of your policy. Just as with your auto insurance (see chapter 1), you can raise the deductible on your homeowners policy and reduce your costs. For example, the minimum deductible on a typical homeowners policy is $250. Depending on your insurance company, you could save as much as 12 percent by increasing that deductible to $500. You could save up to 24 percent by increasing a $250 deductible to $1000.

## * Purchase Your Home And Auto Policies From The Same Insurer

Many companies that sell homeowner's, auto and liability coverage will take up to 15 percent off your premium if you buy two or more policies from them.

## * Insure Your House But Not Your Land

The land your house sits on isn't at risk from dangers such as high winds, theft, or fire covered in your homeowner's policy. So there's no reason to include the land's value when purchasing a homeowner's policy. If you do, you'll end up paying a higher premium than you should.

## * Take Advantage Of Home Security Discounts

Most insurers offer discounts of 5 percent or more for a smoke detector, burglar alarm, or dead-bolt locks. Some companies offer discounts of up to 20 percent to homeowners who install sophisticated sprinkler systems and burglar alarms that ring at the police station or other monitoring stations. Since these systems are expensive, and not every system qualifies for a discount, it's a good idea to ask your insurer for recommendations before you purchase any security device.

## * Kick the Tobacco Habit

Besides being bad for your health, smoking also presents a risk to your home. According to the Insurance Information Institute, smoking is to blame for more than 23,000 residential fires a year. It's that risk that motivates some insurers to offer lower premiums if all residents in a house are non-smokers.

## * Don't Pay For Coverage You Don't Need

While your policy should cover major purchases and/or additions to your home, you should make sure older possessions are still worth including in your policy.

Insurance industry insiders recommend that you compare the limits of your homeowner's policy and the value of your possessions "at least once a year."

### * Get A "Loyal Customer" Discount

Many insurers reward customers who have maintained their policies for several years with reduced premiums. If you've kept your coverage with the same company for three to five years, you may be eligible for a discount of up to 5 percent. If you remain a policy holder for at least six years, your premium may be reduced by as much as 10 percent.

### * Ask About Discounts For Senior Citizens

Some insurers offer discounts of up to 10 percent to homeowners who are at least 55 years old and retired.

You can get more information about homeowners insurance by contacting your state insurance department (see chapter 1). You also can call the National Insurance Consumer Helpline at 1-800-942-4242.

## "Casing" Your Home Security

Once you have home insurance your "castle" is secure. You have no need to worry about the moods of mother nature or thieves who may covet your belongings. After all, you're paying for protection.

It'd be nice if things in the real world worked that way. Unfortunately, they don't. High winds still can rip the roof off your home and crooks can steal your belongings. And while a good home insurance policy covers you against such losses it can't prevent them from happening.

Actually, nothing can prevent high winds and other "acts of nature" from causing damage to your home and property. That's a risk every homeowner has to live with. Theft, however, is another matter altogether. You can take action to discourage thieves from entering your home and avoid the loss of valued property and potential danger to you and your family. In fact, law enforcement authorities say that you can be the "single most important deterrent to residential burglary."

How serious a problem is residential burglary? According to a recent national study, more than 6.5 million such burglaries occur every year. That's the equivalent of one out of every twelve households. Over 700 burglaries occur every hour— one every five seconds. The victims of those burglaries reported losses of over 1.5 billion dollars— an average of $526 per burglary. Those figures reveal that residential burglary is indeed a real and present danger for most homeowners. It's a danger that requires immediate preventive action.

The first step toward making your home more secure against would-be burglars is to recognize that your home could be an easy target. You can do that by "casing" your home security. Honest answers to the following home security survey can help you determine whether or not you have any problems to correct.

## — Home Security Survey

**yes**  **no**

[ ]   [ ]   Are there trees or shrubs around doors or windows that a burglar could use for cover?

[ ]   [ ]   Are any entrances to your home— both front and back— unlighted?

[ ]    [ ]    Are any openings to your home (sky-lights, vents, crawl spaces) unprotected?

[ ]    [ ]    Are any entrances, including garage and inside doors, unlocked?

[ ]    [ ]    Are your exterior doors secured with dead bolt locks (with a minimum one- inch throw)?

[ ]    [ ]    Are all of your exterior doors strong enough to withstand excessive force (at least 1 1/4 inch thick)?

[ ]    [ ]    Are sliding doors and windows secure against forced locks and/or lifting out of their frames? Could a burglar slide such a door open from the outside and climb in?

[ ]    [ ]    Do you have a peephole viewer on the main entrance door?

[ ]    [ ]    Have you secured double-hung windows with removable nail pins or extra locks to prevent them from being jimmied?

[ ]    [ ]    Do you ever leave your house keys with your car keys when your car is parked?

[ ]    [ ]    Whenever you leave home for an extended period, can strangers tell you're gone?

[ ]      [ ]      Do you have a burglar alarm that would activate if an intruder broke into your home?

If, after answering the above questions, you find any areas where security is weak or nonexistent, you should correct the problem(s) immediately. Here are several ways you can beef up your home security:

* Trim trees and shrubbery away from doors and windows. This is a good way to eliminate a would-be burglar's cover.

* Install outside lighting in back and front of your house to eliminate dark areas around doors and windows.

* Keep doors and windows locked as much as possible. Nearly one-quarter of break-ins are unforced entries.

* Make sure all outside doors are solid core in construction, or metal clad. Hollow doors give way easily to force. Also see that all door frames are of solid construction and are firmly attached to the house structure.

* Install non-removable hinges (available at most hardware stores) on any outside doors that require hinges. All outside doors also should have securely mounted deadbolts with one inch throws, which are difficult to pry or jimmy.

* Install a wide-angle lens peephole in the main entrance door. This will allow you to see visitors without opening the door. Also demand identification from all unfamiliar visitors including those who are wearing uniforms.

* Give sliding glass doors special security attention. To prevent both panels from being lifted up and out of the tracks,

secure the stationary panel with a screw from inside into the door and frame. The top track should have small screws protruding down so the door barely clears them.

Wedge a locked sliding door with a swinging metal rod to discourage entry if the lock is picked or broken. You also can wedge a sturdy wooden rod (such as a broom stick) into the bottom track.

* Prevent entry through double hung windows by drilling a hole, sloping downward through the top of the bottom sash and into (but not through) the bottom of the top sash. Insert a removable pin or nail in this hole to prevent a burglar from opening either sash. Also make sure that all casement window latches work properly. They should be strong and tight fitting.

* Before taking a trip, ask someone to watch your home, collect your mail and papers, and mow the lawn. Also use automatic timers for lights and a radio. The over-all effect will give your home a "lived-in" look and make potential burglars think you are home.

* Install an alarm system. Consider the choices and select an affordable system (keep in mind that price doesn't always indicate quality) that provides adequate protection. The system should protect all points of entry into your home. Contact your local police or sheriff's department for help in determining the best system for your home (and budget).

While no home is burglar-proof, taking these home security measures can frustrate a burglar by reducing or removing his/her opportunities. Simple, practical crime prevention techniques can be a homeowners best protection.

You can get additional information about home security by contacting the Insurance Information Institute (110 William Street, New York, NY 10038) and asking for a copy of the free brochure "Home Security Basics."

## Real Estate As An Investment

If you're looking for an income-producing investment you might consider real estate. You don't have to be a millionaire to get into the market, and unlike other investments, such as stocks, bonds and mutual funds, real estate provides a "hands-on" tangible asset that you can become involved with personally. When you own a piece of property you have direct control. You can renovate, landscape, add rooms and make any number of changes and improvements that can add to your property's value and appeal. In addition, as an investment, real estate can generate a steady income, appreciate in value, and allow you to take advantage of several substantial tax benefits.

The residential market, including single-family homes, as well as multiple-unit buildings such as condominiums and cooperatives, all can be relatively inexpensive ways for beginners to get into the real estate market. The success of this type of investment depends on several factors, including location, condition, available utilities, demand, and local economic factors and cycles. If you consider buying such real estate, you'll need to research all those factors thoroughly in order to make an informed investment decision. Regardless of the potential for profit, there also are risks involved in investing in real estate.

More experienced investors may step up to larger properties such as commercial buildings (office buildings, shopping centers, etc.) and industrial property (warehouses, manufacturing plants, etc.). This type of real estate investment, while a potential source of great wealth, also provides increased risk and requires an expertise usually possessed by more advanced investors.

Whether or not real estate is the right investment for you depends on many factors. Obviously, you'll need not only the capital to invest, but be willing to accept the risks involved as well. You'll also need to determine whether or not you're cut out to be a landlord. You'll be responsible for dealing with tenants, and maintaining your property— either doing maintenance work yourself or hiring someone to take care of it for you.

Besides money, you'll need to invest a lot of time and patience. Investing in real estate does not work well with a sedentary lifestyle. If you have the money, time, patience, and desire for a tangible, profitable investment, real estate may be the right choice for you.

The National Association of Realtors, the trade group for real estate agents, offers several helpful consumer-oriented publications including "If You're Thinking Investment, Think Real Estate." For a copy of this publication, contact the association at 430 N. Michigan Avenue, Chicago, IL 60611; (800) 874-6500.

## The Best Starting Place— Single-Family Homes

If you want to begin investing in real estate, you might consider starting with a single-family home. This is a good way to begin, especially if you don't have a lot of upfront capital to invest. The upfront costs required to purchase a single-family home are relatively low, and mortgage financing is usually available at affordable terms.

If you're looking for a long-term investment— 10 years or more— a single-family unit can provide substantial returns. On the other hand, short-term investment in such

property may not provide much potential for capital appreciation. Like all investing decisions, you'll need to consider
the risks involved and whether or not you're willing to wait
a few years to realize any appreciable returns on your
investment.

If you do decide to invest in single-family housing,
make sure you choose properties that are priced low
enough to ensure that your rental income can cover operating expenses and mortgage payments.

## Condos, Co-ops and Rehabs Can Get You Into The Market

While single-family houses often are recommended
for first-time investors, there are other ways to get into the
market, as well. Condos, co-ops and rehabs or fixer-uppers
also offer potential financial rewards as investment property.

### * Condos

Buying a condo— apartment units contained within a
group-owned building— will afford you, as the owner, all
the tax advantages of investing in real estate and home
ownership. Generally, condominium units cost less to buy,
and in most cases are easier to maintain than equivalent
single-family homes.

When you buy a condo, you receive a deed. You own
the unit you live in or rent, and ownership of common elements, such as entrances, elevators, yards, parking and
recreation facilities is shared with other unit owners. You'll
be responsible for your share of a monthly maintenance fee
for the upkeep of such areas, and within limitations, you'll
also be free to mortgage your unit or sell it.

If you're a first time investor, you might consider purchasing a condo and turning it into a rental unit. If you purchase the right property at a reasonable price, your investment can pay off handsomely. However, you have to be careful to buy a property that can generate enough rental income to cover your ownership costs and bring you a profit on your investment.

### * Co-ops

When you purchase a co-op, you get shares of stock in the corporation that owns and manages the building. The number of shares depends upon the size of your condo unit. As a shareholder, you don't actually own any property— the corporation owns it all, including all common elements— and you'll be responsible for a monthly maintenance fee based on how many shares you own. Your monthly fee is a portion of the principal and interest on the building's mortgage, taxes, and maintenance costs. The co-op is governed by a shareholder-elected board of directors, who approve the sale of any unit and enforce by laws and rules to operate the building.

For many people, the appeal of investing in condos and/or co-ops is the cost. Generally, this type of real estate is less expensive than single-family houses, and maintenance is usually taken care of by an owner's association (you do have to pay monthly maintenance fees as your share of maintenance). Condos and co-ops also may provide you with better security than a single-family unit.

While both condos and co-ops can get you into the real estate market, you should enter only after careful consideration. Before buying either, you should do your homework, and be as certain as possible that any rental income is enough to cover ownership costs. Investigate the property's location and make sure it's in a convenient area with stores and public transportation nearby. Inspect your unit and the entire complex, including common areas, carefully, looking for potential and existing problems. You also should check the financial background of the owner or builder, especially if the units are new. Your area BBB can tell you whether or not there are any outstanding complaints against the owner or builder.

### * Rehabs

This type of investment isn't for everyone, but for some first-time investors it can be the ideal way to get into the market. If you're good at carpentry, electrical wiring, and making other repairs, or you can act as your own general contractor, this type of property can be a profitable investment. You can build equity in such property in a relatively short period of time and, in some cases, you can buy rehabs without a cash down payment.

Generally, when you want to buy a home which is in need of repair or modernization, you're required to obtain financing first to purchase the dwelling; additional financing to do the rehab work; and a permanent mortgage when the work is completed to pay off interim loans with a permanent mortgage. The U.S. Department of Housing and Urban Development's 203(k) program is designed to make things a little easier on the borrower. Under this program, qualified borrowers can get just one mortgage loan at a long-term fixed (or adjustable) rate, to finance both the acquisition and the rehabilitation of the property. To provide money for the rehabilitation, the mortgage amount is based on the "projected value" of the property when the rehabilitation has been completed, taking into account the cost of the work.

You can get more information about HUD's 203(k) program— eligibility requirements, maximum mortgage amounts available for investment property, etc.— by contacting an FHA-approved lender in your area. Names of 203(k) approved lenders in your area can be obtained from your area HUD Field Office.

Finding homes to rehab involves checking advertisements in area newspapers for "handyman specials" or "fixer-uppers." You should check each potential rehab thoroughly before you invest. The cost of needed renovations on some properties will be so great that they negate any profits you can expect to make. Make sure you have a good idea how much the renovations will cost before you make a commitment. Also make sure you know how to do the job. While rehabs can be appealing, they also can result in major headaches if you're not fully prepared to handle what will be required of you.

How you choose to cash in on your rehab investments calls for careful consideration. Once the necessary repairs and renovations are complete, you can choose to sell or rent the property. Either way, done properly, you can begin receiving returns from your rehab investment in a relatively short period of time.

## Stepping Up To Commercial Properties

Office buildings, shopping centers, industrial real estate and other commercial properties offer investors opportunities for substantial gain. However, the risks, especially for beginners, generally are much greater for this type of investment. That's largely because buying and managing become more complicated with larger properties. It takes experience in real estate investing along with a willingness and the financial resources to take on the risks.

To reduce the risks, you might want to consider investing in commercial property indirectly through a limited partnership or real estate investment trust (REIT). As a member of a limited partnership, you pool your investment capital with a group of investors to invest in large properties. Obviously this method of investing will cost you less and therefore reduce your risk. However, as a limited partner, you'll have less control over the property than if you were sole owner.

A REIT is a corporation which invests in real estate or mortgages. Since REIT shares trade on the stock exchange, you can get into the real estate market by purchasing a few shares of stock. This is a relatively easy and inexpensive way to invest in commercial properties without excessive risk. You also can sell your investment in exchange for cash in just a matter of days. However, REIT's also have their drawbacks, including a vulnerability to bad real estate markets.

Regardless of what type of real estate you decide to invest in, you'll need to do your homework and be aware of the risks. If you're patient, and can get the right property at a reasonable price, you'll be able to turn your investment into a profitable venture.

## * State-By-State Housing Agencies

### — Alabama:

Alabama Housing Finance Authority,
P.O. Box 230909, Montgomery, AL 36123-0909.

### — Alaska:

Alaska Housing Finance Corporation,
P.O. Box 101020, 235 East 8th Avenue,
Anchorage, AK 99510; (970) 561-1900.

### — Arizona:

Arizona Department of Commerce,
Office of Housing Development,
1700 West Washington, Phoenix, AZ 85007;
(602) 280-1365.

## — Arkansas:

Arkansas Development Finance Authority,
P.O. Box 8023, 100 Main Street, Suite 200,
Little Rock, AR 72203; (501) 682-5900.

## — California:

California Housing Finance Agency,
11211 L. Street, 7th Floor, Sacramento, CA 95815;
(916) 322-3991.

California Dept. of Housing and Community
Development,    P.O. Box 952050;
Sacramento, CA 94252-2050; (916) 322-1560.

## — Colorado:

Colorado Housing and Finance Authority,
1981 Blake Street, Denver, CO 80202;
(303) 297-7427.

## — Connecticut:

Connecticut Housing Finance Authority,
40 Cold Spring Road, Rocky Hill, CT 06067;
(203) 721-9501.

## — Delaware:

Delaware State Housing Authority,
Division of Housing and Community Development,
18 the Green, Dover, DE 19901; (302) 739-4263.

## — District of Columbia:

DC Housing Finance Agency,
1401 New York Avenue, NW, Suite 540,
Washington, DC 20005; (202) 408-0415.

## — Florida:

Florida Housing Finance Agency,
2571 Executive Center Circle East,
Tallahassee, FL 32399; (904) 488-4197.

## — Georgia:

Georgia Residential Finance Authority,
60 Executive Parkway South, Suite 250,
Atlanta, GA 30329; (404) 679-4840.

## — Hawaii:

Hawaii Housing Authority,
1001 North School Street, P.O. Box 17907,
Honolulu, HI 97817; (808) 848-3277.

## — Idaho:

Idaho Housing Agency, 760 W. Myrtle,
Boise, ID 83702; (208) 336-0161.

## — Illinois:

Illinois Housing Development Authority,
401 N. Michigan Ave., Suite 900, Chicago, IL 60611;
(312) 836-5200 or (800) 942-8439.

## — Indiana:

Indiana Housing Finance Authority,
One North Capitol, Suite 515, Indianapolis, IN 46204;
(317) 232-7777.

## — Iowa:

Iowa Finance Authority,
100 East Grand Avenue, Suite 250,
Des Moines, IA 50309; (515) 281-4058.

### — Kansas:

Kansas Office of Housing, Department of Commerce, 400 S.W. 8th, 5th Floor, Topeka, KS 66603; (913) 296-3481.

### — Kentucky:

Kentucky Housing Corporation, 1231 Louisville Road, Frankfort, KY 40601; (502) 564-7630 or (800) 633-8896.

### — Louisiana:

Louisiana Housing Finance Agency, 5615 Corporate, Suite 6A, Baton Rouge, LA 70808-2515; (504) 925-3675.

### — Maine:

Maine State Housing Authority, (207) 626-4600; (800) 452-4668.

### — Maryland:

Department of Housing and Community Development, 45 Calvert St., Annapolis, MD 21401; (301) 974-2176.

### — Massachusetts:

Massachusetts Housing Finance Agency, 50 Milk Street, Boston, MA 02190; (617) 451-3480.

### — Michigan:

Michigan State Housing Development Authority, Plaza One, Fourth Floor, 401 South Washington Square, P.O. Box 30044, Lansing, MI 48909; (517) 373-8370 or (800) 327-9158.

— **Minnesota**:

Minnesota Housing Finance Agency,
400 Sibley Street, St. Paul, MN 55101;
(612) 296-9951 or (800) 652-9747.


— **Mississippi**:

Mississippi Home Corporations,
510 George Street, Suite 107 Dickson Building,
Jackson, MS 39201; (601) 359-6700.


— **Missouri**:

Missouri Housing Development Commission,
3770 Broadway, Kansas City, MO 64111;
(816) 756-3790.


— **Montana**:

Montana Board of Housing,
2001 Eleventh Avenue, Helena, MT 59620;
(406) 444-3040.


— **Nebraska**:

Nebraska Investment Finance Authority,
1033 O Street, Suite 218, Lincoln, NE 68508;
(402) 434-3900.


— **Nevada**:

Department of Commerce, Housing Division,
1802 N. Carson Street, Suite 154,
Carson City, NV 89710; (702) 687-4258.


— **New Hampshire**:

Housing Finance Authority,
P.O. Box 5087, Manchester, NH 03108;
(603) 472-8623.

## — New Jersey:

New Jersey Housing Agency,
3625 Quakerbridge Road, Trenton, NJ 08650-2085;
(609) 890-1300.

## — New Mexico:

Mortgage Finance Authority,
P.O. Box 2047, Albuquerque, NM 87103;
(505) 843-6880 or (800) 444-6880.

New Mexico State Housing Authority,
1100 St. Francis Drive, Santa Fe, NM 87503;
(505) 827-0258.

## — New York:

State of New York, Executive Department,
Division of Housing and Community Renewal,
One Fordham Plaza, Bronx, NY 10458;
(212) 519-5700.

New York State Housing Authority,
250 Broadway, New York, NY 10007;
(212) 306-3000.

## — North Carolina:

North Carolina Housing Finance Agency,
3300 Drake Circle, Suite 200, Raleigh, NC 27611;
(919) 781-6115.

## — North Dakota:

Housing Finance Agency,
P.O. Box 1535, Bismarck, ND 58502;
(701) 224-3434.

## — Ohio:

Ohio Housing Finance Agency,
775 High Street, 26th Floor, Columbus, OH 43266;
(614) 466-7970.

## — Oklahoma:

Oklahoma Housing Finance Agency,
P.O. Box 26760, Oklahoma City, OK 73126-0720;
(405) 848-1144 or (800) 256-1489.

## — Oregon:

Oregon Housing Authority, Housing Division,
1600 State Street, Suite 100, Salem, OR 97310;
(503) 378-4343.

## — Pennsylvania:

Pennsylvania Housing Finance Agency,
2101 North Front Street, Harrisburg, PA 17105;
(717) 780-3800.

## — Rhode Island:

Rhode Island Housing and Mortgage Finance
Corporation, 60 Eddy Street, Providence, RI 02903;
(401) 751-5566.

## — South Carolina:

South Carolina State Housing Financing
and Development Authority,
1710 Gervais Street, Suite 300, Columbia, SC 29201;
(803) 734-8836.

## — South Dakota:

South Dakota Housing Development Authority,
P.O. Box 1237, Pierre, SD 57501; (605) 773-3181.

— **Tennessee**:

Tennessee Housing Development Agency,
700 Landmark Center, 401 Church Street,
Nashville, TN 37219; (615) 741-4979.

— **Texas**:

Texas Housing Authority,
P.O. Box 13941 Capitol Station, Austin, TX 78711;
(512) 472- 7500.

— **Utah**:

Utah Housing Finance Agency,
177 East South, Salt Lake City, UT 84111;
(801) 521-6950.

— **Vermont**:

Vermont Housing Finance Agency,
One Burlington Square, P.O. Box 408,
Burlington, VT 05402; (802) 864-5743.

Vermont State Housing Authority,
P.O. Box 397, Montpelier, VT 05601-0397;
(802) 828-3295.

— **Virginia**:

Department For the Aging,
700 East Franklin Street, 10th Floor,
Richmond, VA 23230; (804) 367-9818.

— **Washington**:

West Virginia Housing Development Fund,
814 Virginia Street, East, Charleston, WV 25301;
(304) 345-6475.

## — West Virginia:

Commission on Aging,
1900 Kanawha Building E.,
Charleston, WV 25305-0160; (304) 558-3317.

## — Wisconsin:

Wisconsin Housing and Economic Development
Authority, P.O. Box 1728, Madison, WI 53701;
(608) 266-7884 or (800) 362-2767.

## — Wyoming:

Wyoming Community Development Authority,
123 S. Durbin Street, P.O. Box 634,
Casper, WY 82602; (307) 265-0603.

**NOTES**

_____

_____

_____

_____

_____

_____

_____

---

> ## CHAPTER 3
> ## Mortgage Guide
> ## How To Borrow Big-Time For Less

---

You've found your dream home and you can't wait to move in. But, first things first. How will you finance the purchase?

You can finance your home with a loan from a bank, credit union, savings and loan, private mortgage company, with seller financing, or various state and national government lenders. There are a number of sources for home loans, providing a wide array of rates and terms, and you have to make the right choice.

Shopping for a home loan is like shopping for any other large purchase— you can save money if you take some time to shop around for the best price. Different lenders can offer quite different interest rates and loan fees and, as this chapter will reveal, a lower interest rate can make a big difference in how much home you can afford.

## Affordability Is The First Consideration

Before you start shopping for your dream home, you need to do some financial soul searching. And that involves figuring out how much you can reasonably afford to pay each month.

Generally, how much home you can afford depends on several factors, including your income, assets, expenses and debts, current interest rates on mortgages, the cash needed for a down payment, and closing costs. Most mortgage lenders expect you to be able to budget 28% to 30% of your gross income for housing expenses (including mortgage payments, property tax, home owner's insurance and utilities). Ideally, your total debts, including monthly housing costs, should not exceed 36% of your gross income. The lower your total debt, the more you should be able to budget for housing expenses.

The following charts, based on a Federal Housing Administration (FHA) formula used by many mortgage lenders, assumes that most people can afford to budget 29% of their gross monthly income to housing expenses, depending on total debt (people with little or no debt may be able to budget over 40% of monthly income to housing). The first chart will give you some idea of the amount you can afford to spend each month on total housing costs, by showing how much 29% of your monthly income is. The second chart shows how much your monthly mortgage payment might be (based on a 30-year fixed-rate mortgage) based on the selling price of the home you're considering.

## — Monthly Income

Locate your yearly income (or an amount close to it) in the "Annual Gross Income" column below. Then read across to find your monthly gross income and what 29% of that figure amounts to. This should give you a good estimate of how much you can spend each month on total housing costs.

| Gross Anual Income | Monthly Income | 29% Gross Income |
|---|---|---|
| $15,000 | $1,250 | $363 |
| $20,000 | $1,667 | $483 |
| $25,000 | $2,083 | $604 |
| $30,000 | $2,500 | $725 |
| $35,000 | $2,917 | $846 |
| $40,000 | $3,333 | $967 |
| $45,000 | $3,750 | $1,088 |
| $50,000 | $4,167 | $1,208 |

## — Mortgage Payment Calculator

The mortgage payment chart listed below is based on a 30-year fixed-rate mortgage and includes monthly principal and interest payments, but not taxes and insurance which may vary from community to community.

| Cost | 6% | 6.5% | 7% | 7.5% | 8% | 8.5% | 9% | 9.5% | 10% |
|---|---|---|---|---|---|---|---|---|---|
| $25,000 | $150 | 158 | 166 | 175 | 183 | 192 | 201 | 210 | 219 |
| $30,000 | $180 | 190 | 200 | 210 | 220 | 231 | 241 | 252 | 263 |
| $40,000 | $240 | 253 | 266 | 280 | 293 | 308 | 322 | 336 | 351 |
| $50,000 | $300 | 316 | 333 | 350 | 367 | 384 | 402 | 420 | 439 |
| $60,000 | $360 | 379 | 399 | 420 | 440 | 461 | 483 | 505 | 527 |
| $70,000 | $420 | 442 | 466 | 489 | 514 | 538 | 563 | 589 | 614 |
| $80,000 | $480 | 506 | 532 | 559 | 587 | 615 | 644 | 673 | 702 |
| $90,000 | $540 | 569 | 599 | 629 | 660 | 692 | 724 | 757 | 790 |
| $100,000 | $600 | 632 | 665 | 699 | 734 | 769 | 805 | 841 | 878 |
| $110,000 | $660 | 695 | 732 | 769 | 807 | 846 | 885 | 925 | 965 |
| $120,000 | $719 | 758 | 798 | 839 | 880 | 923 | 966 | 1,009 | 1,053 |
| $130,000 | $780 | 822 | 865 | 909 | 954 | 1,000 | 1,046 | 1,093 | 1,141 |
| $140,000 | $839 | 885 | 931 | 979 | 1,027 | 1,076 | 1,126 | 1,177 | 1,229 |
| $150,000 | $899 | 948 | 998 | 1,049 | 1,101 | 1,153 | 1,207 | 1,261 | 1,316 |

Using the above charts as an example, if 29% of your gross income is $725, that means you should be able to afford $725 a month on total housing expenses, including mortgage payments, taxes, insurance, and so on. You should look for a mortgage that leaves you plenty of room to meet your other housing expenses.

When you begin shopping for a loan, ask several potential lenders to help you estimate how much your total costs will be. Otherwise, you could end up saddled with a mortgage you can't really afford.

## Lower Your Mortgage Costs By Avoiding "Points"

With today's competitive market, more and more lenders are offering deals to reduce mortgage costs. Among the potential bargains are "no-points," low-cost loans. Such a loan can be especially advantageous for first-time buyers who may not have the cash to pay points, or buyers who want to put more money into their down payments.

Since each point (also known as loan origination fees) is equal to 1 percent of the principal of your mortgage, and points usually are collected at closing, a no-point loan can save you hundreds or thousands of dollars in up-front costs. For example, if you get a mortgage for $80,000, one point means you pay $800 to the lender; with two points, you'd pay the lender $1,600. The amount you save on initial mortgage costs, depends on the size of your loan and the number of points you avoid.

The main drawback to minimizing your up-front costs by avoiding points is higher interest rates. Generally, the lower a mortgage's initial costs (no points) the higher its interest rate. On the other hand, if you pay points, you'll get a lower interest rate. According to industry insiders, the general rule of thumb is: Pay points to get a lower mortgage rate if you plan to stay in your house more than four years. Your total savings on interest payments should more than make up for your up-front costs. However, if you don't plan to stay in your home for several years, your best deal may be a no-point loan which will pay off immediately. In that case, you might consider asking your lender if you can have the option of paying fewer or no points in exchange for a higher interest rate.

## Jumping On The Refinancing Bandwagon

If you've been thinking about refinancing your current mortgage to get a lower interest rate, now may be the time to act. As of this writing, rates on 30-year fixed-rate loans have plummeted to nearly 7 percent. Depending on the interest rate on your old mortgage, refinancing at the current rate could save you hundreds of dollars a year.

Generally, refinancing is recommended when interest rates go down at least 2 percent below the rate you're paying currently. However, you may benefit from mortgage refinancing if you can obtain a rate that is at least 1.5 percent less than your current rate. Obviously, if you have a double-digit interest rate on your current mortgage, you can save a bundle of money by refinancing at a rate well below 8 percent. But for other homeowners the question of refinancing may be more difficult.

In order to determine whether or not refinancing is worthwhile, you need to consider the costs involved. You should compare the up-front costs— title insurance, legal fees, document fees, appraisal fees, points, etc.— of the new loan with the amount you'll save in monthly payments each year. If the closing costs are low, and your savings will exceed your costs in two to three years, it may pay you to refinance for an interest-rate deduction of as little as 1.5 percent.

If you do decide to refinance, you also might consider switching from a variable-rate (if that's what you have now) to a fixed-rate loan. While your monthly payments may not drop, they'll be stable for the life of your new loan. And you can refinance again if rates drop even lower.

To learn more about refinancing, order a free copy of "Refinancing Your Home" from the Federal Trade Commission, 6th Street and Pennsylvania Avenue, Washington, DC 20580.

## Don't Overpay Your Mortgage

If you're not careful and you don't shop around for the best rates and terms, you could end up overpaying your mortgage by thousands of dollars. The first step in avoiding overpaying is to determine which type of mortgage meets your needs. If you lack cash, you'll probably want a loan that requires little or no down payment. If your income is average or below, you may want financing with small monthly payments. If your income is above average, you may prefer financing with low interest but higher monthly payments. Once you determine the type of mortgage you need, you can begin shopping for the best rates.

While the interest rate is the primary factor in determining how much your mortgage will ultimately cost, there are several other factors that could help you avoid overpaying, as well. Prequalifying for a mortgage, locking in the best rates, minimizing closing costs, avoiding prepayment penalties, and accelerating your payment schedule, also can help you reduce your cost for a home loan.

## * Prequalification

Lenders follow certain guidelines in deciding whether to lend you the mortgage money you need to buy a home. Generally, a lender will expect you to spend no more than 28% of your gross monthly income on total housing expenses, including mortgage payments, taxes and insurance. Your housing costs, plus your other long-term debts, such as car payments should not exceed 36% of your gross monthly income.

Considering those guidelines, check with potential lenders before you begin shopping for a home and find out whether or not you would qualify for a loan. Then you can begin focusing your attention on homes you can realistically afford.

## * Locking In The Best Rate

When shopping for a mortgage, you're looking for the most favorable interest rate and the lowest points and other up-front charges. In most cases, the terms you are quoted by various lenders may not be the terms available to you at settlement weeks or even months later. Between the time you apply and settlement, the cost of mortgages may change and you could receive less favorable terms.

Lock-ins on rates and points may offer you a way to ensure that the terms you apply for are what you get at settlement. A lock-in is a lender's promise to hold a certain interest rate and a certain number of points for you for a specified period of time, usually while your loan application is being processed. If your interest rate and points are locked in, you should be protected against rate increases while your loan is being processed. The protection could affect whether or not you can afford the mortgage. However, a locked-in rate also could prevent you from taking advantage of rate decreases, unless your lender is willing to lock in a lower rate that may become available during the specified time period.

When considering paying for a lock-in (most lenders will charge you a fee for a lock-in agreement), find out whether or not the lender also will be willing to give you a lower rate in the event of a rate decrease. And be sure to get the lock-in agreement in writing. Verbal agreements can be hard to prove in the event of a dispute.

### * Closing Costs

Many lenders are willing to offer lower interest rates on mortgages that include points. If you're planning to stay in a home you buy for more than four years, you'll lower your ultimate mortgage cost by paying points to get a lower interest rate.

Lenders also are required to provide borrowers "Good-Faith" estimates of the charges and fees they may be expected to pay at settlement. Make sure your lender provides such an estimate, including charges for property appraisal, title insurance, credit reports, and other items. Study the items on the estimate sheet carefully. There may be extra fees you haven't been told about, and others, such as title insurance which you may be able to purchase at a lower cost from another source.

### * Prepayment Penalties

If possible, avoid lenders who impose penalties if you decide to pay off a mortgage ahead of schedule. Some lenders charge prepayment penalty fees of 2 percent to 3 percent on the original loan amount for early payoff. If you're planning to move, trade in your old mortgage for a lower-cost new one or pay off your new loan within three years, watch out for a prepayment penalty clause before you submit an application for a loan.

### * Accelerated Payments

You shouldn't have to pay extra if you make biweekly payments that help you reduce interest and pay off your loan faster. However, some lenders will charge a fee of several hundred dollars for arranging an accelerated payment plan. You can avoid such a fee by making extra payments yourself without the lender's "help."

Depending on the amount of your loan and its duration, you can pay it off years earlier and save thousands of dollars.

## Mortgage Secrets

Shopping for and getting the home loan you want requires a great deal of preparation on your part. As already noted, there are several ways you can cut the costs of a mortgage if, of course, the loan is approved. The loan approval process itself can be a harrowing experience, especially for first-time homebuyers. It generally begins with an initial meeting between the prospective homebuyer and the lender to discuss the potential loan.

Often, homebuyers prefer to meet with lenders before they begin house hunting. That way they can determine in advance what price range they can realistically afford and the mortgage amount for which they can qualify. This step in the process, called prequalification, can save you (and the lender) a lot of time and trouble by making certain you are focusing in the correct price range.

Whether or not your initial meeting with a lender is for the purpose of prequalifying or to actually submit an application for a home loan, there are certain things you can do to make the process proceed as smoothly and as rapidly as possible. Many industry insiders say the secret to speeding up the application process is a borrower's thorough preparation for this initial meeting.

For your initial meeting with a lender, you should come prepared with the following items:

* A purchase contract for the house (if you have one);

* Your bank account numbers and the address of your branch bank;

* Copies of your checking and savings account statements for the past six months;

* Evidence of other assets, such as bonds and securities;

* Pay stubs, W2 withholding forms, tax returns for two years, or other proof of employment and income verification;

* Balance sheets and tax returns, if you're self employed;

* A list of all credit card account numbers and the approximate monthly amounts owed on each to show the amount of revolving debt, or canceled checks for rent or utility bill payments, to show payment history;

* Information on other consumer debt, such as car loans, student loans, etc.

Having this information on hand when you meet with the lender will show him/her you are serious and responsible and will help speed up the application process. Unless you're meeting to prequalify for a mortgage, you'll probably have to pay an application fee and an appraisal fee when you submit a loan application. This is required only after the seller has agreed to your offer.

In deciding whether or not to approve the type and amount of mortgage you want, a lender will focus on two key factors: your ability and willingness to repay the loan. Your ability to repay the mortgage is verified by your current employment and yearly income. Most lenders prefer for you to have held a job with the same employer for two years or longer. It's also a plus if you've been in the same line of work for several years.

Your willingness to repay is determined by examining how the property will be used. For example, will you be using the house as your primary residence or will you just rent it out? Your willingness to pay also is related to how you met past financial obligations. That's why the lender will need to see your credit information or rent and utility bills.

The thing to keep in mind is that each applicant is handled on an individual basis. Your application will be approved or rejected on its own merits. If the loan makes sense, lenders are likely to do all they can to see that you qualify. The secret to approval is being well-prepared and presenting a reasonable proposal.

## Help For Those Hunting Low Mortgage Rates

The first step in shopping for the best mortgage rates is locating sources of up-to-date information. Two of the best sources for locating low mortgage rates are newspapers and reporting agencies.

### * Newspapers

The real estate or business sections of your local newspaper will likely feature a list of current rates from area lenders. Such listings usually feature the interest rate plus points. For example, a listing of 9 + 1, means a 9% loan plus 1 point.

### * Reporting agencies

For a fee, mortgage information services or title companies can provide mortgage rate information. Title companies compile these rates as a customer service. National or multi-state rate reporting agencies also can provide the latest rate information. If no local source for current mortgage rates is available, you might consider the following mortgage rate reporting services:

— **HSH Associates**, (800) 873-2837. This company tracks loan rates and offers the "Homebuyers Mortgage Kit." The kit provides a survey of lenders in your local area, as well as a 44-page booklet that explains the mortgage process. The kit costs $20. If you have a computer, HSH also offers the latest rates on disk.

— **National Mortgage Weekly**, (800) 669-0133 in Ohio and Michigan; (216) 273-6605 elsewhere. This reporting service tracks mortgage rates in the midwest. Cities covered include Columbus and Cleveland, Ohio, as well as Detroit, MI. Over 80 lenders in each market are surveyed. The weekly costs $4 per issue.

— **Gary Myers & Associates**, (800) 472-6463. This company tracks mortgages in 60 major cities. Their report on mortgage rates in Chicago includes 150 lenders. Reports from other cities provide information on up to 80 lenders per market. The cost for a one-city report is $22 per issue.

Another way to find the lowest rates is to hire a mortgage broker. Brokers buy mortgages at wholesale from banks, savings and loans and other lenders and mark them up to sell retail. A good mortgage broker will shop among several lenders to get you the best deal possible on a loan that meets your needs.The rate a broker charges is based on a percentage of the loan amount— typically 0.5 to 1%. However, the commission is negotiable, especially on larger loans.

The National Association of Mortgage Brokers can help you find a mortgage broker in your area. You can write to the association at 1735 N. Lynn Street, Suite 950, Arlington, VA 22209.

A reputable real estate agent should also be able to tell you which lenders offer the best terms in your area.

## Big Savings On Mortgage Interest

The best way to save on mortgage interest is to shop around for the lowest rates. Since the market is extremely competitive, lenders often will offer lower-than-market rates to attract business. That makes it a money-saving idea to contact several lenders and compare rates and terms based on the type of mortgage you want.

There are several ways you can shop for a low-interest home loan (see "Help For Those Hunting Low Mortgage Rates" elsewhere in this chapter). You can visit your public library and check the real estate or business sections in metropolitan newspapers for a general idea of the market. Or, if you're willing to spend $10 to $30, a professional reporting service can provide you with up-to-the-minute information on interest rates available from area institutions.

Since lenders are so competitive, interest rates can vary by one percent or more among financial institutions. For example, one lender might offer a 30-year fixed-rate loan at 8% plus a flat fee of $200. Another lender might offer the same 30-year fixed-rate loan but at a lower rate of 7% with two points. You may choose to pay higher points to get the lower interest rate, if you plan to stay in your house for more than four years.

You also can save on mortgage interest over time by paying down your principal early. There are several ways to do this. You can make small prepayments of, say $20 to $25 a month toward principal. These monthly payments will reduce your balance, and since the lender computes interest due on your outstanding balance each month, you'll reduce the amount of interest you owe. The nice thing about principal prepayments is that you can send any amount you choose each month, depending on how much you can afford.

A growing equity mortgage is a rapid payoff mortgage you may choose in order to save on mortgage interest. This type of mortgage features a fixed interest rate and increased monthly payments each year which reduce principal. Bi-weekly payment mortgages also eliminate some of your mortgage interest by paying down on principal. If you can afford to make the extra payments, you can realize great savings on mortgage interest with either of these mortgage loans.

The Mortgage Bankers Association of America, the trade group of mortgage bankers, offers several publications, including "A Self-Test: How To Save Half On Interest Costs." To get a copy, write to the association at 1125 15th Street, NW, Washington, DC 20005.

## Saving On Mortgage Insurance

If your down payment is less than 20 percent of the purchase price of a home, you must buy private mortgage insurance (PMI) on a conventional loan. This type of insurance protects the lender in the event of default. If you default on your payments, resulting in foreclosure, the mortgage insurance company reimburses the lender all or part of its losses.

You can pay PMI in one of two ways: (1) by making premium payments which are added to your monthly mortgage interest payment or (2) by making a "lump-sum," one-time premium payment at closing. If you plan to keep your mortgage for only a short time, monthly premiums may be your best option. However, if you plan to keep your mortgage for several years, paying the one-time premium may save you money in the long run. Most lenders will let you add the cost of mortgage insurance to your total loan amount so your closing costs won't increase.

Another way to save on mortgage insurance is to keep track of your home's value and your loan balance. Over time, your property should appreciate and your loan balance should decrease. Once you have at least 20 percent equity in your home you can drop the mortgage insurance policy. Be aware, however, that you may have to pay for a new appraisal to document your property's higher value before you can discontinue your PMI premiums.

## Don't Forget To Deduct Mortgage Points

Closing costs when buying a home may seem excessive, but the IRS offers a tax break for homebuyers that can make the expense more palatable. Points (loan origination fees) paid on mortgages for buying a home generally are fully deductible in the tax year paid. For example, say you obtained a 30-year mortgage and paid $1,500 in points—you can deduct the full $1,500 on your tax return the year in which the points were paid.

As a buyer, you also may be able to deduct points paid on your behalf by the seller. For tax purposes, the IRS allows a buyer to treat seller-paid points as if he/she had paid them. A buyer can then deduct the points in the year paid.

If you're replacing an existing mortgage or refinancing, points paid on your second mortgage can not be deducted fully in the year paid. Instead, you must spread the points over the life of the mortgage. Generally, you can deduct an equal portion in each year of the mortgage. For example, if you take out a 30-year refinancing mortgage and paid $3,000 in points you can deduct $100 (1/30 of the points paid) on your yearly returns over the term of the loan. there is however, an exception: If you refinanced and used some of the money to improve your main home, points paid on that portion are fully deductible in the tax-year paid.

For additional information on deducting mortgage points, call the Internal Revenue Service at 1-800-829-3676 and order Publication 936, "Home Mortgage Interest Deduction." It's available free of charge.

## Choose Your Mortgage Type Carefully

It used to be relatively easy to choose a mortgage. There weren't too many variations— not much to choose from. Things are different now. Stiff competition among lenders has led to a continually increasing number of choices. Instead of a "one type of-mortgage-fits-all" policy, lenders now offer mortgages in a wide range of combinations of interest rates, duration, and fees. There are literally scores of loan packages to choose from.

Which loan is right for you depends on a number of factors including how long you plan to live in the house and how much you can reasonably afford in monthly payments. Most lenders offer several types of mortgages and, with careful study, you should be able to find one that provides the best deal for you.

Here are several of the most common options:

## — Conventional Mortgages

### * Fixed-Rate Mortgage

With this type of mortgage, your interest rate stays the same for the term of the mortgage, which can be 15 or 30 years. Your principal and interest payments remain stable, making it easier to plan a monthly budget. A fifteen-year fixed rate mortgage requires a down payment or monthly payments higher than those required on a 30-year loan. If you can afford the higher payments, a fifteen-year fixed-rate loan will save you interest and help you build equity.

The main drawback to a 30-year fixed-rate loan is that initial interest rates tend to be higher than with other types of loans. Also new fixed rates are seldom assumable.

### * Adjustable-Rate Mortgage (ARM)

With an ARM, your initial interest rate and monthly payments are lower than with a fixed-rate. However, your rate and payments can change either up or down, depending on where interest rates are going. If rates are going up, your monthly payments are likely to increase as well, sometimes significantly.

Many borrowers are attracted to ARMs because the starting interest rate is generally below market. When considering this type of loan, find out the "cap" or the maximum interest rate that can be charged during the life of the loan. Also ask how often the rate might change. An ARM may be a good idea if you plan on staying in your home for only a few years.

### * Balloon Mortgage

With a balloon mortgage, monthly payments are based on a fixed-rate. The loan is usually for a short term and payments may cover interest only with the principal due in full when the loan reaches term. While it's true that you get low monthly payments with a balloon mortgage, you're not likely to build any equity until the loan is fully paid. Also, the loan must be paid off or refinanced when due. If refinanced, the loan could be at a higher rate.

### * Assumable Loan

You may be able to find a home with a mortgage loan you can "assume" from the previous owner. In that event, the lender will transfer the old loan on the home to you. An assumable loan can be a great deal— featuring lower monthly payments, and the paperwork usually is not very complicated. It also can make your home more attractive to buyers when (or if) you want to sell.

By law, many mortgages are no longer assumable. Proceed with caution if you are offered a mortgage which the seller represents as "assumable."

## — Government Home Loan Plans

### * FHA-Insured Mortgage

With this type of loan, the Federal Government insures the lender against loss in case the home buyer defaults on the loan. An FHA-insured mortgage can be a good deal for people who can't afford the usual 10% to 20% down payment required by most lenders. With an FHA-insured loan, you may be able to purchase a home with as little as 3% down.

### * VA Loan

With a VA loan, the Department of Veterans Affairs guarantees the lender against loss due to default. To qualify for a VA loan, you need to be active in the military, a veteran or a surviving spouse. This loan doesn't always require a down payment and the charges are generally lower than conventional rates.

These are just a few of the many different methods lenders have devised to help you pay for a home. Each plan has its own advantages and disadvantages. You should study each offer thoroughly before making a commitment. Being stuck with a mortgage that you can't afford can take all the pleasure out of owning your own home.

The Federal Trade Commission (FTC) offers a helpful publication on choosing a mortgage. To order the free booklet, "The Mortgage Money Guide," contact the FTC, Public Reference Section, 6th and Pennsylvania Avenue, NW, Room 130, Washington, DC 20580. You also can get helpful information from the Mortgage Bankers Association of America, 1125 15th Street, NW, Washington, DC 20005. Ask for "How To Shop For A Mortgage."

## Avoid This Mortgage Trap

Most professionals advise buyers to be wary of financing based on negative amortization. While the payments might be lower than in other types of home loan agreements, they're not enough to cover the monthly interest charges. When that happens, the interest that is left unpaid is added to the principal, which means that each month, the borrower pays interest on an increasingly higher amount.

Negative amortization can be a home-financing trap because the debt actually keeps increasing rather than decreasing. That can be an especially serious problem if the size of your debt grows to exceed the equity in your home. You also could end up owing a lot of money in a balloon payment at the end of the loan or losing your home because you're unable to repay what you owe.

Despite the attractive low monthly payments, you may be better off to avoid a negatively amortized loan. The long-term consequences of such financing may eliminate any benefits you gain with lower payments. Instead, you may consider waiting to buy a home until you can afford the higher monthly payments with a typical home loan or check out low cost loans available from the FHA or Veterans Administration.

## Try For A "Seller Take-Back" Mortgage

One way to get a mortgage at below market-rate interest is to find a seller who is willing to finance all or part of a first or second mortgage. Generally, owners who are having trouble selling their homes are more open to financing such a "seller take-back" mortgage and at rates as much as two percentage points below market rates.

Under such an arrangement, the seller acts as your lender. You make monthly mortgage payments to the seller rather than to a lending institution. Since sellers usually charge lower than market-rates, you secure a low-cost loan while the seller earns a fair return on his/her property. Should you default on the loan, the seller takes back the house.

Typically, seller-financing uses a balloon payment method wherein repayment of a large part of the principal is deferred, resulting in low monthly payments. While that can be an enticement for many buyers, a balloon mortgage requires full payment when the note matures or refinancing at market rates, which could sharply increase your debts. If you're financially prepared for such eventualities, a seller take-back mortgage can be a viable home-financing option.

## FHA-Insured Reverse Mortgages

Wouldn't it be nice if instead of you making monthly mortgage payments to a bank, the bank made monthly mortgage payments to you? In effect, that's exactly what can happen when you assume a reverse mortgage. Here's how it works: instead of borrowing against the equity in your home and paying interest, you arrange with a lender to convert some of your equity to cash while you retain ownership. You'll be paid in a lump sum, in monthly advances or through a line of credit. And you can use the money for any purpose.

While assuming a reverse mortgage can be an especially good deal if you're retired and own your own home free and clear, there are some caveats to consider. First of all, interest rates on this type of loan might be higher than rates on other types of loans. In the long run, the interest (which is not deductible on your taxes until you repay the loan in full) can increase considerably, and there may be significantly less equity for you and your heirs in the future. In addition, application fees, points and closing costs also might be higher than other types of loans.

On the plus side, a reverse mortgage can be a good way to tap into your home equity if you don't have several heirs expecting to split a large estate when you die. It allows you to convert your home's equity into cash without selling or giving up your home. You can use the money for anything you want and not worry about paying it off unless you sell the home or move permanently. The reverse mortgage also comes due when you die, at which time your heirs must pay off the loan. And the payments you receive from a reverse mortgage are considered "nontaxable" income.

If you decide to pursue a reverse mortgage, you'll have three basic types to choose from: lender-insured, uninsured and FHA-insured. While each has it's advantages (and disadvantages) an FHA-insured reverse mortgage may be the best option for many people. With an FHA-insured reverse mortgage you're not required to pay off the loan as long as you continue to live in the house. You also can change the way you receive payments from monthly advances to a line of credit at any time at minimal or no cost. And the FHA guarantees your payments even if the lender defaults.

If you qualify for an FHA-insured reverse mortgage, you'll be required to make a small down payment, as well as up-front loan origination and insurance fees. Your local FHA office and/or real estate agent can give you current information about FHA-insured reverse mortgages.

You can get additional information about reverse mortgages— how they work and which institutions currently grant them, by contacting the National Center For Home Equity Conversion, 7373 147th Street West, Suite 115, Apple Valley, MN 55124.

Information also is available from the Department of Housing and Urban Development (HUD), 451 Seventh Street, S.W., Room 9282, Washington, DC 20401.

## Buying Mortgages As An Investment

When you're buying a home of your own, a mortgage is a long-term investment. Even though you may never sell your home and realize a capital gain, your investment pays off by allowing you to own a home of your own. For many people, that's enough of a return. However, if you're looking for a real estate investment that offers the prospect of high returns, you might consider buying other people's mortgages.

One way to invest in mortgages is to buy into second mortgages, which are loans made to homebuyers to facilitate a sale. Sellers who "take back" second mortgages in order to sell their properties may, in turn, be willing to sell these second mortgages at substantial discounts, especially if they want their money right away. Often, home-sellers will offer secondary-market second mortgages through advertisements in newspapers, and in some cases they may hire real estate brokers to help them locate investors willing to buy their mortgages.

If you have a fairly large sum of capital to invest, you can buy into such second-mortgage loans and earn a relatively high interest payout. Typically, with a second mortgage, the borrower makes monthly payments only on interest. As the lender (and investor) you'll get your principal back when the loan expires. The interest rate is negotiated by the lender and the borrower.

Even though the returns on such an investment are relatively high, you shouldn't jump into the market without first taking several common-sense precautions. After all, buying into a second mortgage means you're taking a risk on a homebuyer who couldn't afford a primary mortgage. You should screen buyers carefully to make sure they are financially able and willing to pay you back, before you buy the mortgages.

Another, less risky,way to invest in mortgages is to buy shares in a mortgage pool. After a bank or a savings and loan issues a mortgage to a homeowner, the loan is sold to a federal agency, which repackages the loan along with thousands of other mortgages it has purchased into mortgage-backed securities pools. Investors are guaranteed interest and principal payments as they come due, regardless of whether or not a homebuyer is late with his/her payment or defaults on the mortgage.

As an investor in a mortgage-backed security pool, you'll be paid interest and principal every month. That's not a bad return on an investment that lets you avoid dealing directly with a borrower. There is a downside, however; generally, it will take a minimum of $25,000 to invest in such a mortgage pool.

If you have the capital, mortgage-backed securities can be a profitable investment. But you should consult with a qualified financial advisor before you begin purchasing shares in such securities.

For more information about mortgage-backed securities, contact the Public Securities Association, 40 Broad Street, 12th Floor, New York, NY 10004-2372; (212) 809-7000. Ask for a free copy of the pamphlet, "An Investor's Guide To Mortgage Securities."

## NOTES

_____

_____

_____

_____

_____

_____

_____

_____

_____

_____

_____

_____

## CHAPTER 4
## DEALING WITH BANKS AND S&Ls

## THINGS BANK DON'T TELL YOU

You may think bank personnel communicate all their policies up front to help their customers make an informed decision. But they don't. Here are some examples:

**\* Mortgages** — What they tell you: If you make a lump-sum payoff of an old low-interest mortgage, they'll offer you a big savings. What they don't tell you: The "big savings" doesn't come from interest, but from principal, and are therefore considered taxable income to you by the IRS. What you can do: Keep the low-rate mortgage, but take the same amount of money the bank is requesting in a lump-sum payment and invest it for yourself at a current higher market rate.

**\* Savings** — What they tell you: They publish the effective annual yields for all their savings accounts. What they don't tell you: Competing money-market funds are only allowed to advertise their simple interest rates, despite the fact that money markets compound interest on a daily basis. So, if a bank and a money-market fund  actually pay the same rate, the banks will be able to advertise a  higher yield. What you can do: Check the weekly financial tables in  the investment newspaper Barron's. They list most of the major money  market funds and provide the current annual effective yields, which  you can use to compare the value of the bank's offering.

**\* Checking Accounts:** What they tell you: Your bank may offer you  immediate drawing power on all deposited checks, so long as you provide collateral in the form of another account. What they don't tell  you: If the "collateral" account happens to be a six-month certificate of deposit, and the check bounces, the bank can cash in your CD  before maturity — in which case, you are liable for the interest  penalty on early withdrawal. What you can do: Ask for an account that  gives you time to cover bounced checks before it withdraws money from any timed deposit. If your bank won't provide this service, find one that will.

Other things they probably won't tell you:

\* Banks will not cash checks dated more than six months previously — no matter how much money is in the issuing account. (U.S. Treasury checks, however, remain valid indefinitely.)

\* If the numerical amount on the check differs from the amount written out in script, the bank will still pay the check — but only  in the amount written out in words.

\* When sending checks through the mail for deposit, write "For  Deposit Only" above your signature on the back. That way, if the  letter goes astray, your endorsement cannot be used by someone else  to cash the check.

## HOW SAFE IS "MONEY IN THE BANK"?

Even though your bank may be reporting profitable quarters, it could still be in fiscal trouble. Some audits have found many of the nation's major banks still have insufficient capital to support their business — with hundreds of lesser banks on the brink of failure. Reason: Their portfolios are loaded with non-performing real estate loans that are either past due, or not being repaid on schedule. And commercial real estate is still showing few signs of making a healthy rebound.

What happens if your bank fails? In the past, when the Federal Deposit Insurance Corp. was forced to close a bank, it was paying off depositors above the federally mandated $100,000 level. But with more and more banks failing and the FDIC's reserve fund hard-pressed to come up with more cash, the policy has changed. If your bank goes belly up and you're a large depositor, expect not a penny more than $100,000.

What can you do? The best thing is to thoroughly check out your bank's health, both by reviewing the bank's own financial statements and by checking with an independent source. Several commercial services can give you a rating on your bank, including:

* Veribanc, Inc., Box 461, Wakefield, MA 01880, 1-800-442-2657, charges $10 to rate one bank, and $5 for each additional institution. The cost is $25 for a more detailed report. (They also rate credit unions.)

* Weiss Research Inc., 2200 N. Florida Mango Road, West Palm Beach, FL 33409, 1-800-289-9222, offers ratings at $15 per bank. For $25 per bank, you can get a one-page summary with a letter rating (A+ through F).

\* The FDIC itself will send you the latest quarterly report on a bank's financial condition for $6 per bank per quarter — but don't bank on getting a quick response. Don't send money with your request; the FDIC will bill you. Write: FDIC, Disclosure Unit, FDIC, 550 17th Street NW, Room F 518, Washington, DC 20429.

If you're checking out the bank yourself, ask a bank officer for a copy of the institution's "call report." This financial document lists capital, profits and loan-loss reserves. Declining profits may mean that losses will endanger the bank's capital. To calculate the bank's capital ratio, divide the equity capital by its total assets. The figure should not be below 5 percent — and 7 percent or higher is preferable.

## WHAT IF YOUR BANK GOES BELLY UP?

On the heels of the savings and loan debacle of the mid and late 1980s, the Chicken Little brigade predicted wholesale bank failures across the land. So far, it hasn't happened. There have, however, been a higher-than-usual number of shutdowns as federal regulators have moved in to head off bank insolvencies.

Still, every time a federal bank shutdown makes headlines, people get panicky. Whether the bank is being closed for an actual insolvency, or to prevent a possible insolvency, many older Americans have Depression-era nightmares, and younger citizens experience their own more modern anxieties. How does this uncertain climate affect you, the depositor? The fact is, even though the Federal Deposit Insurance Corp. estimates that under half of 1 percent of the nation's banks will likely fail, your bank could be one of them. However, once you know how the FDIC rules operate — what they protect, and what they don't — you'll sleep better.

In fact, you'll realize that even a bank failure need not be  catastrophic for you. It doesn't even have to be a major headache.  Here's why: If your bank is closed by the FDIC, your deposits (including both principal and interest due) will be covered up to the   maximum of $100,000. This maximum applies to all individual accounts,  even if the amount is split between savings and checking in the same  name at the same bank. Anything over that amount in just one name is  not insured. In addition to the individual $100,000 limit, two or   more people can have joint accounts separately insured to $100,000.  (Each co-owner of the joint account must be given equal withdrawal  rights and must have filled out a signature card.)

Thus, a couple can have two separate $100,000 accounts — both  fully insured — and they can have a jointly owned $100,000 account   at the same bank. Total: $300,000 in protection. (Prior to December  1993, a husband and wife could hold insured deposits up to a total of $500,000 using a combination of individual, joint and trust accounts.   In addition, with a complicated combination of insured accounts held  separately or jointly by a husband, wife and two kids, deposits could  be protected up to $1.4 million at one bank.)

**Caution:** With the recent changes in banking law, if the qualified  beneficiary of a trust account has an individual account at the same  bank, the amount in that individual account is calculated toward the  $100,000 limit. Thus, a testamentary trust account where husband and  wife are both grantors and joint beneficiaries would be treated by the FDIC not as a trust account, but as a joint account. In the event  of bank failure, money in such an account would be added to any other  joint accounts held by the couple.

**Another caution:** IRA or Keogh accounts held at the same bank are  also be eligible for up to $100,000 of insurance protection. However,  even though these accounts are technically held by a trustee on your  behalf, the December 1993 regulatory revision states that they must be lumped in with all your other accounts at the same bank when it  comes to determining your total balance for coverage, with respect to  the $100,000 insurance limit.

So, what happens if — in a worst-case scenario — the bank goes  belly up? Depositors normally get their insured funds back within 10  business days. To facilitate this, however, it's important they have copies of all account documents establishing their ownership of all  deposited funds. In a more likely scenario, a failed bank will be  taken over by a healthy bank, and all accounts will remain open. The  only threat may be a lowering of CD interest rates to the level of  passbook savings. The takeover institution can also legally close out  CDs and return the money.

**The bottom line:** No depositors have ever lost a penny of FDIC insured funds, so long as they observed all the coverage rules outlined  above. In fact, even most funds in excess of $100,000 have even been  covered during past insolvencies. That was because, in the past, the FDIC tried to keep depositors of failed banks "whole," paying off at  least 85 percent of deposits over $100,000. More recently, however,  federal bank authorities have resolved to reduce bail-out costs by  strictly adhering to the $100,000 insurance cap. As a result, hundreds of millions of dollars in accounts over the ceiling at insolvent  banks have been forfeited.

Here are two typical horror stories, which could happen to even  the most careful depositor:

* A businessman maintained a $90,000 balance in his account, but he deposited another $75,000 just long enough to cover a check he was writing to the IRS. Unfortunately, before the IRS check had cleared, the FDIC took over the bank and found a total balance in his account of $165,000. Result: The businessman lost the uninsured $65,000 portion of the deposit.

* A couple sold their house, depositing the proceeds — $285,000 — until they could write a check for a new property. They should have divided those funds into three wholly insured accounts, but they didn't want to go to all that trouble just for a short time. Result: The bank went belly up with the whole amount sitting in one account, and the couple lost $185,000.

The moral of both stories: Make sure you have full FDIC coverage in all accounts at all times. More details are available in a free federal booklet, "Your Insured Deposit," c/o the Federal Deposit In- surance Corp., Attn: Consumer Affairs, 550 17th St. NW, Washington, DC 20429.

## IS A BANK ACCOUNT REALLY NECESSARY?

Almost everyone has some type of conventional bank account — but it's possible you could get along quite nicely without one. The alternative: Open an asset-management account with your stock broker. With such an account, you usually receive:

* A money-market fund that serves as your interest-paying checking account, but with higher interest rates than conventional banks or S&Ls. The checks are accepted anywhere a regular check would be. Some accounts even offer bill-paying services, so you can have your paycheck deposited and regular monthly bills paid automatically.

\* A debit card that can be used for many purchases — gas, groceries, etc. These cards can be used anywhere a bank ATM card would  be accepted, including overseas. Drawback: Your bank probably gives  you free ATM trans- actions at its own branches, whereas the usual ATM  fee for a brokerage house debit card is around $1 per transaction.

\* A margin account. This special account serves as a cred- it line,  allowing you to borrow against the value of your stocks, bonds and mutual funds, but at a lower interest rate than those charged by most  bank credit cards.

\* A brokerage account. You can buy and sell stocks, bonds and  other securities within your account, and any interest, dividends or   capital gains go into your money-market account. Caution: Since your  regular funds may be inter- mingled with your investment reserves, you  could wind up losing money needed for normal living expenses.

All these services are recorded in a single monthly statement.  There can be other charges, depending on the brokerage company, but   they're usually lower than the total monthly fees charged by banks.  Some leading asset- management accounts include:

\* Schwab offers a low-cost bank alternative account called Schwab- One. To open one, you'll need $5,000 cash or eli- gible securities. The  account has no annual fee, unlimited free checking and a no-fee Visa  card. If you live in California or New York, Schwab offers funds that  are free of state and local taxes. Beware: If your balance drops below $5,000, you pay a $5 penalty unless you made more than two security trades during the last 12 months. You pay lower commissions with  Schwab, but since they are a dis- count broker, you won't get any personal investment advice.

* Merrill Lynch, a full-service broker, offers the Capital Builder Account. For a $5,000 minimum investment, you'll receive a no-fee Visa card and lower interest rates on your debit card. Downside: No commission-free mutual fund purchases.

* Fidelity Investments has the Ultra Service Account. For slightly more money — $10,000 to be exact — you will be charged no annual fee, have unlimited free checking and a no-fee Visa Gold debit card. You have a choice of keeping your funds in a taxable interest-bearing account, a national tax-exempt fund or one of seven state tax-free funds. Like Schwab, however, you get no investment advice.

Unfortunately, unlike most bank checking and savings accounts — which run pretty smoothly overall — there can be problems with some of the asset-management accounts. These include mistakenly bounced checks, incorrect information on automatic withdrawals and returned checks. It's also more difficult to get your broker to take the time to deal with your routine money problems, as opposed to taking security orders. On the plus side, your funds on deposit with a brokerage firm are insured (against default or fraud, but not investment loss) up to $500,000 by the Security Investors Protection Corp. (SIPC), not just $100,000, as with the FDIC or FSLIC. Still, you should weigh the facts carefully before opting for an asset-management account over a regular bank account.

## HOW TO CORRECT YOUR BANK'S MISTAKES

Unfortunately, even preferred bank customers sometimes find that the bank has made an error — and, unlike the game of Monopoly, it's rare when it's "in your favor." Most of them go against you — and, even if they don't, the bank will quickly rescind your good fortune when it finds the error (though they're not so quick to correct the ones in their favor). So, what do you do when the bank makes a mistake? Here are some steps you can take in correcting bank errors:

* Talk to the appropriate bank officer and see if the problem can be resolved. Take in as much documentation as you can find to support your position, including canceled checks, deposit receipts, ATM receipts, account statements or loan papers and payment books.

* If you don't get satisfaction, go a step higher and talk to the branch manager (or, if it's a local bank, the president). That person should have the authority to solve most problems.

* If that doesn't work, write a letter explaining the problem to the bank's consumer affairs department or corporate headquarters. Include copies of your documentation, as well as any written explanations from bank personnel as to why they can't — or won't — correct the problem. (You'll likely have to ask for these latter items since most bank officers and branch managers will try to get by with a verbal response to your complaint.)

* If you still can't get satisfaction, send another letter, with copies of everything you've amassed so far, to the appropriate regulatory agency.

* If all this fails — and you're still convinced you're right — take the bank to small claims court. If you can convince the judge the bank did make an error, you can win a judgment for damages and costs up to $10,000. (Some states have lower limits, $1,500 to $3,000 on small-claims awards, but that should still be enough to cover most routine banking disputes.) If the amount is larger — or you think there

might be fraud involved — you can also contact a regular lawyer or the media. They can apply much more pressure than can you as an individual.

Whatever you do, keep your cool. Explain your case in a reasoned, business-like manner and you'll get a better response at all levels. Go in ranting and screaming, and you'll likely be written off as a crank — or escorted out of the bank by a security officer.

## SHOPPING FOR LOANS — THE SMART WAY

Purdue University's Credit Research Center estimates than less than half of those borrowing $5,000 or more compare rates before taking out a loan. They don't shop around. Maybe they think it's too much trouble, too much math. But it's well worth the effort. Here's a quick shoppers guide to the loan market:

* **Home-equity loans.** Many people shy away from these, afraid to put their equity at risk (and, you should scrutinize any agreement — some permit the bank to seize your property if you miss even a single payment or are late several times in a row). However, for people with sufficient emergency funds and the financial discipline, home equity loans have definite advantages. You may be able to borrow up to 80 percent of your home's value, minus the balance on your mortgage. Interest rates are variable, but are usually lower than on other types of loans. However, the key advantage is that the interest charges are tax deductible. Note: home-equity loans may involve closing costs, as when you first got your mortgage. Some banks advertise no-fee equity loans, but the savings may be illusory if the interest rate is higher than that offered by other banks.

**\* Consolidation loans.** You've heard ads for these — combine all your monthly bills into one "easy-to-make" payment. And the monthly payment may indeed be lower than the sum of all your separate bills, due to the longer repayment schedule. However, rates are generally relatively high — and you'll pay substantially more over the longer term of the new loan. Plus, you can get right back into trouble if you fail to change your spending habits. Thus, these should be avoided unless you have no other alternative — and you're sure you have the discipline to trim future expenses.

**\* Education loans.** Shopping for college loans is essential, since there are so many kinds. And comparisons should start at least a year before you'll need the money. There are need-based loans for low income families, as well as low-cost education loans offered by banks and others based on the credit worthiness of middle-income borrowers. Terms vary drastically, as do repayment and interest-compounding schedules and insurance fees. A free government book, The Student Guide, is available if you call 1-800-433-3243. Note: Loans taken out by the student rather than the parents usually offer more attractive rates.

**\* Auto loans.** Some dealers have been known to inflate the price of a car if you mention you're looking to finance elsewhere. To head this off, get a quote for the best loan deal at a bank or credit union, then go to the dealer to settle on a cash price for the car. The dealer may still come up with a financing package, but if it's not better than your bank's, just leave a deposit. Then take out your loan elsewhere and return later with a check for the balance. Regardless of who handles your financing, you can probably get a better rate if you up the size of your down payment. Lower rates also attach to loans of three years or less. Avoid four or five-year schedules. If you sell the auto before it's paid off and don't get enough to cover the balance, you'll end up paying the dealer for a car you no longer have.

**\* Personal loans.** The interest rates on these any-purpose loans depend on your credit rating or the type of security — e.g., a car or other valuable property. To reduce it further, have your payments automatically deducted from your checking account. If you don't have a checking account at your lending institution, consider opening one. It may get a fraction of a point deducted from your interest. Note: If you can't get a loan from banks, try your company's credit union.

**\* Other sources.** Some insurance policies offer loans for a low one-time fee, with the amount borrowed deducted from the cash value of the policy when paid up. You can also withdraw money from an Individual Retirement Account without penalty if you redeposit the full amount in another IRA within 60 days.

## SECRETS FOR GETTING THAT LOAN

One of the lingering effects of the S&L crisis and the subsequent banking scare has been a credit crunch. Put another way, instead of lending money to their credit-worthy customers, banks have been bolstering their own balance sheets by buying government bonds. That's fine for the banks, but what about would-be borrowers desperate for money to start a business, fix up property or finance a kid's college education? If you're one of these, are you just plain out of luck?

No. Not if you have an acceptable credit history, a persuasive reason for needing a loan and — perhaps most important — are willing to pursue an aggressive strategy for prying the bucks out of the loan officer's hands. Here are some tips on getting that loan:

* Research the bank's lending policies and your credit. Call anonymously and ask which credit-rating service it uses in reviewing loan applications. Then ask that agency for its latest copy of your credit report. If you find any errors (which show up nearly half the time), you'll have a chance to get them fixed. Perhaps you delayed payment on a bill over a disputed charge. That could show up on your record and adversely affect your loan application. The advance peek allows you either to get the item removed or to prepare a convincing explanation for the loan officer. Note: It should be obvious, but if your credit report does not reflect a particular financial problem in your recent past, don't raise the issue. What the bank doesn't know can't hurt you.

* Prepare a financial statement. This document shows your income, assets, personal investments and so forth. Even if you're not in the market for a loan, it's a good idea to have a financial statement on file with your bank. If you do apply later on, your loan officer may rank you considerably higher because of the statement. Banks provide blank forms for personal financial statements. If you need help filling out any part of it, ask your accountant. A financial statement, by the way, is not a place for exaggeration or truth-bending. You may, however, use high-end estimates for the value of such assets as your house and anticipated future income. If expecting a raise or bonus, for instance, put down a maximum-range figure.

* Personal contact. Any ongoing relationship you can develop with bank officers can only help later on in securing a loan. A banker is more likely to decide in favor of a person he or she knows than for a faceless name on an application. Begin with a get-acquainted appointment with a loan officer, then follow up by casual contact as you conduct your daily business with tellers and bookkeepers. Better yet, diversify your contacts. Otherwise, the officer you have carefully cul- tivated may be transferred to anoth-

er branch or another city. Get to know as many folks in the bank as possible — and in other banks and lending institutions, including your credit union.

* Be careful dealing with non-traditional lenders. Because of the credit crunch, many would-be borrowers have been driven to less well— known sources of personal funds. If you have doubts about a private lender or small loan company, check with the Better Business Bureau or the state attorney general's office.

* Shop around. Loans are like most anything else in the marketplace: You should always comparison shop — and it doesn't have to be an ordeal. A few phone calls can get you terms, rates and fees. Generally, smaller banks are more eager to accommodate borrowers than are gigantic institutions. You'll find that most lenders, large or small, prefer standard installment loans, rather than single-payment, simple-interest notes. Whenever possible, you should try to negotiate the latter. Here's why: Interest charges on single-payment, simple— interest notes are only on the balance at any given point in time, while standard installment loans charge interest on the original balance throughout the term of the loan.

## QUICK AND PAINLESS LOANS

It's often said the only way a bank will loan you money is if you can demonstrate you don't need it. Unfortunately, there's too much truth to this. Bank loan departments require applicants to fill out endless forms and put up substantial collateral. However, there's another kind of loan that only requires you to walk into the bank — almost any bank. This is a cash advance or line of credit on your Visa or MasterCard.

Getting the cards in the first place is far easier than getting a  regular bank loan. You can do it by mail. Once you have the card, if  you later lose your job, retire or land in financial trouble and need  a cash-advance loan, you can get it. The bank won't put you through  the third degree. How does it work? Just walk into the bank (not necessarily the card-issuing bank), show them your credit card with a second form of ID (usually a driver's license) and fill out a simple  cash-advance form. Then take your cash and walk. You can even do it  by mail. Request a cash-advance form. This works just like a check,  only with your credit card account number on it. Fill it out for any  amount up to your available credit limit and use it to pay bills, or  deposit it to your savings or checking account.

Be aware, however, that these loans should be strict-ly the court of last resort for borrowers. Cash advances on your credit card cost  the going interest rate — up to 22 per-cent — plus a fee, typically  from 2 percent to 5 percent of the amount borrowed. If you must fall  back on this type of loan, at least compare credit card rates and annual mem-bership fees, and then use the card offering the best deal.

## A BANK BY ANY OTHER NAME MAY BE A CREDIT UNION

Credit unions, unlike banks, are non-profit coopera-tives. That  means they can often pass savings on to their members in the form of   lower interest loans or higher deposit interest rates. For instance:

* Car loans. When it comes to new car loans, banks are taking a  back seat to the nation's credit unions. In fact, the race isn't even  close. An average four-year bank loan for a new car will cost more  than 10 percent. Most credit union rates are currently running around  7.5 to 8.5 percent.

* Services. More and more credit unions are offering a package of  customer-oriented services, including credit cards. If yours does, or  you can join one that does, chances are you'll beat the bank rate on  credit cards by a hefty margin. Example: Bank cards often charge 18  percent or more, while many credit unions now offer cards with rates  in the 12 to 14 percent range.


* Unsecured personal loans. The credit union average on unsecured  personal loans is around 13.5 to 14.0 percent. At banks, you can expect to pay substantially more — 16 to 17 percent.


* Interest rates on savings. Current rates of return on money-market accounts and CDs are still pretty discouraging, but you can almost always do slightly better at your credit union than at your bank  or S&L. Bank money-market accounts at most banks now pay around 2.75  percent, while credit unions average 3.25 percent. For short-term CDs  (30 to 60 days), the gap is around a full point: Banks, 3.50 percent,  credit unions 4.50 percent.


## NOTES

_____

_____

_____

_____

---

## CHAPTER 5
# KEYS TO CREDIT
# AND CREDIT CARDS

## DOING A CREDIT CHECK ON YOURSELF

**B**een turned down for a loan recently? If so, you can — and should — find out why. And don't fall for one of those come-on ads  offering your credit report for a small charge. You can get it free  — and fix it.

First, if you're turned down for a loan, your bank must tell you  what credit reporting agency it used — and how to contact it. The  report is free — if your loan application was within the last 30  days. Once you get the report, if you find an error, you can challenge the information. The bureau will investigate. If they find the  item you questioned is indeed wrong, they must remove it by law. Ask  them also to send a corrected report to any creditor who queried them  about you within the past six months.

What if the creditor maintains its information is correct? If so, they must insert your correction or amplification (not exceeding  100 words) in your report. And, you're also permitted to attach a letter of explanation or protest regarding the suspect data.

---

If your loan turn-down was more than 60 days prior, the reporting agency doesn't have to supply a free copy of your report. However, you can still get one free — from TRW. TRW, one of the three major credit reporting agencies, will send you one free copy of your report per year, no matter what your status. Here's the address:

TRW Consumer Assistance
Box 2350
Chatsworth, CA 91313-2350

To apply, send them the following information: Name, address (plus addresses for past five years), Social Security number, birth date, spouse's name, plus a copy of either a driver's license, phone or utility bill. You can also request a copy of your report by calling 1-800-422-4879.

The other two major credit reporting agencies — Trans Union and Equifax — both charge for copies of their reports once you are beyond the 60-day turndown limit. Trans Union charges $8 per report, and you can order by calling 1-800-851-2674. Equifax charges $15 (except in states that mandate lower fees), and you can request a report by calling 1-800-685-1111.

## IF YOU FIND A MISTAKE

Once you get a copy of your credit report, review it carefully. If you find a mistake, contact the credit agency immediately and request a review. The credit bureau will then go back to the business that reported the information and ask for a clarification. If the erroneous entry isn't confirmed, it must be removed from your file within 60 days.

In addition to reviewing what is in your credit file, you should also note anything that might be missing — at least if the missing data reflects positively on your borrowing habits. As much information as most credit files contain, there are also a surprising number of gaps — and it is your right to request that any positive information be added. You will have to supply details of the missing material to the credit bureau, complete with the name of the creditor and when the loans were paid or if the accounts are still open and current. By law, the credit agency must verify the information you've supplied and update your file within 20 days.

Your credit report will also contain a list of every business or lender that has requested a copy of your file in recent months — or, in some cases, recent years. That can also be a problem since too many inquiries will make it seem you are either on a buying spree or intent on getting as much credit as possible — both of which can cause a potential lender to reject your credit application. If you didn't authorize the inquiries — or if you feel they are out of date — you have the right to request their removal. And, even if you did authorize an inquiry, you have the right to add a note to the file explaining why (perhaps a potential lender changed terms on you at the last minute, forcing you to seek an alternate loan source). Preventive measure: If you have a number of inquiries on your file and don't want to go to the trouble of having them removed, simply note on any new credit applications that you have also applied for other recent loans, explain the reasons why and note whether you got the credit or not.

## ASK FOR — AND GET — A RATING UPGRADE

If you find something you don't like on your credit report, don't get mad at the credit agencies. Remember, they don't set credit ratings — they merely report the information provided to them by your creditors. Thus, if you want a black mark removed from your file, you will have to satisfy the creditor, not the credit agency. Assume, for example, that you had some problems with payments on a new washer and dryer and, as a result, the appliance store has given you a poor rating. If you have since gotten back on schedule with your payments, you should go to the store and ask to see the credit manager. Introduce yourself, and then explain that you could use some help. Tell him that though you had some payment problems in the past, your more recent payments have been on time. Outline why you had the earlier problems — and why those same problems won't recur. Then tell the credit manager it would be a great help to you and your family if he or she could update the store's credit report on you, upgrading your rating. In most cases, unless the manager is a real hard case, your request will be granted. And, once you get the upgraded, other potential creditors who check your file will have no way of knowing there was ever a problem.

## GETTING RID OF INSTALLMENT DEBT

Americans are sinking deeper and deeper into debt — saving less and spending more. Some in this predicament hope for a dramatic turnaround in the national economy that will miraculously lift them out of their financial sinkhole. Others wisely realize that since they got themselves into debt, they have to get themselves out. The question is, how can it be done?

One theory is to gradually ease up on spending and increase debt payments. This also seems to be the theory the U.S. government uses to deal with its massive deficits. And guess what? It doesn't work. However, most accountants and financial planners agree that drastic debt problems require drastic solutions. Anything less is doomed to end up on the trash heap of good intentions and no followthrough. Here is some three-gulp austerity medicine that has been proven to work:

**1.** Slash all spending. You can't get out of a hole if you keep digging it deeper. That means delaying all major purchases and as many minor ones as you can. Cut maintenance expenses and all frills. Read library books or watch free TV (as opposed to paying for expensive cable hookups). Haul out the ironing board and avoid dry cleaners. Don't even go to the mall. You get the idea. Reduce your life style before it reduces you — to bankruptcy.

**2.** Pay cash or don't buy. In most instances, credit card and consumer loans are how you accumulated installment debt. And the escalating interest on these loans, as you've surely seen, can keep you from ever getting even. Stop using your credit cards. Cut them in half if you have no will power (although you can keep the accounts open). If you don't have the cash for something, don't buy it.

**3.** Pay down debts as fast as you can. Your austerity program should soon start providing you more money with which to pay bills. However, even that may not be sufficient to catch you up. If you're already getting late fees and overdraft charges, consider more drastic options to fund your debt reduction payments, such as:

* Ask your employer for more overtime opportunities.
* Change your W-4's to reduce the withholding tax and increase take-home pay.
* Look for a second job.
* Ask relatives for a shortterm bail-out loan.
* Cut unnecessary coverages on your auto insurance.
* Consider terminating cash-value insurance and switching to cheaper term insurance.
* If you have a 401(k) or other retirement plan, take out a temporary loan. Many plans offer these penalty and interest free.
* Hold a yard sale.

Best strategy on making payments: Rather than just increasing your monthly installment payments on larger debts, continue to make the minimum payment. Then, separately, make an unscheduled payment specifically to reduce the principal. That way you will also reduce subsequent interest charges.

What about home equity loans? Home equity loans, equity lines of credit or a total refinance are other cash-raising alternatives — available if your credit rating hasn't taken too much of a beating. Equity credit lines generally run 10 percentage points below the interest charged by credit cards, so it makes sense to switch your debt off the plastic and to this kind of loan. Refinancing and home-equity loans may also work for you, but both entail hefty upfront charges.

What about consolidation loans? These commercials loans are con- stantly advertised as the solution to your bill-paying woes. The idea is to combine all your debts — with the usual exception of mortgage and car payments — and loan you enough money to pay them all off. Afterward, you'll make only a single monthly payment to the loan company — which, because of longer-term financing, is less than the total of the payments you had before. The loan companies make this sound like a financial lifesaver — and many people in dire financial straits swim straight for it. However, unless there's no other alternative, these kinds of bill-consolidation loans should be avoided — for two very simple reasons:

* Interest rates are too high, reflecting the risk of lending to folks in financial trouble.
* The long-term financing means a cumulative increase in total interest charges.
* You may be extending what's only a short-term problem.

If you have loans due to be paid off in a few months, a consolidation loan will extend the debt for many additional years. As a result, if you do opt for a consolidation package, you should probably exclude any loan with fewer than a year's worth of payments remaining.

If you feel you just can't raise the money to meet your monthly obligations, a better solution than a consolidation loan involves making minimum payments on longer term debts and send in extra on shorter term ones until they're paid off. By eliminating some smaller debts, you'll start decreasing your monthly payouts — and may soon have them down to a manageable level.

## CUTTING THE COST OF PLASTIC MONEY

You can save $100 or more a year on credit card charges by following these four tips:

**1.** If you're paying more than 15 or 16 percent interest on your card, ask your bank to put you into a lower interest-rate program. They DO have lower interest rates available — and most banks will offer it to you rather than lose your business.

**2.** If your bank says no, shop around. Call 1-800-845-5000 (Bank- card Holders of America) for a free list of cards with low interest rates or no fees. Another source: Send $5 for the monthly CardTrak newsletter, at Box 1700, Frederick, MD 21702. Or call them at 1-800-344-7714. Some bank cards actually charge less than 9 percent, though some may require impeccable credit records, or offer minimal credit lines.

**3.** A bank card with a low rate is critical if you carry a large balance. The grace period isn't important because it's probably forfeited on a revolving balance. However, if you always pay off the monthly balance, you're better off with a card that has no annual fee and a grace period of 25 to 30 days.

**4.** If you often get cash advances, make sure your bank doesn't charge high fees for this service. And compare the cash advance fees to store purchase fees.

**Additional tips:** Avoid making minimum payments. Smaller payments cost more in the long run. If you don't plan to pay your bill in full, send your payment in as soon as the bill arrives. Paying early will reduce the average daily balance, cut interest compounding and reduce total finance charges. Also, make big purchases the day after your card's closing date. As long as you pay your balance in full, you'll give yourself a grace period of nearly two months.

## BEST NO-FEE CARDS

If you pay off your monthly credit card balance every month, you should be using no-fee, long grace period cards. Here are several banks that have no-fee cards with 25-day grace periods:

* Consumer National Bankcard, 1-800-862-1616. Offers 25-day grace period.

* Amalgamated Bank of Chicago, 1-800-365-6464.

* USAA Federal Savings Bank, 1-800-922-9022.

* AFBA Industrial Bank/KBC Card Services, 1-800-776-2265.

If you don't want to call all over the country in search of a no-fee credit card, there's also one place you can check right in your own hometown. Sears charges no annual fee for its Discover card, gives you a 25-day grace period and you can apply at any Sears store. You also get a 5 percent rebate on all purchases made with the card. However, if you don't pay your bill in full each month, you'll more than pay for both the rebate and the lack of an annual fee because of the card's high 19.80 percent fixed interest rate.

## NO FEE – AND TRAVEL BENEFITS, TOO

The American Automobile Association (AAA) offers its members a no-fee Gold MasterCard that also features a variety of extras — including free American Express Travelers Cheques. The card offers a 25-day grace period, has a variable interest rate that's currently pegged at 16.8 percent and each purchase earns bonus points that you can redeem for Auto Club products and services. In addition, the card offers purchase protection, free auto rental collision damage waiver coverage, checking and instant-cash privileges and full protection against liability if your card is lost or stolen (with most cards, you're at risk for the first $50).

## PROFIT FROM CREDIT CARD WARS

Not long ago, some small and aggressive lenders declared war on the big guns of the credit card industry. As a result, interest rates finally began to come down — into the single digits, in many cases, with no annual fees and substantial credit lines. And smart consumers began to profit from this surprising competition among the purveyors of plastic credit. If you're paying more than 16 percent on your credit card balance, it's definitely time to look for a lower rate.

If you transfer your present credit card balance to one of these issuers of bargain plastic, you may be able to lock in a single-digit interest rate for up to a year. Afterward, though, your rate may rise again to 16 percent or higher. However, you can still enjoy substantial savings in the interim. For instance, you could save $360 a year on an average balance of $4,000 by switching from a 17.9 percent card to an 8.9 percent card. And, you may be able to do even better — depending on your credit history. People with better records can qualify for a better rates at some banks.

The plastic wars have had an effect on even some of the industry giants. Citibank, for instance, has been forced by consumer demand to offer lower card rates in order to compete with smaller banks that have ridden aggressive credit card operations to surprising growth. A few of the smaller banks offering single-digit plastic are Simmon's Bank in Arkansas, Oak Brook Bank of Illinois, People's Bank in Connecticut and AFBA Industrial Bank of Virginia.

**Caution:** Some banks offer low-rate cards, then slip in expensive extras or tricky exceptions. For instance, some banks have been known to charge interest not on the actual balance due, but on the amount available to borrow. In other words, although you only charge $300, your interest may be calculated on your total credit line of $2,500. That's why you must always to read the fine print of any credit card agreement.

## DON'T FALL FOR CREDIT CARD EXTRAS

In the high-fee, high-interest plastic wars, credit card issuers will try almost anything to get you to use their product instead of someone else's. You've probably already been bombarded through the mail or over the phone with some of these so-called credit card "enhancements" or "extras." Examples: Catalog shopping discounts, guaranteed medical insurance, travel offers and on and on. You can bet your bottom dollar that with just a little bit of shopping around, you can beat all these so-called deals.

## CREDIT CARD INSURANCE IS A MAJOR RIP-OFF

Of all the bad types of insurance marketed today, absolutely the biggest waste of money is credit card coverage — designed to make payments on your plastic debt should you lose your job or become dis-abled. Though the marketing brochures do a good job of obscuring the fact, it is outrageously expensive. The premiums run between 50 and 75 cents per $100, which sounds reasonable. However, when you apply that to the total outstanding balance, the actual costs can mount up quickly. For example, if you have an average outstanding balance of just $2,000, your annual insurance premium at a rate of 75 cents per $100 would be a whopping $180! In addition, most of this insurance provides really poor coverage. For example, it usually pays only the minimum monthly payment — meaning the interest only, or the interest plus a small percentage of the principal — not the full balance. And it usually does that only after a waiting period of 30 to 45 days — which is longer than most disabilities last. Finally, since the premiums are billed to your credit card account, you end up paying extra interest, raising the total cost still further.

## KNOW YOUR CREDIT CARD RIGHTS

Credit cards offer considerable convenience, but using them can also subject you to certain abuses if you don't know your rights. Here are four potential problem areas:

**1.** Surcharges for credit card use. If a merchant posts a price, he cannot add on an extra fee if you want to pay with a credit card. Such surcharges are specifically prohibited by both Visa and MasterCard, as well as by American Express in most states. (Many stores build credit card processing charges into their prices, meaning they can give you a discount for not using a credit card.)

**2.** Purchase minimums. Despite posted signs at many firms — particularly restaurants — requiring that you purchase at least $5 or $10 before using your credit card, such practices are prohibited by Visa, MasterCard and American Express (in most states).

**3.** ID demands. Though many stores ask for your driver's license number, phone number or address when you buy something with a credit card, you are not obligated to provide the information. In fact, California, Delaware, Georgia, Maryland, Minnesota, Nevada, New Jersey and New York have specific laws prohibiting merchants from requiring such information.

**4.** Credit card requirements when cashing checks. Many stores demand that you have a credit card before they will allow you to cash a personal check. However, while they may legally ask to see a card, they cannot force you to give them the card number — and you should never allow them to write it on the check. For one thing, it opens the door for fraudulent use of your credit card account. For another, the card number does the merchant no good since Visa, MasterCard and American Express all prohibit member stores from assessing a charge against your credit card to cover a bounced check. They also refuse to go into their billing files to help a merchant locate you in order to collect on a bounced check. Each of the states mentioned in No. 3 have laws prohibiting this practice — as do Florida, Iowa, Kansas, North Dakota, Ohio, Virginia and Washington. If you'd like more information about credit card rights, write Bankcard Holders of America, 333 Pennsylvania Ave. SE, Washington, D.C. 20003, or call 1-800— 553-8025.

## WHEN YOU SHOULD WITHHOLD CREDIT CARD PAYMENTS

When you use a credit card to buy goods or services that prove  substandard, you may be able to legally withhold your payments to the  card issuer for those items. That's because the Fair Credit Billing  Act permits credit card companies to reclaim such disputed amounts  from merchants, even after credit card slips are signed — but only  when certain conditions of purchase are satisfied. Here are the five  conditions that must be met before you can withhold payment:

**1.** The purchase must have been made within your home state — or  within a 100-mile radius of your residence.

**2.** The amount of the disputed charge must be in excess of $50. (Note: Conditions 1 and 2 are waived if defective goods were purchased from the same company that issued the credit card or from one  of its corporate affiliates — e.g., you buy a defective television  from Sears using a Discover card.)

**3.** You must have tried to settle the matter first with the merchant.

**4.** You must notify the card issuing institution that you have  already tried and failed to settle the dispute and that you will be  withholding payment. After getting your notice, the card issuer will  credit your account in the amount of the charge, then bill the amount  back to the merchant.

**5.** You must dispute the charge before you pay your credit card  bill. Once you send in a check, you're stuck with the merchandise.

## FREE CREDIT CARD REGISTRATION

With crime rates rising, it's almost certain that, at some time or another, you're going to have a wallet or purse stolen — and, if you're like most Americans, it's going to be full of credit cards. That makes credit card registration essential. These services, which maintain lists of all your card numbers and the issuing institutions, will handle all the notification chores for you if your cards are lost or stolen. That means you have to make just one call — to them. Many also cover you against excess liability due to unauthorized card use. Of course, these services usually come with a price — usually around $20 a year, but sometimes as much as $35 or $40 annually.

However, because the credit card business is so lucrative, many smaller specialty card issuers — such as department stores and oil companies — are offering these services free in an effort to entice consumers to use their cards rather than the "Big Four" (Visa, MasterCard, American Express and Discover). For example, BP — the big international oil company (BP stands for British Petroleum) — offers holders of its BP Horizon card free registration services for both credit cards and important documents (driver's license, Social Secur-ity card, passport, etc.). To get an application for a BP card, call BP Customer Service at 1-800-321-9555.

## BEWARE OF LOAN-AGREEMENT TRAPS

Any time you take out a loan, you will be asked to sign a credit contract. If you want the loan, you won't have any choice in the matter. However, that doesn't mean you should ignore dangerous clauses that appear in many loan agreements. Some examples:

* **Lien provisions** — These give the lender the right to seize your home (except in homestead states), car, boat or other valuable items of personal property if needed to pay off an overdue debt.

* **Wage-garnishment clause** — This gives the lender the right to attach part of your salary to satisfy a delinquent loan.

* **Acceleration clause** — This allows a lender to call the entire note if you miss a single payment.

* **Confession of judgment** — This waives your right to defend yourself against foreclosures, repossessions or seizures by the lender.

* **Assumption of legal fees** — This states that you will pay any attorneys' fees the lender may incur in collecting an overdue loan.

If you spot any of these traps in the fine print of your loan document, attempt to have them stricken — or at least modified — before signing on the dotted line.

## PAY EXTRA PRINCIPAL AND SAVE

Lenders and credit card companies love people who make the minimum payment each month. Why? Because that ensures the loan term is extended as long as possible, enabling the creditor to collect the maximum amount of interest. For example, assume you have a $2,400 balance on a credit card with an 18 percent rate. The minimum payment might be calculated based on interest (0.015 percent per month x the balance), plus 1/60th of the principal (a six-year payoff term). If  so, your initial payment would be $76 — or $36 in interest (0.015% x  $2,400 = $36), plus $40 in principal ($2,400/60 = $40).  That means more than 47 percent of your monthly   payment was interest and only 53 percent went to retiring your debt.  No wonder you can't seem to get ahead of your bills! If you make the  minimum payment, the same circumstances will prevail the following month, with the balance falling to just $2,360 and the minimum payment dropping to just $74.73 ($35.40 in interest and $39.33 in principal).

If, however, you make a payment in excess of the minimum, every   penny of the additional money goes toward principal, which quickly  shortens the payoff time — saving you hundreds or even thousands in extra interest charges. For example, if you take the above situation and pay just $50 more than the minimum each month, you will cut your payoff term roughly in half and save about $1,050 in total interest payments. Payoff strategy: Don't try to divide your money so you can make extra principal payments on all your debts. Instead,  concen-trate your extra payments on those loans or bills that carry  the highest interest rates. This will save you more in interest charges than if you spread your money around.

## GO FOR A SHORTER TERM

If you don't have the discipline to make extra principal payments on your own, you can force the issue on installment debts by taking  the shortest loan term possible. In other words, rather than financing a new car for 60 months, finance it only for 36 months. The monthly payment will rise only slightly, but the interest savings will run  into the thousands. As a general rule, try not to finance anything  for more than 36 months. If the loan amount is under $3,000, cut the  term to 24 months — and, if it is under $1,000, finance for only a  year. This strategy will cost you a little more in the short term, but your total borrowing cost will fall dramatically over the life of your loans — freeing up money that can be used for savings, investments or merely an improved lifestyle.

## GETTING CREDIT FOR YOUR BUSINESS

Lenders have a natural aversion to small business owners, simply because they often have an erratic cash flow and lack a proven income stream. Many also have the bulk of their assets tied up in their companies, meaning there is little security available for new loans. However, there are some strategies you can adopt if you own a small business and need to improve your credit worthiness:

* List yourself as an employee of the business rather than the owner — and have an accountant verify your income for the lender.

* Incorporate your business and pay yourself a salary, verifiable by W-2 forms instead of your business tax returns. Arrange for a contact person whom the lender can call to confirm your employment with the company (your bookkeeper or accountant will often do this).

Though it may seem silly, this will make you much more appealing to lenders — even though your actual financial status is absolutely the same.

## BANKRUPTCY — TO FILE OR NOT TO FILE?

Declaring bankruptcy is the ultimate financial safety net, since it provides temporary protection from harassing creditors, who otherwise might sue or garnish your wages. However, it's still a drastic step and exacts its toll in several ways.

First, bankruptcy remains on your credit record for 10 years, making it nearly impossible for you to obtain credit during that time. Also, good bankruptcy attorneys don't come cheap. They can charge from $350 to $1,500 or more if your case is complicated.

The most severe form of consumer bankruptcy, Chapter 7, requires you to sell most of your property (with the possible exception of your house) to pay off your debts. Chapter 13, on the other hand, allows debts to be rescheduled if you have a steady job, less than $350,000 in secured debt and are a good risk to eventually pay off your bills.

Bankruptcy alternatives: If you're not in desperate financial circumstances and feel you can "restructure" your debts, talk to a credit counseling service. They can negotiate on your behalf with creditors to set up a repayment plan both sides can live with. To locate a reputable counselor near you, call the National Foundation for Consumer Credit Counseling, 1-800-388-2227. Beware: There are a lot of rip-off artists in this field, so be sure to go through the CCC rather than answering a newspaper or TV ad.

## DON'T LET BILL COLLECTORS BULLY YOU

In tough economic times, it's natural for folks to fall behind in paying their bills — especially victims of layoffs or costly illnesses. Unfortunately, tough times also tend to bring out the ugliness in debt collectors. And some collection agencies resort to tactics that are not only aggressive, but downright illegal — such as using intimidating or abusive language, leaving threatening phone messages, telling a third party about the alleged debts or repeatedly calling debtors at work.

In fact, there are even uglier tactics. The Federal Trade Commission has had complaints from people who've had collectors show up on their doorsteps, armed, claiming to be cops and threatening arrest. Other threats (besides garnishing of wages and filing a lawsuit) include having the debtor's name appear in the paper.

Debt collectors are within their rights to demand payment and ultimately take you to court — but you have rights too. The Fair Debt Collection Practices Act doesn't permit them to harass you. Examples of harassment are calling a debtor before 8 a.m. or after 9 p.m. — unless the debtor gives explicit permission. Coercive threats, especially of violence, are absolutely forbidden, as is use of profanity. And, you can turn off those intrusive phone calls — whether they are technically abusive or not — just by writing a letter to the collection agency requesting them to stop calling you. By law, the agency cannot phone again except to notify you of the next step in its collection procedure.

Besides telling the agency to stop contacting you, you may also wish to refer them to your attorney. Thereafter, the agency must deal with the lawyer. And, a collection agency cannot legally threaten you with immediate arrest or publishing your name. It can inform you if it intends to garnish your wages or seize your property, but these must be actual intentions, not threats.Warning: When dealing with collectors, never agree to write a post-dated check for what you owe. Collection agents often make this "suggestion," but if you're unable to cover the check, they can then threaten criminal charges.

If you're having trouble with meeting a debt obligation, the best approach is to go straight to the people you owe and strike a deal with them. Most creditors would rather negotiate a payment schedule — even reducing the amount — than turning your account over to an agency. Such a negotiation may also safeguard your credit report. If you dispute the debt (or the quality of goods or services received), you should definitely bring your complaint to the creditor's atten- tion. Remember, as a consumer you have 30 days after first being con- tacted to contest the debt in writing. Note: Although it's not widely known, even collection agencies will compromise — sometimes dramatically — on the amount you must pay. You can also call 1-800-388-2227 to contact the nearest national Consumer Credit Counseling Service center and get someone to serve as an intermediary between you and your creditor or collection agency.

As a last resort, you can also sue a debt collector for up to a year after the date you believe your rights were violated. In fact, you can sue for damages, court costs and attorney's fees.

**NOTES**

_____

_____

_____

_____

_____

---

CHAPTER 6

# BEST DEALS ON INSURING
# LIFE AND HEALTH

---

## LIFE INSURANCE — HOW MUCH DO YOU NEED?

A rough formula for calculating how much life insurance you need is to multiply the annual gross salary of the chief wage earner by a factor of five. (Two-income families should calculate five times the annual gross salary of both spouses.) However, a more sophisticated formula requires some simple arithmetic. Compile a figure based on the following factors, and you'll have a fairly precise estimate of just how much life insurance you need:

**1.** List current yearly living costs. Include mortgage or rent payments, food costs, loan payments, utilities, clothes, transportation and so on. Add costs of services you'd have to pay to replace in case of death — housecleaning, laundry, child care, and so on.

**2.** Add up yearly income. Don't list income that would be lost in the event of the death of the person to be insured. Include income from spouse, investments, Social Security, pension benefits and annual income from any current insurance policies.

**3.** Subtract "1" from "2" to find out how much additional annual income your family will require. If "2" is greater than "1," you've got too much insurance. For every $5,000 your income exceeds costs, decrease your coverage by $100,000.

**4.** Calculate how much insurance you'll need to make up any annual income shortfall. The formula is the reverse of the one used for over insurance — i.e., for each $5,000 of needed yearly income, you need $100,000 in insurance. For example, if your family income will fall short by $20,000 should you die, you need $400,000 in insurance.

**5.** Add additional cash requirements. In addition to annual costs, calculate one time lump sum requirements, such as funeral costs, consumer loan payoffs, children's future education expenses, etc. If you leave these needs out of your insurance package, they will have to be met by reducing family expenditures.

**6.** Add last two figures together to calculate the total insurance death benefit required.

**Note:** Most financial analysts agree insurance policies are great for providing protection against loss, but are poor investment tools. Example: Whole-life policies may advertise high fixed rates of return, but the guaranteed rate of return is invariably much lower — probably below the inflation rate. You can usually do better with Series EE U.S. Savings Bonds.

## CREDIT LIFE INSURANCE: JUST SAY NO

These policies are offered as a way to pay off your loans in the event you die before making all the payments. This may sound good, but unfortunately the actual payouts on such policies average less than 3 percent of the premiums collected.

Another indication that they are not what they seem is how they are offered. You probably won't be presented with such a policy when you're applying for a loan and are scrutinizing all papers carefully.  It'll show up in your mailbox weeks or months later, when you're less vigilant, and the literature will make it seem like a minor add on to protect your credit. These are definitely not a good deal — except for the bank or loan agency selling them.

## YOU MAY NOT NEED LIFE INSURANCE

Though a sales agent will never admit it, not everyone needs life insurance. People who can do without personal coverage include non-income producing spouses with no dependents, young singles and retirees  without dependents whose holdings are small enough to avoid estate taxes when they die. Self-employed individuals should also make sure they have adequate disability or income replacement insurance before  spending a lot of money on a life insurance policy. Exception: If you  are young and single, but plan to marry and raise a family later, you  may want to take out a small policy now to ensure you'll be insurable  in the future. Pass the insurance physical now, and you will be able  to later renew the policy or convert it to a different type without having to take a new exam.

## WHAT IF YOU CAN'T PASS THE PHYSICAL?

If you have health problems and have failed one or more life insurance physicals, there's no reason to give up on getting the  coverage you need. The key is to find an independent agent who knows  the health standards of a number of different insurance companies.  How can he or she help? Simple. Although you may not know it, health standards vary substantially from company to company. Thus, the independent agent can ascertain your specific problem and identify the company with the most lenient standards in that particular area. For example, many companies will refuse a middle-aged, 6-foot man who weighs more than 250 pounds. Others will insure him, but will add a substantial surcharge on the premium. However, a few will accept such a person without an extra charge, so long as he has no other obvious health problems. The independent agent can compare standards and find those companies.

Good agents also know how to word applications so your health problems are presented in the most favorable light. Alternative: If your health problems are so bad even a good independent agent can't find a policy for you, there's a good chance that you can still get coverage under a group policy. Many social clubs, fraternal orders, professional associations, churches and other organizations offer group policies to their members. If you can't get insurance any other way, you may do well to join such a group — the membership fee will be a small price to pay to get the coverage you need.

## INSURANCE COMPANY RATING FACTS

To give you a better idea of why you might be turned down by a life insurance company, here's a list of interesting health, life style and longevity facts the insurers have come up with, based on reviews of mortality statistics and actuarial probabilities:

* The most dangerous kind of obesity is when a person's abdomen is larger than his or her expanded chest.

* Smokers at all ages have death rates more than twice as high as non-smokers.

* The death of both parents before age 60 increases by one-third the child's mortality risk.

* Suicide rates are much lower among overweight people, but being lean generally increases one's lifespan.

* Living alone is far more dangerous to your health than being in a stable relationship.

* Rich people live longer — probably because they get better medical care, hygiene and nutrition.

* Getting insurance is almost impossible for those who have a stroke after age 60, but a stroke before age 60 becomes a diminishing  mortality factor the longer the person lives uneventfully after it.

* Nearsighted people are prone to anxiety.

* Obsessive-compulsive people are more susceptible to depression  and suicide in later life.

* Severe drunkenness — once a week or even once a month —  dramatically increases mortality risk factors.

* Involvement in kinky sex increases the likelihood of violent  death or suicide.

* Doctors have found a correlation between susceptibility to fear and blood coagulation associated with phlebitis.

* Insurers charge 1 applicant in 250 a surcharge because of occupation. Only 1 in 10,000 is refused outright because of an occupational hazard.

* Among the best insurance risks — farmers, college teachers and  ministers.


## SWITCH INSURANCE COMPANIES AND SAVE

As long as you remain in good health, you may save money on your  term life insurance by switching companies every three to four years.  The reason: Many companies offer the first four or five years of term coverage at a reduced rate in order to attract new business, then recover the difference with higher-than-average premium hikes on subsequent renewals. Using this strategy will take a little time every few years, but it could save you 25 to 30 percent on your life insurance  premiums. Inconvenience: You'll probably have to get a new physical  each time you switch — but then you should get a physical exam at  least that often anyway.

**Cautionary notes:** Don't drop your existing coverage until you've been approved for the new policy, just in case you should fail the physical. Also, be sure the new policy you switch to offers guaranteed renewal, just in case health problems should develop that would prevent you from getting new coverage.

## WHEN YOUR INSURER WON'T PAY

Ever try to collect from an insurance company — any kind of insurer? Then you know how they hate to pay claims. Suddenly you're not their treasured customer and loyal premium payer, but an adversary. And, the adjustors don't sound anything like those friendly folks who sold you the policy. Remember, insurance companies don't fatten their profits by paying claims. They do it by disputing claims and finding  loopholes in the policy they sold you. Fortunately, there are a few  things you can do to shift the odds in your favor should you have to  fight to get a claim paid. Here are four:

**1.** Ask your agent what your claim is worth. If he or she won't  tell you, ask a negligence lawyer.

**2.** Be prepared to accept a reasonable discount. You can use a  lawyer to negotiate or do it yourself (to save legal fees). A small  financial incentive may be all it takes to get the insurer to settle  your claim.

**3.** If you incur heavy out-of-pocket expenses due to pain and suffering, it may be worth it to hire a lawyer to point out claimable losses you're not aware of.

**4.** If your company continues to stall your claim, complain to the state insurance regulatory agency — or take them to court. In fact, when you're not getting action, the mere threat of suit may be just what it takes to get a really hard-ball company to take you seriously.

One of the best ways to prevent problems is to follow the proper procedures before you file a claim. Here are some guidelines:

* The instant the injury, accident or property loss occurs is the time to begin accumulating documentation to help support your claim. Start a folder and file copies of all medical reports, police or fire inspection reports, all communication with insurance company personnel (written, fax or phone), along with receipts, repair or replacement estimates. Xerox all documentation proving ownership.

* Keep duplicates in a second folder. Any time you send something to the insurance company, keep a copy in this folder.

* Keep abreast of your policy conditions. Double check all your relevant policies — including the fine print. Make sure you know what kind of documentation will be required in case of a claim. The more you play by the company rules and supply the correct paperwork, the more likely you'll get a quick and fair settlement.

* Exercise a proper amount of patience. Claim periods vary — especially disability claims — and get longer depending

on circumstances (such as continuing police investiga-
tions). Normally, routine claims should be settled within the
following limits:

— Life insurance claims, two to three months.

— Health insurance claims, 45 days.

— Homeowner's insurance claims — 10 days to two
weeks.

— Business insurance claims — two to three weeks.

— Automobile injury liability claims — three to four weeks.

— Automobile personal-injury claims — two to three
weeks.

— Auto property-damage liability claims — 10 days to two
weeks.

— Automobile collision claims — one week to 10 days.

## DISPUTING YOUR PROPERTY INSURANCE COMPANY

Too many homeowners have crawled out after some
natural catastro- phe only to get flattened again by their
insurance carrier. Here are  the kinds of nasty aftershocks
that can happen — and what you can do  about them:

* You're offered an inadequate settlement for your losses.
This could mean your claims adjustor was merely incompetent or blatantly  unfair. And, since most states do not
have licensing requirements for insurance adjustors, either
one is a distinct possibility. Also, many adjustors base
assessments on surface appearances, but don't have the
expertise to diagnose structural damage. You have every
right to ask  for another adjuster. You should also talk with
neighbors whose property suffered similarly, especially any

with the same insurer. Discuss in detail how your various claims are being handled. If you're still unhappy with the settlement being offered, complain to the company. Surprisingly, this often results in more equitable payouts.

* You discover your coverage isn't enough to rebuild your house. This is a frequent complaint. In fact, two-thirds of U.S. homeowners are not adequately insured for the serious losses they could face. Often this underinsuring is traceable to a sales pitch or company advertising that glossed over unpleasant realities. For instance, if you're only insured for the market value of your house, you may not receive a settlement sufficient to rebuild — the actual replacement value. A local building contractor, not an insurance company sales agent, can best estimate adequate replacement value. What can you do after the fact? Don't hesitate to go back to the insurer and complain that the policy they sold you didn't provide the coverage that was promised. After the devastating 1993 firestorms in Southern California, hundreds of homeowners won additional settlements after making exactly that complaint to their insurers.

* You dispute the kinds of repairs your insurer deems adequate. Again, this is a frequent area of controversy. The insurer's assessment people — contractors, engineers or whatever — obviously tend to come up with fixes that will cost the company as little as possible. To counter, you should hire your own experts — contractors with experience in the particular type of damage repair. Take those estimates back to the insurer company, highlighting any discrepancies in cost or materials. If you and the insurance company remain at odds, you can request a third party be brought in to mediate.

* You discover your "guaranteed replacement" policy has a limit that renders it insufficient. Unfortunately, there's not

much you can do about this after your house has been clobbered. The time to act is beforehand — switching to a policy that guarantees unlimited replacement coverage.

* Your home is adequately covered, but its contents aren't. Most policies base coverage of belongings on a percentage of the house's value — and use that figure as a ceiling on settlements. This may apply even though your policy offers guaranteed unlimited replacement coverage. For instance, if your house is insured for $200,000, and the contents have a coverage ceiling of 75 percent, you can recover only $150,000 for them. The solution is to increase your home coverage. If your insurer refuses the additional coverage, ask them to at least raise the cap on the contents. If that is also denied, shop for another insurance company.

* You wait too long to sue your insurer. This can happen if your policy contains an internal one-year limitation on lawsuits, and you weren't aware of it. If this happens to you, you're probably out of luck. Check your policy carefully.

* You discover additional losses after an initial settlement. If this happens, don't think it's too late because your case has been closed. There may be a legal time limit on suits, but you can always go back to an insurer to show additional damages. Many have done so, and collected more money.

## SINKING LIFEBOATS — WHEN INSURERS FAIL

Bank and S&L failures have been much publicized and frightening. This is true even though federal bank authorities have stepped in and made good the losses of all depositors — up to $100,000. But, recently some major insurance companies have rolled belly up — through bad investments or bad fiduciary management. The result: Many holders of  whole-life policies and annuities have lost partial value — being  forced to accept settlements or around 55 cents on the dollar — and  discovered they had very few rights. In many of these instances there  were guaranteed state funds established to protect policyhold- ers, but  most such funds took the pragmatic position that they weren't obliged  to make up the principal losses of pol- icyholders who accepted early settlements.

The best insurance against the potential failure of your insurance company is knowledge. You need to know what is likely to happen  if your company fails. This way you will know the appropriate steps to take before anything has happened — and to guard against it hap- pening — and, afterward, to protect yourself during a crisis. Risk  also varies, depending on the type of policy:

* Death benefits are rarely at risk. If a failing insurer can't make good on these obligations, regulators will. However, such policies routinely allow you to cash them in while you are still alive,  and that option may be lost in event of a fail- ure.

* Variable life policies and variable annuities are not at risk, no matter what happens to the underwriter. The full value will be  available to you. That's because the premiums you pay for these funds  are invested in separate accounts, which are protected from the insurer's creditors.

* Health insurance policies are usually totally at risk. You will  be left with no coverage at all — and may not be able to recover any  prepaid premiums.

\* Disability policies — or others that provide ongoing pay-ments — will generally also be a total loss. The periodic payments will  stop at the moment the insurer fails, and you'll go on the list with  all the other creditors when you try to recover prepaid premiums.

If your insurance company fails, you obviously need to talk to  your agent, your accountant and to a lawyer or financial planner. You  need quick, accurate and situation-specific advice in several areas:

\* Should you take out a new life insurance policy right away?

\* Should it provide the same coverage, or perhaps more?

\* If so, will you qualify for such a policy?

\* How do you go about seeking return of prepaid pre-miums?

\* How do you get new health or disability coverage if you can't  pass the medical conditions for a new insurer?

With certain types of coverages, you may be able to apply for a  hardship withdrawal from the failed insurer. You may qualify if:

\* You have medical bills but no health insurance.

\* You are permanently disabled or have a terminal illness.

\* You are being evicted from a nursing home or hospital.

\* You can prove the money is needed to pay for college tuition.

These withdrawals by-pass all settlements and pro-vide 100 cents on  the dollar. However, if you don't qualify for a  hardship withdrawal, earlysettlement arrangements are probably the best way to go. Afterward, you can file a claim with the state guaranteed fund for the  amount you were denied in the settlement.

You should also determine immediately how much cash value remains  in your policy? (This amount is reduced by loans you've taken against it.) Don't, however, stop making premium payments just because you don't have sufficient cash value. You don't want the policy to lapse  — and, even though you may be denied immediate access to the policy's full cash value, you are still insured.

When you do start looking for new insurance, you want to make  sure the new company you choose is healthier than your former one.

Select only insurers rated C-plus or above by Weiss Research. (You  can get a rating by calling 1-800-289-9222. The charge is $15 per  rating — money  well spent if it saves you from going  with another shaky outfit.) Also, consider no-load and low-load insurance as well as full-commission insurance. Finally, don't put all your insurance eggs in one basket — no matter how secure the basket looks in the company sales literature. It's best to spread your total insurance needs among two or three strong companies.

## SIDESTEPPING INSURANCE PITFALLS

Some insurance salespeople can sound like pulpit-pounders. They  make their policies sound like the only road to financial salvation.  Not only will they provide death benefits, you'll be told, but they  will give you secure, tax-deferred investment earnings. Then, flipping glossy bar charts at you, they will explain how your monthly premiums will gradually build into a sizable estate. Now, how about giving equal time to what the salespeople won't tell you:

* Life insurance isn't for everyone. If you want to guard your family's assets and lifestyle against the death of a wage-earner, you need it. But, if you don't have dependents, assets or debts, you probably don't need it.

* Insurance agents will try and sell anyone breathing on the investment angle of a whole-life policy. But, taken strictly as investments, whole-life policies don't stack up. You'd be better off with a 10-year Treasury note. The yields are comparable, but the Treasury note gives complete security of principal, an interest rate guarantee and the ability to sell your T-note on the open market at any time. Life insurance companies, on the other hand, penalize policyholders who try to cash out in the first 10 years — often as much as 10 percent of the cash value in surrender fees. And, as far as security of principal, insurance companies can and do fail. If it happens to you, payoffs can be delayed for years — or forever.

Shopping for insurance the low-pressure way: If you have a family and financial obligations, you do need insurance. But you don't need to deal with high-pressure, commission-hungry salespeople. Try these alternatives:

* You can get free quotes on term life policies by calling Select-Quote, 1-800-343-1985; TermQuote, 1-800-444-8376; or InsuranceQuote, 1-800-972-1104. These services make their money if you subsequently buy one of their products.

* Send a check for $13.95 to National Insurance Consumer Organi- zation, 121 N. Payne St., Alexandria, VA 22314, for a guide detailing reasonable rates and restrictions based on age and gender.

## DOUBLE INDEMNITY CAN BE A BARGAIN

A double-indemnity clause is a provision in an insurance policy that doubles the face value in the event of accidental or violent death. For young families, a double-indemnity clause can provide the additional coverage needed without a substantial increase in premiums. The reason is that most people calculate total potential need without considering the likelihood of why they might have to collect on a policy. A young father might feel he needs $500,000 to adequately protect his family, even though such a policy would be a huge strain on his budget. What he overlooks is that the greatest life risk he faces at his age is from an accident. Thus, he could cover his greatest risk by simply buying a $250,000 policy with a double indemnity clause. This might add only $10 or $15 to the annual premium, but would increase coverage to $500,000 for an accidental death. Caution: If you do get a double-indemnity policy, make sure there aren't too many exclusions with respect to the greatest risks you face (e.g., we've seen some that apply to accidents in public carriers, but not to accidents in your own car).

## PREPARING FOR CATASTROPHIC MEDICAL COSTS

The time to prepare for a possibly catastrophic medical emergency is before it happens. Of course, these are things no one wants to envision or deal with. For instance, few want to decide in advance where they wish to die — at home or in a hospital — but the resolution of that one issue can save (or cost) tens  of thousands of dollars. And the fact remains that, on average, half  of all medical costs are incurred in the last five days of a person's  life.

Some health insurance policies have provisions to cover catastrophic illness. Premiums on these policies are lower than average since  they have a large deductible — usually from $5,000 to $20,000. That  is because they are designed only to pay very large medical claims —  those that can ravage an estate in a frighteningly short period of time. The trade-off: For older adults, policies with lower deductibles designed to pay off smaller hospital and doctor bills can run  $5,000 to $8,000 in yearly premiums — and the policyholders remain unprotected from catastrophic costs.

These issues are sensitively and sensibly discussed in "150 Ways  to Be a Savvy Medical Consumer," by Charles B. Inlander, President,  People's Medical Society, 462 Walnut, Allentown, PA 18102. Cost: $5.

## A COST-SAVING HEALTH-INSURANCE TRICK

Fear of a chronic or disabling illness that could erase a family's assets is another reason many people cite for buying excess insurance. However, you can provide additional low-cost protection for  your family against such an occurrence by simply buying an "excess"  major medical policy with a deductible equal to the maximum benefit under your current health plan. Because of the high deductible, the  premium cost will be much more reasonable than if you bought a full— coverage policy for the same total amount.

## PREMIUM SAVINGS — 10 INSURANCE POLICIES TO AVOID

One insurance industry expert estimates that 10 percent of the  money spent Americans spend on insurance is thrown away. How can you tell if a particular policy is a smart bet — or a foolish waste of  money? Here are two rules of thumb:

\*   Avoid single-risk policies — ones that cover only a specific disease or type of accident. Comprehensive policies make more sense.

\*   Never insure against minor losses you can cover yourself.

To be more specific, here are 10 types of policies you'll almost  never get good value from — and thus should not waste money on:

**1. Mortgage-protection insurance.** It's understandable you might  fear a job lay-off, which could cost you your house, and therefore  buy a policy to step in and make your mortgage payments or up to a  year. However, premiums for such policies are generally much too high  for the amount of coverage.

**2. Clunker collision coverage.** If your car is more than five  years old and your collision costs more than 10 percent of the car's  market value, drop it — and save 20 percent to 40 percent on your  premiums. Note: For an estimate of your used-car's value, check the  public library for the "Older Used Car Guide" or the "Official Used  Car Guide."

**3. Extended auto-service contracts.** Most auto experts agree these   policies are a bad deal. The items covered rarely have problems during the years of the contract.

**4. Trip cancellation insurance.** Travelers who buy non-refundable tickets often go for this, worried some emergency will cause them to miss a flight. However, such policies often have tricky exceptions — and odds are the airline will sell you a new ticket for an extra $25.

**5. Credit insurance.** This is a standard add on every time you get a loan from a finance company, auto dealer or bank. It's supposed to cover your payments in event of death or disability — but, in most cases, the price tag is grossly inflated. Most financial advisers recommend you instead beef up your savings account enough to deal with several months of payments. If the debt is a major one, it makes more sense to cover it with your life and/or disability policies.

**6. Term insurance for a child.** The agent's pitch here is that, for about $200 a year, you protect your child and guarantee that he or she will be covered in the event of disease. However, unless your child is a breadwinner (McCauley Culkin, for instance), you probably don't need insurance.

**7. Wedding insurance.** Granted, weddings tend to be major investments, and the expenses involved in a sudden cancellation can be substantial. However, such policies are expensive, too, and may be duplicated by your homeowner's policy or the liability policy of the wedding site. Even if it's not, this still isn't a smart bet.

**8. Flight insurance.** These are usually last-minute impulse purchases from airport vending machines. Before you drop the coins, however, think it over. Do you buy extra insurance every time you get in your car, which is far more dangerous? Spend the bucks on a souvenir instead.

**9. Rain insurance.** This is like wedding insurance. You shell out a few bucks to your property insurance agent as a hedge against rain washing out some outdoor event you're staging. However, such policies generally cost a sizable fraction of the proceeds they're protecting. Better to plan a rain check or an alternate indoor site.

**10. Home warranties.** Builders and real estate agents sometimes trot out these policies — supposedly protecting you, as the buyer, against major defects. Lots of buyers are going for them, but they come with lots of exclusions and don't come cheap — up to $500 a year is pretty standard, plus $100 whenever the contractor comes by to fix something. And, the coverage is worthless if the builder goes out of business — something that happens all the time.

## TV INSURANCE ADS — BUYER BEWARE!

In spite of how good — or how cheap — the announcers make it sound, most insurance advertised on TV and sold by phone or mail is a bad deal. The rates quoted (i.e., "a dollar a week") are usually for a minimum base policy (sometimes as little as $1,000 face value), meaning it will cost substantially more to get enough coverage to offer even modest protection. In addition, even when the policies do offer substantial face value for the premium, they tend to have multiple exclusions that eliminate coverage in the most common circumstances.

Firms that provide mail order health or accident policies are even worse — with bad records for denying claims or excluding illnesses. Another Trap: Low introductory rates that are quickly raised once you are dependent on the coverage. The best course is to avoid these companys, but if you feel tempted, check with your state insurance commission to make sure the company is licensed and has not built up a thick file of complaints.

## YOU COULD BE COVERED AND NOT KNOW IT

Insurance is automatically built in to a number of financial contracts, membership agreements and other documents. Here are several types of insurance coverage you may already have — or get when you make certain purchases — and not even know about:

* Your homeowner's policy will usually cover lost luggage, stolen purses or wallets and property taken in a car break-ins. It may also cover unusual accidents — such as damage by vandals or motor vehicles — and property lost or damaged while moving.

* If you buy an airline ticket with most major credit cards, you automatically get from $25,000 to $100,000 in free travel life insurance.

* American Automobile Association (AAA) members have automatic hospital and death benefits if hurt in a car accident.

* Membership dues for many fraternal organizations and service clubs entitle you to minimum life or health insurance benefits under group policies.

* If you are in a car accident, you may be able to collect twice on your injuries, first via your health insurance and again through a medical payments provision in your auto policy.

* Family health policies usually continue coverage for children, even if they are away at college. Check before you buy separate policies for them. Many colleges and universities also include a small amount of automatic life and/or health coverage in their tuition or mandatory fees, and others provide free health services for full-time students at on campus infirmaries.

---

## CHAPTER 7

# INVESTMENT AND
# WEALTH-BUILDING GUIDE

I nvestment is the key to successful wealth building. Almost no one — with the possible exception of authors, actors, sports figures and a few top corporate executives — can get rich simply by working for money. The only chance at wealth most of us have is to work hard enough to set aside a little extra cash — over and above what it takes to live on a day-to-day basis — and then let that cash go to work for us, earning more cash, which will also go to work, earning still more cash, which ... ad infinitum. If we follow that pattern — and invest the cash wisely — most of us can achieve a relative level of wealth given a little bit of time. Of course, the hardest part of that equation is the phrase "invest the cash wisely." The investment world can be highly confusing, and it's also full of pitfalls. However, with a little study, a little effort and a lot of patience, almost anyone can become reasonably proficient at the art of investing. And, the information contained in this section will help you learn to do just that.

## THE BEST STARTING PLACE — MUTUAL FUNDS

Once you've put aside enough money to cover your basic living needs, as well as savings equal to three to six months worth of income as a contingency against emer-

---

gencies, you're ready to move up in status from "saver" to "investor." And, for most people, the best place to start investing is with mutual funds. Funds offer a variety of advantages individuals can find nowhere else. These include:

* **Professional management.** Mutual fund operators are experienced professionals with access to top research and the latest in economic and market information. They also have large staffs to provide constant portfolio supervision.

* **Diversification.** The average price of all stocks on the New York and American stock exchanges is around $35 a share. Thus, if you wanted to build a diversified portfolio of only 10 to 12 specific stocks, buying in round lots (100 shares), you'd need $35,000 to $40,000 to do so. By contrast, you can diversify across scores or even hundreds of stocks in a mutual fund with an investment as small as $100.

* **Economies of scale.** Because funds deal in quantity, they get the best rates on commissions and other fees, which helps offset management expenses and enhance returns.

* **Simplified supervision.** Fund staff members keep track of portfolios, record transactions, enter stock splits, collect stock dividends or bond interest payments, reinvest funds or mail out checks, compile year-end tax summaries and provide a variety of other services — meaning you can keep track of your investment with a review of just one regular statement.

* **Ease of investment** and reinvestment of dividends. Regular investments can be made in small increments, and dividends can usually be reinvested automatically with no charge to you.

**\* Switching privileges.** If your fund is part of a family of funds — as most now are — you can usually switch from one type of fund to another as market conditions change, often with transaction charges (although most funds now limit the number of switches per year).

**\* Variety.** There's a fund designed for nearly every type of investor objective you can imagine, making it possible to tailor your fund investments to meet your personal goals.

Unfortunately, this latter attribute also creates something of a problem — which mutual fund do you choose? Consider that there are only 2,534 individual stocks listed on the New York Stock Exchange, but there are now over 3,750 different mutual funds, about 65 percent of which invest primarily in U.S. or foreign stocks. The others concentrate on bonds and/or money market securities, with some focusing on more specialized areas such as precious metals, commodities, etc.

The list is steadily growing too, as fund managers seek out new ways to put the soaring volume of incoming investor money to work. According to the Investment Company Institute, a trade organization of mutual fund managers, more than $155 billion flowed into equity mutual funds in 1993 and 1994, bringing total assets of equity funds to almost $600 billion. And, the influx of cash seems likely to continue as more and more people recognize the wealth-building potential of long-term investment in stocks — which, over the past 75 years, have outperformed all other investment forms by a margin of almost two to one.

Obviously, the mushrooming number of new funds makes selecting the best one for your individual needs more difficult. However, with a little extra effort and a good plan for evaluating both past performance and future prospects, you can be successful in finding quality mutual funds with a proven history of solid returns and steady growth.

## EVALUATING MUTUAL FUND PERFORMANCE

Mutual funds in America are big business. In fact, most analysts agree that the current $1 trillion-plus in mutual fund assets is now THE driving force behind price movements in the U.S. financial markets. This is particularly true in the equity sector, where fund managers have a ever-increasing amount of cash to throw at a stable or even shrinking supply of stocks. However, of more importance to you as a potential mutual fund buyer is the tremendous amount of money the fees on these assets generate for fund operators, sales people and others involved in the business. Management fees alone — which are charged by all mutual funds and average about 0.5 percent of assets managed each year — amount to around $5 billion annually.

And that doesn't even include front-end sales commissions (which can run as high as 8.5 percent of the amount invested), redemption fees (as much as 6.0 percent) or any of the other optional fund charges, such as 12b-1 fees. All told, it is estimated mutual funds generate annual fees and sales commissions in excess of $25 billion!

With that kind of money at stake, it should come as no surprise that you are likely to be overwhelmed by full-page newspaper and magazine ads, glitzy marketing brochures, varied promotional gimmicks and high-powered sales pitches when you begin shopping for equity mutual funds. How do you handle this barrage? Our advice is simple: Ignore it all — except as a starting point for your own research. If you see an ad for a fund that sounds appealing, don't just take the stated claims at face value. Check them out yourself. Verify that the fund's performance as stated is accurate and that it covers a long enough period to have real meaning, rather than just representing a single-year (or single-quarter) blip in an otherwise weak record. (The top-performing funds one year have a distressing tendency to turn in less than stellar showings the following year.) Make sure the fund's sales commissions and fees are competitive — or, better yet, lower than average. This is vital as an 8.5 percent load doesn't just cost you 8.5 percent. Your remaining capital — that left to work for you after the commission is deducted — has to grow by 9.29 percent (8.5/91.5 = 9.29%) just to get you back where you started. That's almost a full year's average appreciation for the S&P 500!

Most importantly, make sure the fund's objectives match your own investment needs. Don't let the promise of high-flying returns lure you into making the wrong choices. The same rules should apply to unsolicited fund recommendations you receive from brokers, financial planners or other commission-compensated financial professionals. While most of these people really do have your best interests at heart, they also depend on their commissions in order to eat — and this pressure sometimes clouds their judgment with respect to your personal objectives. There's nothing revolutionary in all of this. It's obviously sound advice, most of it based on simple common sense — but how do you follow it?

Most experts advise taking a seven-step approach, starting with a group of several potential funds that you have identified as being in the class that meets the investment objective you are trying to fill. These can be funds that came to your attention through advertisements or broker recommendations — or you can select your initial group of purchase candidates from the regular fund performance tables carried in a variety of leading financial publications, most of which break the funds down by category. These same tables should provide a lot of the information you need to begin your evaluation, but you should also request a prospectus for each of the funds you are considering, as well as a copy of the fund's latest annual report to share-holders. If you have a sizable sum of money to invest — or merely want to be especially thorough — you may also want to subscribe to one of the mutual fund rating services or one of several newsletters devoted exclusively to funds. (Note: If you'd like to check these services out, but don't want to spend the money on a subscription, most major public libraries take one or more of the publications, which you can review free in their reference sections.)

Once you have the necessary information at hand to make your fund evaluations and comparisons, you can start narrowing down the list of potential purchase candidates using the following seven steps, with the key factors to consider ranked in order of importance:

1. The 10-year annual compounded return of each fund.

2. The five-year annual compounded return of each fund.

3. Each fund's simple return for the most recent year.

4. The "variability" of each fund (i.e., the degree to which the fund outperforms or underperforms its own longer-term average compounded return during any given short-term trading period).

5. Each fund's "return per unit of risk," which is computed by dividing the fund's long-term average compounded return by its variability rating, as determined in No. 4.

**6.** The quality and experience of each fund's manager — and its investment advisor if that responsibility is handled by a different person or organization. (Fund management can be even more important if a fund has changed managers recently. In such cases, its five and 10 year compounded returns are probably suspect — especially if they are higher than the fund's return for the most recent year. That's because they were produced largely through the efforts of a different person, who may have had better stock selection skills or a different investment philosophy. As a result, you may do better by choosing a fund with a slightly lower long-term average return but an experienced manager over one with a higher long-term return but a fairly new manager.)

**7.** Each fund's sales commission (or load) and its expense ratio. Evidence is mixed on whether load funds perform better than no-load funds. Thus, if you have a choice between a load fund and a no-load fund with comparable performance records, you should probably select the no-load fund. With respect to expense ratios (total fund operating expenses expressed as a percentage of total assets), you should generally avoid funds with ratios in excess of 1.25 percent — and a 1.00 percent limit is better.

Obviously, you'll save yourself some time if you eliminate weaker contenders as you work your way through the evaluation process. If you get to the final step and don't have any funds left from which to choose, you can always go back and further examine some of the ones you dropped earlier. Hopefully, though, you will wind up with two or three top-flight funds still in the running, giving you the luxury of being able to pick and choose.

## A BARGAIN WAY TO TRY MUTUAL-FUND NEWSLETTERS

If you think you might like to subscribe to a mutual fund newsletter, but aren't sure which one, Select Information Exchange offers low-cost trial subscriptions to a variety of publications. One recent trial offering featured 25 different mutual fund letters or reports for just $29. To order, write SIE, 244 West 54th Street. New York, NY 10019, or call 1-212-247-7123.

## FUNDS CAN TAKE YOU OVERSEAS, TOO

One mistake too many American investors make is keeping their money at home. That makes little sense since roughly 95 percent of the world's population resides elsewhere — most in the so-called Third World nations. With the fall of Soviet communism, most of these nations are moving toward free-market economic systems, and will likely be the primary source of economic growth in the 21st century, producing big profits for those who invest there now at bargain prices. Unfortunately, making such investments can be difficult (some markets even restrict access by foreigners) and fraught with risk, both financial and political. However, by choosing the right investment vehicles — shares in closed-end, single-country funds traded on American stock exchanges — the process can be greatly simplified and many of the risks substantially reduced.

The first step in choosing such a fund is selecting a country of opportunity — one that offers the most investment potential with the least amount of danger. Here are some basic guidelines on what to look for:

* The country should be emerging from communism, socialism or some other restrictive government system into full-blown democracy,   a necessity for free-market growth and expansion.

* It should have a rapidly expanding population base, signaling  larger potential markets in the future.

* It should show signs of rising incomes, which will mean more  consumer spending and growing interest in Western-style products —  which, in turn, will mean growth in local industries that will have  to expand to supply consumer needs.

* The entire country should have an "upgrading economy" — meaning one that is becoming more intertwined with the rest of the world,  as signaled by participation in international economic pacts, trade  treaties and global financial systems. Adoption of generally accepted banking and accounting standards and passage of laws offering protections to consumers and investors are also helpful signs.

Obviously, identifying such countries will require a monitoring  not just of the financial media, but of the international news pages  in your daily newspaper and in monthly news magazines. An occasional trip to the library to check out foreign publications from the  region can also prove helpful, although you'll quickly find that a lack of quality information is one of the leading risk factors. Once  you have selected an area or country of interest, the next step is to  decide on your preferred method of investment. As we noted above,  direct investment in individual foreign stocks is risky in most cases  — and virtually impossible in some. However, there are attractive   alternatives. A number of major U.S. mutual fund companies have  regular international funds that focus specifically on Third World  markets or on distinct geographical areas, such as Southeast Asia, Eastern Europe or Latin America. These "open-ended" funds provide both profit potential and international diversification — but most of them are broad-based (not focused on a single country) and thus fail to provide a pure play on any given foreign market. For that reason, we prefer "closed-end" single-country investment funds.

There are currently more than 120 of these funds specializing in the stocks of more than 25 nations. Their managers and analysts have the time and expertise to carefully review economic and business conditions within their target country and select the best local companies. They also have the foreign governmental, banking and financial connections needed to quickly and economically buy and sell stocks in those companies. Finally, they offer the ultimate in convenience for American investors since their shares are listed on leading U.S. exchanges (or trade over the counter), meaning they can be bought and sold through your local broker — just like ordinary stocks. As a bonus, they frequently sell at a discount to their true net asset value — meaning they offer added appreciation potential.

To identify one of these 120 or so funds in which to invest, you should first check out a list of the markets on which they are available. The best way to do this is to get a copy of the Monday edition of The Wall Street Journal, which has a special weekly listing of all closed-end funds by type, complete with current price, net asset value and percentage premium or discount. Then select a few countries that you feel might offer good opportunities and begin familiarizing yourself with news events and economic conditions in those nations. As a starting point, you might select China, Indonesia, the Philippines, Malaysia, Taiwan and India, plus any others that interest you (don't pick more than 10 countries as you won't be able to find time to do the research on more than that).

You should also start watching price and volume patterns for the closed-end funds investing in those countries in order to get a feel for how they trade (the Journal will provide this information). That's because volatility is a major factor with these funds, and you want to buy only after a large price pullback (such as the one in many Latin American markets after the Mexican peso crisis in early 1995) — preferably one that results in the fund's price being discounted to its net asset value. As an example of the volatility, con- sider that the Taiwan Fund (TWN) had a 1993 trading range of $17.25 to $39.75 — more than $22 a share — even though its actual net value per share varied by only about $2.50, closing slightly above $18. Your goal — once you've picked out the countries to watch and gotten a feel for the funds representing them — is to buy on the pullbacks (e.g., closer to the Taiwan Fund's discounted $17.25 price), and then sell when the shares rebound, climbing to a price that represents a substantial premium to the actual net asset value (e.g., closer to the Taiwan Fund's inflated $39.75 price). Do that with a fair degree of consistency and you'll get both healthy profits and international diversification, which protects against higher inflation or a weaker economy here at home.

## USE CLOSED-END FUNDS FOR OTHER SECTORS, TOO

Closed-end funds can also be valuable tools for investing in other areas — from bonds and government securities to precious metals and mortgages. In fact, a high-quality mortgage investment fund is a great way to enhance returns on the fixed-income portion of your portfolio since these funds normally average yields from 1.5 to 2.0 percent higher than Treasury bonds or high-grade corporate bonds when held for the long term. In addition, unlike most debt securities, which have a fixed coupon rate, the yields on mortgage funds tend to fluctuate in response to changing market interest rates, thereby reducing volatility. Safety is also relatively high because most of the mortgages in which these funds invest are guaranteed by agencies of the U.S. government (such as the VA and FHA). The fund shares are also more liquid (remember, closed-end funds trade like stocks) than many individual debt securities — especially regular mortgages. Many of these funds also have a projected maturity date — i.e., a date in the future on which the fund will be liquidated and the assets returned to shareholders at a target unit price (usually around $10 a share). This enables investors to better plan both their cash flow and the availability of funds to meet future needs.

Among our favorite funds in this class is are the American Adjustable-Rate Term Trusts, a group of finite-life closed-end funds with currently scheduled maturity dates in each year through 1999. To help you see of how these funds work, we'll briefly describe the American Adjustable-Rate Term Trust of 1999, which trades on the NYSE (symbol: EDJ). According to the fund's statement of objectives, it is "a diversified closed-end fund that seeks to provide a stream of current income, plus a return of capital equaling $10 per unit or more at the trust's termination in September 1999." The fund began in 1992 with a 16.5 million share offering at an initial price of $10 per unit. The 1999 trust invests a minimum of 65 percent of its assets in U.S. government guaranteed mortgage-based securities backed by pools of adjustable rate mortgages (including modified pass-through certificates issued by agencies such as the Government National Mortgage Association, or Ginnie Mae). The other 35 percent of the fund's assets can be invested in zero-coupon bonds, fixed rate securities or government and corporate debt securities — which, if not backed by the govern- ment or its agencies, must have quality ratings of AA or better. As of mid-1994, the fund was providing a current yield of 6.37 percent, with scheduled monthly dividend payments of 4.2 cents a share (a total projected annual dividend of 51 cents a share). The shares were trading at a price of $8-1/8 ($8.125) — a substantial discount to their estimated net asset value of $9.61 a share. To buy the shares, you can either ask your local broker to get you a prospectus, or call the fund management company direct at 1-800-866-7778 and ask them to send you one. (The prospectus should also cover other funds in the group, just in case you're interested in one that matures in a year other than 1999.) Once you've reviewed the prospectus to make sure the fund really meets your needs, just call your broker to order.

## FUNDS CAN HELP SPEED WEALTH BUILDING

Mutual funds — regular open-ended ones rather than the closed— end type — are ideal vehicles for speeding your wealth building efforts because they allow you to easily reinvest your earnings, as well as add new money to that which is already working for you. One of the best strategies to accomplish this latter goal is dollar-cost averaging. This is a process of regular investment that lets you build up your holdings without having to worry about trying to time market tops and bottoms. Here's how it works:

Let's say you invest $100 a month in a fund with an initial share price of $10. You buy 10 shares the first month. The next month, the price doubles to $20, so you buy five more shares — still investing $100 a month. In succeeding months, say the fund goes back to $10 a share (you buy 10 more shares), falls to $5 (you buy 20 shares), then back to $10 (you buy 10 more). In five months, you've picked up 55 shares for a total cost of $500. The price began at $10 and ended at $10. No profit you think? Wrong. You actually paid an average of just $9.09 a share, including the 20 shares you picked up at $5. So you have 55 fund shares at $10, worth $550. You've made $50.

Dollar-cost averaging doesn't guarantee that you'll beat the mar- ket, but it does position you to take advantage of market movements and helps speed the growth of your fund holdings, as well as lowering the average unit cost per share.

## AVOIDING THE ANNUAL MUTUAL FUND TAX BITE

Most mutual funds announce their annual distribution of dividends and capital gains in December. The distribution is taxable — but you can avoid the liability if you make your fund purchases just after, instead of just before, the announcement date. Here's how it works: Suppose you buy 100 fund shares at $10 per share. The next day the fund announces a $2-per-share distribution in dividends and capital gains, reducing the share value to $8. You can accept the payout in cash or use it to buy additional shares, but you must pay tax on the distribution (on the $200 payout, you'd pay $56 in the 28 percent tax bracket). If you had waited until after the distribution to make your fund purchase, you could have had the same number of shares for $800 and skipped the tax. Since the actual announcement date for distributions varies from fund to fund, be sure to ask for the specific date before making your purchases.

## EASY PICKINGS IN THE STOCK MARKET

Many potential investors are scared of the stock market — not only because of the risk involved, but because it's like learning a foreign language, full of strange jargon. Or maybe a gambling game they just can't figure out. They want an ABC-simple stock-selection system — one that doesn't require computer analysis or studying annual reports. And, there such a system is available. It was developed by money manager Michael

O'Higgins (see his book, "Beat the Dow," HarperCollins, 1991). Over the past 20 years, it's averaged a 21.7 percent return on investment, outperforming the Dow Jones Industrial Average by a wide margin — and, in 1994 (when the S&P 500 returned just 1.32 percent), it returned 7.98 percent. Here's how the technique, known as the "Flying Five" strategy, works:

On Jan. 1, you rank all 30 Dow stocks from highest to lowest in order of their dividend yield. (These figures are published in The Wall Street Journal and other financial newspapers). From the 10 stocks with the highest yield, you then pick the five with the lowest share prices, buy those five and hold them for one year. That's all! Next Jan. 1, you start the process all over. Some stocks you may end up holding, others will be new.

Is the system foolproof and guaranteed? Of course not. One year, 1990, four of five stocks selected by this method performed badly and the yield was down 15 percent for the year. The system also doesn't tell how much of one's total investment to apportion to the stock market, how much to bonds, and so forth. That being said, it's a still a pretty remarkable formula.

A variation — actually a forerunner of the above strategy, first outlined in the 1960's book "Beating the Dow" (HarperPerennial, $10) — involves buying an equal dollar amount of the 10 Dow Industrials stocks with the highest dividend yield. This strategy has beaten the performance of the full Dow Industrials list and the S&P 500 in 16 of the past 20 years — averaging an excess gain over those indexes of about 6 percentage points. In 1994, it produced a return of 4.07 per-cent vs. the S&P's 1.32. Commissions can be a drawback with this technique since you have to restructure your holdings each year. However, there's even a way around that — investors with as little as $1,000 can buy  shares of the Select 10 Unit Trust (a closed-end fund) managed by Merrill Lynch and also sold by Dean Witter, Prudential Securities, Smith Barney and PaineWebber.

## HANDICAPPING A GROWTH STOCK

Every stock investor's dream is to find a quality growth stock  and then ride it to huge profits over a period of several years. Unfortunately, that's difficult to do — but there are some criteria  that can help, devised by Benjamin Graham, considered the father of  modern security analysis. His selection methods are time tested and  have proven effective in choosing low-risk stocks poised for signi- ficant appreciation. They are divided into two segments — risk criteria and reward criteria — detailed as follows:

### The Reward Standards

**1.**  The company must have an earnings/price (E/P) yield at least  twice that of the current yield on AAA-rated bonds. The E/P yield —  the reciprocal of the better-known price/earnings (or P/E) ratio —  is determined by dividing a company's current per-share earnings by  its current per-share price. It is expressed as a percentage, which  can then be used to make a direct comparison to bond yields. For  example, if AAA-rated corporate bonds currently have a yield of 7.5  percent, Graham would require a company to have an E/P yield of 15  percent (.075 x 2 = .150, or 15.0 percent). (The current average  yield for AAA-rated bonds is listed weekly in most major financial  publications. If you have trouble finding it, it is always included  in the "Market Laboratory/Bonds" section  near the back of Barron's financial weekly. The number you want is the listing for "Best Grade  Bonds.")

**2.** The company's current price/earnings ratio must be less than 40 percent of the highest P/E ratio the stock has had over the past five years.

**3.** It must offer a dividend yield of at least two-thirds the current AAA-rated bond yield.

**4.** It must have a stock price below two-thirds of the company's tangible book value per share.

**5.** The stock price must be below two-thirds the company's "net current asset value."

### The Risk Standards

**1.** The company's total debt must be less than its book value.

**2.** It must have a current ratio greater than 2.00. (The current ratio is a measure of a company's liquidity determined by dividing total current assets by total current liabilities.)

**3.** The company's total debt must be less than twice its "net current asset value."

**4.** The company must have shown a compound annual earnings growth rate over the previous 10 years of at least 7 percent.

**5.** There must be stability in growth of earnings — i.e., the company can have no more than two declines of 5 percent or more in year-end earnings over the previous 10 years.

Obviously, Graham's standards for determining undervalued stocks are extremely high — requiring in-depth analysis of a company's financial condition and earnings history, as well as its recent stock price performance. However, in the years since Graham first laid down these guidelines, repeated studies have shown they do identify sharply undervalued stocks with minimum downside risk — a fact verified by the performance results of mutual fund managers and professional investors who use them to select new holdings for their portfolios.

## FINDING STOCKS THAT WILL DOUBLE IN PRICE

There's only one absolute in selecting stocks: If a company isn't making money — or at least showing a pattern of steadily shrinking losses (in the case of R&D firms and start-up firms) — it cannot pass profits on to shareholders. And, without the hope for profits, there is no reason to own the stock. That translates into a lack of buying demand, without which a stock simply cannot go up — much less double in price. Thus, before you make any stock purchase, you must evaluate the company's earnings. If they are flat, or have been falling, the likelihood of a major price advance is remote. Likewise, if a company is losing money, there is little chance of its stock making a major upmove until it becomes profitable — the exceptions being takeover candidates with no earnings, but lots of assets and certain technology and health-care research firms, whose stocks often advance on expectations of large future returns.

As a rule, the best opportunities lie in companies that have shown at least five consecutive quarters of solid earnings — and five quarters of steady earnings growth is even better. Most market analysts place heavy emphasis on the price-to-earnings (P/E) ratio — and if earnings are rising, stock prices will almost invariably follow. For example, if a company in an industry group whose members normally have P/E ratios of around 20 earns $1 per share, its stock  price should be around $20 (20 x $1 = $20). If earnings subsequently  rise to $2.00 per share and the same P/E norm prevails, the stock can  be expected double in price to $40 (20 x $2 = $40). If it doesn't,  the stock would be considered undervalued. In fact, one of the most popular methods of finding stocks likely to double is to search out  issues with P/E ratios below those of other stocks in the same industry or market sector — the expectation being they will soon rise in  price to bring their P/E ratios in line with the rest of their group.

Following are three stocks that could be good candidates to double in price in the next 12 to 18 months, based on recent earnings  growth patterns through year-end 1994:

**1. CDP Technolgies** (Nasdaq: CDPT), an on-line information company  specializing in medical care and health services data. The company  lost 6 cents a share in 1991, but earnings have grown steadily since,  with profits hitting 16 cents a share in 1994. The stock's 1994 high  and low were $11 and $5.75, respectively, and it has been trading recently in the $9.50 to $10 range. Write the company at 333 Seventh  Ave., 4th Floor, New York, NY 10001, or call 212-563-3006 for a prospectus and annual report.

**2. Printronix** (Nasdaq: PTNX), a manufacturing company that speci- alizes in making high-durability computer printers designed for continuous use in factories and other facilities where it's essential to churn out a steady stream of such things as labels, bar code stickers and shipping invoices. The company lost $2.76 in 1991, cut  the loss to 76 cents in 1992, made a profit of 58 cents in 1993 and improved to a healthy $1.24 in earnings in 1994. The stock has been  trading in a recent range of $25 to $27 after having hit an all-time high of $29 in mid-1994. Write the company at Box 19559, Irvine, CA 92712 or call 714-863-1900 for a prospectus and annual report.

**3. Ecogen** (Nasdaq: EECN), a biotechnology firm specializing in agricultural growth enhancement products — some of which are already being marketed and sold (unlike the products of most other biotech firms, which are still in the conceptual or developmental stages). The company has yet to make a profit, but has reduced its loss from $1.26 per share in 1992 to 32 cents a share in the latest 12 months. Recently trading at about $3 a share, near the bottom of its 52-week range (which saw a high of $8.25), this stock seems destined to not only double — but perhaps triple or even quadruple in the months to come. Write the company at 2005 Cabot Boulevard West, Langhorne, PA 19047, or call 215-757-1590 for a prospectus and annual report.

# DO STOCK SPLITS OFFER BUYING OPPORTUNITIES?

Many investors view stock splits as a sign of prosperity at a company and use splits as a signal to purchase new (or more) shares. However, according to Al Goldman, chief strategist for A.G. Edwards, stock splits aren't necessarily a good thing. He says that, while many good companies split their stocks to make them more affordable, a lot of bad companies also use stock splits as a way to promote themselves. Warren Buffett, the highly regarded chairman of Berkshire Hathaway (which trades at the incredible and obviously unsplit price of $15,700 a share), goes even further, saying he generally ignores splits. "[Stock splits] don't make a company worth any more money, and they impose slightly more transaction and listing costs," says Buffett. Our recommendation: Avoid stocks that split when they're only trading at $10 or $20 a share. The only valid reason to split, and thus the only time it's a good buying signal, is when the split brings the price down into a more attractive buying range — say from $50 a share down to $25.


## PLAYING THE TAKEOVER GAME

Another reason many investors buy shares in a company is because they think it's a possible takeover target. Although the action is more subdued now than it was in the leveraged-buyout frenzy of the mid-1980s, plenty of companies are still being taken over every year — and plenty of shareholders are making large profits on the deals. So, how do you pick out potential takeover targets?

The first step is to identify companies that are severely undervalued relative to either their assets (book value) or their earnings potential. Once you've found some likely candidates, watch so-called 13D filings with the Securities & Exchange Commission (SEC), reported in most financial newspapers and many newsletters, and also available directly from the SEC. Both companies and individuals must file 13D reports within 10 days of making a stock purchase that brings total holdings in a company to a level greater than 5 percent of shares outstanding — a good sign that further purchases, or a takeover bid, are likely to come. To find out how to get copies of 13Ds, call the SEC office in Washington, New York, Chicago or Los Angeles. If you're more serious, there are also a couple of firms, Bechtel Information Services (1-800-231-3282) and Disclosure Inc. (1-800-638-8241), that will monitor 13D filings for you, watching for specific companies to appear on the lists.

# The Good Life Money Book

## BUYING STOCKS WITH NO COMMISSIONS

Once you're a shareholder, certain companies allow additional  share purchases through what are called a Dividend Reinvestment Plans  (DRIPs). Your initial share purchase must be made through a broker,  but after that, you can reinvest dividends and buy additional shares  (in some cases, up to $10,000 worth per year) directly from the company, paying only a small stock transfer and registration fee. Here  are a list of stocks that offer DRIPs, along with contact phone numbers to call for more details:

Bell Atlantic1-800-631-2355

Bell South1-800-631-6001

Chevron1-800-221-4096

Corning1-716-258-5833

Delta Air Lines1-404-765-2391

Dominion Resources1-800-552-4034

Duke Power1-800-438-0142

Federal National Mortgage1-212-613-7147

Fifth Third Bankcorp1-513-579-5300

GTE Corp.1-800-225-5160

General Electric1-617-575-2900

General Re.1-800-524-4458

Intel1-408-765-1480

ITT Corp.1-201-601-4202

Jastens1-612-450-4046

Merck1-908-594-6627

3M1-612-450-4064

New Plan Realty1-617-929-5445

Pacific Telesis1-800-637-6373

SCE Corp.1-800-347-8625

Texaco1-914-253-6072

Utilicorp1-212-791-6422

Washington REIT1-301-652-4300

Waste Management1-312-461-2544

In addition to those on the above list, there are roughly 800  other companies with DRIP programs. A newsletter
that covers these  companies is The MoneyPaper, 1010
Mamaroneck Ave., Mamaroneck, NY  10543. The company also produces a "Guide to Dividend Reinvestment
Plans," available for $15 by calling 1-800-633-1116, and
provides  low-cost brokerage services on stocks with
DRIPs.

## TREASURY SECURITIES MINUS TRANSACTION FEES

If you're more interested in safety and short-term liquidity than  long-term growth, then U.S. Treasury bills may
be for you — and you  don't even need a broker to buy
them (or the longer-term T-notes and  T-bonds). You can
buy them directly from the government, through your  nearest Federal Reserve Bank office. To get details on buying
U.S. Treasury securities — or to actually purchase them —
call the Federal Reserve Bank headquarters in your area at
one of the following  numbers. Ask for information on the
Treasury Direct program:

* District  1 —    Boston, MA, 617-973-3810

* District  2 —    New York, NY, 212-720-6619

* District  3 —    Philadelphia, PA, 215-574-6675

* District  4 —    Cleveland, OH, 216-579-2490

* District  5 —    Richmond, VA, 804-697-8372

* District 6 — Atlanta, GA, 404-521-8653
* District 7 — Chicago, IL, 312-322-5369
* District 8 — St. Louis, MO, 314-444-8703
* District 9 — Minneapolis, MN, 612-340-2075
* District 10— Kansas City, MO, 816-881-2409
* District 11— Dallas, TX, 214-922-6770
* District 12— San Francisco, CA, 415-974-2330

## A BASIC PRIMER ON BOND INVESTING

With interest rates on the rise, bond prices have come down sharply from their highs in late 1993 and early 1994. Many analysts think bonds are now near a bottom and that this is a good time to buy. However, many people shy away from bonds because the don't understand exactly how the markets work. If you fall into that class, here are some basic facts to remedy the situation:

A bond is just a long-term, debt-based security. In other words, it is a loan to the bond issuer — unlike a stock, which represents a share of ownership in the issuing company. When you buy a bond, you are literally lending money — in most cases, the "face" or "par" amount — to the issuer, be it a corporation, a government or some other agency or institution. In return, you receive a certificate — the bond — which represents the issuer's promise to repay the debt and make periodic interest payments on that loan. (Note: In most instances these days, investors don't actually receive the certificate. Rather, they are merely listed as owners on account books maintained by the issuer and/or their brokerage firm.)

Bonds are, by definition, "long-term" loans. To be called bonds, they must have a term to maturity of five years or more. Debt securities with maturities of less than five years — and, in the case of U.S. government securities, less than 10 years — are called notes, bills or other names. And, unlike some types of debts, such as auto loans, they are "securities" because they are designed to be bought and sold in the open market. As a security, every bond issued must carry with it a statement, known as the "bond indenture" or "deed of trust," that spells out the conditions of the agreement between the bond issuer (borrower) and the bond buyer (lender). This agreement specifies, among other things:

* The amount the bond issuer has to repay when the bond matures. Known as the "face value," "par value" or "principal," this amount is usually $1,000, though some government bonds have larger face values ($5,000 to $1 million).

* The interest rate. Called the "coupon," this rate is set when the bond is issued and remains in force until maturity (except in the case of so-called "floating-rate bonds"). The interest rate is not preset by the issuer, but rather is determined by market conditions and the issuer's credit rating at the time the bond is offered to the public. The actual dollar amount of the annual interest payment can be quickly determined by multiplying the bond's coupon by its par value. For example, a $1,000 bond with a coupon of 8-1/4 percent would return $82.50 per year ($1,000 x 0.0825 = $82.50).

* The schedule of interest payments. Bonds typically pay interest every six months, with payments usually made on either the first or fifteenth of the month.

* The length of the loan. Called the "term" or "maturity" of the bond, this names the date when the bond issuer must repay the face value or principal to the bond buyer. Maturities can range from as little as five years (a short-

term bond) to as long as 50 years (a long-term bond). Corporate bonds have widely varying maturities, depending on the needs of the issuer at the time the bond is offered; government bonds typically have maturities of 15 to 30 years.

* The collateral. Many bonds are secured by actual physical or financial property, such as a mortgage on real estate or a claim on income from a package of investments. Others, particularly so-called "municipal" bonds, issued by state and local governments, are secured by a pledge of general or specific tax revenues or a claim on income produced by the project the bond offering is designed to pay for (a toll road, stadium, sewage treatment plant, etc.). Federal debt securities are backed by the "full faith and credit" of the U.S. government. However, most corporate bonds are unsecured — backed only by the general assets and projected earnings power of the company. Such bonds are referred to as "debentures" and can carry varying levels of risk, depending on the creditworthiness of the issuer.

Bond certificates may also contain a variety of other provisions, depending on specific features of the individual issue, including:

* **Call provisions** — Conditions under which the bond issuer can pay off the loan early.

* **Refunding provisions** — Circumstances under which the bond issuer may, at maturity of the current bond, offer a new bond issue to pay off the money due on the old one.

* **Rate-adjustment provisions** — Full description of the rules for changing the interest rate or coupon on floating-rate bonds.

\*   **Discount provisions** — An explanation of the terms under which  some bonds are offered at a price lower than their face value.


\*   **Sinking-fund provisions** — Details of plans under which certain  bond issuers set aside a pool of money designated for partial early  redemption of outstanding bonds.


## THE BENEFITS OF BOND INVESTMENT

You should now have a basic understanding of bonds — But why invest in them? What advantages do they have that aren't available with  stocks? Essentially, there are six reasons for investing in bonds —  income, capital gains, seniority, safety, leverage and selection —  though not all are exclusive to debt securities. Here's a brief look  at each of these motivations:


**\* Income.** Many people seeking income buy stocks that pay dividends. However, there is no guarantee that even major companies will  not lower — or even eliminate — their stock dividends during hard  times. And, in order to get those dividends, you have to take the  risk that the price of the stock may fall, leaving you with a capital  loss larger than the value of the dividends received. By contrast,  bonds offer a steady — and guaranteed — stream of income. Unless a  company goes bankrupt (or restructures its debt, in which case new   securities will be issued in exchange for existing bonds), it must  make interest payments to bondholders at the stated coupon rate under  the terms spelled out in the original bond indenture. If the bonds  are held to maturity, there is also no risk of capital loss because  the issuer must redeem them at full face value. This fixed flow of  income — and the guarantee that the principal underlying it will be returned intact (barring bankruptcy) — is the primary reason most  people buy and own bonds.

**\* Capital gains.** Though it is impossible (again barring bankruptcy) to suffer a capital loss on bonds bought at issue and held to maturity, there are several ways to make capital gains on bond holdings. In some cases, lower rated bonds are issued at a discount to make them more attractive to buyers. This gives investors who hold them to maturity a guaranteed capital gain in addition to the regular interest payments. In addition, when the current market interest rate is above the coupon rate of older bonds, many bonds can be purchased in the secondary market at a discount. If held until maturity, or until interest rates fall, those bonds can then be cashed at face value or sold at a higher price, again generating a capital gain. Finally, if a bond is bought at face value and market interest rates then fall, the price of the bond will rise to a level above face value — i.e., it will trade at a "premium" — and it can be sold in the secondary market, again producing a capital gain.

**\* Seniority.** This is a legal term denoting the preferred status of bonds as debt securities. As mentioned above, seniority ensures interest payments on bonds will be made before any dividends can be paid to holders of either common or preferred stocks. It also provides that, unlike dividends, bond interest payments are made on a pre-tax basis — meaning you get paid even before the IRS gets its due. Finally, depending on the terms of the original offering, bond indebtedness is sometimes also given seniority over claims of other creditors in the event of financial troubles or bankruptcy. (Bonds without this seniority provision are known as "subordinate debentures" and should be avoided by risk-conscious investors.)

**\* Safety.** As with nearly all investments, there are some risks in bond ownership. However, as a general rule, bonds offer considerably more safety and predictability than stocks or other investment vehicles. The seniority provision accounts for some of this added safety, but there are also other factors. For one thing, the main reason bond prices change is the movement of market interest rates, and those rates tend to move in a fairly steady fashion, following well-established trends most of the time. This makes price changes for bonds more orderly and predictable than price changes for other investments. The "pull" of the bond's face value — i.e., the fact it can always be cashed in at par when it matures — also tends to limit price swings. In other words, when interest rates go up, bond prices fall, but at a steadily decreasing rate. Finally, bonds are closely monitored and regularly rated for safety by agencies such as Moody's and Standard & Poor's. Thus, if you stick to highly rated ("investment grade") bonds, the odds of an unpleasant surprise are far lower than with stocks.

* **Leverage.** As is the case with stocks, bonds can be purchased on margin, meaning you do not have to put up the full face value to buy them. However, although stocks require a deposit equal to at least 50 percent of their total value, bonds can be bought with a much smaller cash deposit (with the exception of so-called "convertibles," which can be exchanged for stocks under certain circumstances and thus also require a 50 percent deposit). Exact margin requirements for federal, municipal and non-convertible corporate bonds are set by individual bond dealers and brokerage firms, but can be as low as 10 percent on U.S. Treasury bonds and 25 percent on high-grade corporate issues. This can be an important consideration for people who want to trade bonds for potential capital gains. However, the majority of people who take advantage of the liberal margin privileges on bonds do so in order to get loans from their brokers, which they use to invest in other securities that offer better returns or greater potential for capital appreciation.

## WHAT TO DO IF BONDS ARE CALLED

Some bonds carry what are known as "call provisions," which means that the bond issuer has the option to return the loan principal to the holders of the securities and stop all interest payments. This unpleasant surprise is most likely to occur when interest rates fall sharply. Once notified of a pending call, the bondholder is faced with finding new bonds of the same or better credit quality — and reinvesting the principal at the current, lower interest rates. So, what do you do? The only way to fully protect yourself is to buy only bonds without call provisions — or to set a plan to sell the bonds well in advance of the "call date" (the first date on which the bond issuer has the right to call the securities). The T-bill alternative: Treasury notes and bonds are almost never callable. You might also consider non-callable municipal and corporate bonds. Caution: When figuring the potential yield to maturity of a callable bond, you must calculate it using the length of time remaining until the call date, not the length of time until the bond's official maturity. This produces a higher projected yield — but one that will fall if the bond is not called (which will usually happen only when market rates are higher than the bond's stated coupon rate).

## GETTING MORE SPECULATIVE WITH PUTS AND CALLS

Options are highly leveraged vehicles that allow investors — or, more often, speculators — to pursue potentially huge profits at an extremely low cost. Options are traded on virtually every type of investment vehicle, from stocks, bonds and market indexes to precious metals, currencies and agricultural commodities. Regardless of the underlying asset, however, there are essentially only two types of options:

**\* Calls** — These options give their owners the right (but not the  obligation) to BUY a specific underlying asset at a set price for a  limited period of time. For example, an April IBM 75 call would give  its purchaser the right to buy 100 shares of IBM common stock at a  price of $75 a share at any time between the date of purchase and the  option's stated expiration date.

**\* Puts** — These options give their owners the right (but not the  obligation) to SELL a specific underlying asset at a set price for a  limited period of time. Thus, an April IBM 70 put would give its purchaser the right to sell 100 shares of IBM stock at a price of $70 a  share any time between the purchase date and the expiration date.

Options offer the potential for tremendous speculative gains because they allow their owner to profit on a point-for-point basis (at  expiration) on any move in the underlying asset's price above a certain level (in the case of calls) or below a certain level (in the  case of puts). This level is known as the "striking" or "exercise"  price of the option. The option buyer pays a "premium" for the op- tion, which mostly covers the value of the time remaining prior to  expiration, plus any real (or "intrinsic") value the option might have at the time of purchase. If the underlying asset fails to move  by a sufficient amount during that time, the option buyer loses most  — or all — of his investment. Because of this, options are known as  "wasting assets" — meaning that, all else being equal, their value  decreases steadily with the passage of time. Most options (about 80  percent of them) expire worthless, meaning holders lose the entire amount they paid for them. This works to your advantage when you  "write" (i.e., sell) options, but against you when you buy them.

In addition to outright speculation, there are at least a score  of additional strategies for using options, including such techniques  as "calendar spreads," "bear spreads," "straddles," "strangles" and others. However, because our space is limited, we'll only discuss three of the most basic strategies, as follows:

\* Locking in profits by buying a put on a specific stock that you own. If you have a nice gain in a stock but don't want to take those profits for any reason (e.g., tax consequences), you can guarantee a set sale price for your shares until you are ready to sell by buying a put option with a striking price at that level. For example, if you bought a stock in June at $25 a share and saw it rise to $41 a share by mid-November, you would likely be quite pleased. However, although you know stocks tend to fall near year's end, you might not want to sell because your gain would be short term and you would incur a tax liability in the current tax year. You could solve your problem by buying a January put with a striking price of $40 a share. This would probably cost you $3 or $4 a share ($300 or $400 per full option), but would guarantee you the right to sell your stock at $40 a share on the third Friday of January — regardless of what happened to the underlying stock (even if it fell to zero). If the price did fall, you'd simply exercise the put and sell your shares at $40, taking your gain in the new tax year and deducting the original cost of your put option from your total profit. If the stock's price continued to rise, climbing further above $40, you'd simply let the option expire worthless, sell your stock at the higher price, savor the tax savings and once again deduct the option cost from your total profits.

\* Hedge your overall stock portfolio by buying put options on a broad-based market index. This strategy is similar to the one just described for individual stocks, but your goal here is not to delay the sale of your stocks. Instead, you want to continue holding your stocks, but make enough profits on your side investment in index puts to offset any paper loss you might incur on the stocks during a general market pullback. The choice of index depends on the nature of your portfolio. If you had largely Blue Chip issues, then you'd want to buy puts on the S&P 100 Index or the American Stock Exchange's Major Market Index. If you held a broad mix of issues, you'd choose puts on the S&P 500. And, if you owned mostly smaller-capitalization issues, you'd buy puts on the NASDAQ 100 index. The term, or lifespan, of the options should be determined based on your expectations regarding the length of the expected market decline. Although it's impossible to recommend the number of options you should buy without knowing the makeup of your portfolio, a good rule of thumb is to buy one put for each $5,000 to $7,500 in stocks you own. Sell the puts, taking your profits, once you feel the downward move has fully run its course.

* Write "covered" call options against stocks you own to generate additional income from your portfolio. This is one of the most popular option strategies, used by even ultra-conservative investors. It involves selling out-of-the-money call options (those with striking prices above the current price of your stocks) and using the premiums received to either increase your portfolio income or lower your effective cost basis in the stock, thus getting added protection against a pullback. For example, if you owned shares in XYZ Corp., which was trading at $58 a share, and you wanted to augment your income, you could sell calls with a striking price of $60 — perhaps collecting $2 to $3 a share for an option with three months of life remaining (depending on the volatility) of the stock. If XYZ is at or below $40 at expiration, you've made a gain of $200 to $300 (less commissions) for each option sold (one full option equals 100 shares of stock) — and you can repeat the process, continuing to collect option premiums so long as XYZ stays below $60. (You can also sell calls with higher or lower striking prices should XYZ's price change.) If, on the other hand, XYZ's price rises above $60 a share, you have two alternatives. You can either buy back the call, taking a small loss, which will be offset by the increase in the stock value (you don't actually lose money until XYZ

climbs above the striking price by more than you received for the call). Or, you can let the stock be "called away" at expiration, keeping the $2 in extra appreciation (from $58 to $60), plus the premium you received for the call.

As for option selection for this strategy, sell only out-of-the-money calls and sell the shortest amount of time possible — preferably under three months (that way you can repeat the process several times a year). However, be sure the options have premiums sufficiently high to warrant the possible loss of appreciation should the stock price rise sharply. We recommend looking for options with premiums high enough to net you a return (after commissions) greater than the current return on risk-free T-bills that mature about the same time as the options expire. Warning: NEVER sell more than one option for each 100 shares of stock you own. This will expose you to unlimited risk on the uncovered option and also require a hefty margin deposit with your broker. Also be aware that commissions generally make this strategy ineffective if you sell fewer than three options — meaning you shouldn't use it unless you own at least 300 shares of the stock.

## THE ABC's OF FINANCIAL PLANNING

In spite of the wealth of information available on the subject, many people don't feel comfortable planning their financial strategies on their own — meaning they may want the services of a financial planner. This is alright, but it's not without peril. For starters, you have to know your acronyms before shopping for a financial planner. There are several professional designations — each of which requires completing a course of study at a registered institution and passing an examination. (Note: Any individual who offers one-on-one financial advice must be registered with the Securities and Exchange Commission or Commodity Futures Trading Commission.) Following are the definitions of the most commonly used industry designations:

**\* CFP** — Certified Financial Planner. This designation denotes that the holder has successfully completed a comprehensive six-part curriculum at the College for Financial Planning in Denver. This license also involves a commitment to continuing education.

**\* ChFC** — Chartered Financial Consultant. This title is given to planners who complete the 10-course program of the American College, Bryn Mawr, Pa.

**\* CLU** — Certified Life Underwriter. This is a designation given those who complete one of several certified courses in insurance law and insurance-based financial planning.

**\* CPA** — Certified Public Accountant. This designation is granted practitioners who finish an approved college-level accounting course and pass a certification exam (similar to the bar exams required by the individual states).

There are significant differences between the functions each performs — and none of them guarantees a superior return on your investment. In fact, according to most informed industry opinion, there is no reason to suppose a financial professional can do better with your money than you can — if you apply yourself diligently. When investigating any of these, clarify your own financial goals first, then inquire about the professional's method of compensation — i.e., commission only, fees and commissions, or fee only. Caution: All good financial planners should coordinate their efforts on your behalf with attorneys, accountants, tax experts and other professionals. Ideally, you should look for an advisor with a range of contacts throughout the financial world, and one licensed to offer investments in limited partnerships and insurance as well as securities.

## POVERTY IS EASY, WEALTH TAKES A PLAN

In case you haven't heard, wealth-building in the '90s is harder than in the '80s — and will likely get more so. The economy remains suspect, profits are slow in recovering, tax rates have been raised (and may not come back down in spite of the Republican congressional coup in 1994's elections), and the deficit is still out of sight. So, what do you do? Make more money; get a second job? Unfortunately, both of these remedies are losing their potency. A second income is rarely enough these days to take care of retirement or a child's future college expenses. And salary cuts are the order of the day, with layoffs, givebacks and downsizing. A better approach is to follow these two tried-and-true wealth-building principles:

**1.** Write yourself a monthly check — and put it in savings or an investment account. How much? At least 10 percent of your after-tax income, if you earn $50,000 or more a year. Don't figure out how much you can afford to save. Pay yourself first, just as if it was rent or mortgage. If you can't do this, your savings will never amount to much — and regular savings, coupled with the growth of your money through investment, is the key to wealth-building. Of course, the earlier you start saving, the better. Saving early is more important than how much you set aside. If you've put it off too long already, don't compound the error. Start today.

**2.** Take advantage of tax laws. This means investing where the Tax Code gives you the biggest break. Remember, every dollar you save in taxes is a dollar added to your tax-free wealth. Here are a couple things to remember:

\* Make your expenses business deductions — vacation, education, recreation, and so on. A home business may do the trick.

\* Put as much money as possible into retirement plans, which give you the power of tax-free accumulation.

## FOUR SECRETS TO BECOMING A MILLIONAIRE ON AN AVERAGE SALARY

Most people think millionaires live like "the rich and famous," but most people would be wrong — again. Many folks who reside in posh neighborhoods and enjoy glitzy life-styles are not wealthy; and an amazing number of millionaires live in modest surroundings with few flashy outward signs of wealth. There's a reason. Wealth isn't what you spend, but what you accumulate. Make a million a year, spend a million a year, and you'll have lived high — but you'll also be broke. So, how do you make a million? Through inheritance — or winning the lottery? Because it can't be through hard work, right?

Wrong. Actually wealth is most often the result of hard work, with the added ingredients of perseverance and self-discipline. The average millionaire (having a net worth of $1 million or more) has lived all his adult life in the same town, in a middle-class neighborhood; has been married once and not divorced; owns a business — a chain of stores, a factory, a service company, etc. — and, in four out of five cases, didn't inherit any of the wealth, but made it by himself. And, how did he make it? Well, another key factor in this profile is that the average millionaire is a compulsive saver and investor. And he probably subscribes to all four of these basic rules for getting and keeping wealth:

**1. Don't concentrate on income**, but net worth — which means most millionaires usually plow what could have been their take-home pay back into their businesses, or into their stock portfolios or other assets. Of course, they know that the more they bring home as income, the more the IRS can take. Wealth isn't taxed, income is.

**2. Invest, don't spend**. Luxuries offer lavish creature comforts, but no financial return. And a rich-and-famous lifestyle, naturally, becomes a serious and escalating financial drain. Insurance and fuel and maintenance costs on a Rolls-Royce, for instance, are a whole lot more than for a Ford Taurus, although both have four wheels and go places, (Sam Walton of Wal-Mart drove a pickup truck). The same common sense outlook applies to fancy food, fancy houses, fancy clothes, fancy vacations. According to some millionaires, the fastest way to spend yourself broke is to buy a big house and then keep up with all the bills. And, said another, if you want to experience the joys of owning your own yacht, just stand in your shower, fully dressed, and tear up $100 bills. Smart wealth builders put their money into investments or their own businesses — not lavish possessions.

**3. Set clear goals**. Working vaguely or without purpose is not something you'll find millionaires doing — or having done. They all knew where they wanted to go ultimately, how much money they wanted to accumulate, and usually had definite intermediate stepping stones along the way and time limits to achieve them. Do you want to retire early? Leave a sizable estate? No matter what your age, start now to develop a plan with a timeline for getting there. Then work backward to calculate how much you need to save each year.

**4. Seek good advice**, and be willing to pay for it. Most self-made millionaires would far rather spend top dollar for legal or financial advice than they would for such things as flying first-class. On the other hand, people who spend foolishly tend to skimp on professional investment counseling. Note: That doesn't mean you shouldn't be on the lookout for hot investment tips.

## LIVE ON LESS THAN YOU EARN

During the high-flying '80s, the operative phrase seemed to be: "If you've got it, flaunt it." Now, in the belt-tightening '90s, that seems to have changed to: "If you've got it, don't make a big deal about it." This downsizing isn't just faddishness. There's a sound financial principle at work — which can be expressed in four words: "Live below your means."

Another way of saying it: Pay off your debt, set aside money for retirement, spend carefully and inconspicuously. For instance, don't go into major debt to buy an impressive car beyond your means. Getting expensive new wheels every few years is one of the biggest money-drainers. Four-year car loans can drive you into endless long-term debt. If you don't like depriving yourself, think of it this way: By simply by replacing your car every 10 years, instead of every two or three, you could save enough to retire five years earlier. Other luxury perks fall into the same wasteful category — eating out at fancy restaurants, compulsive credit card shopping, "Rich-and-Famous" vacation get-aways, etc. There are wiser and better things to do with your money.

If your family earns upward of $50,000 a year, you should be setting aside 10 percent of that gross amount — or more — in savings. That can be in a combination of instruments, including company retirement plans. Better yet, kick that contribution level up to 15 or 20 percent. This is not only a way to be frugal, it's a way to get rich. (If you're middle-aged, that 20 percent savings level is probably critical — unless you are one of those rare folks who's been systematically preparing for your retirement since your first job.)

You can cut spending in some big-ticket areas by some simple expedients. For instance, over the life of a house mortgage, you can save thousands of bucks by simply making bi-weekly half-payments instead of paying the total once a month. The trick here is that you make the equivalent of just one extra monthly payment per year, with the result that your loan will be fully paid off in 18 to 21 years instead of 30. Your commuting expenses can be slashed by simply arranging to live near your work. If you can't do this, you should definitely carpool or use public transportation. The cumulative savings will be dramatic.

Impulse shopping may not seem a big budgetary problem, but if you sit down and run the monthly numbers, you may be in for an unpleasant jolt. Solution: Carry only a single emergency credit card — and try not to use it. Daily lunch expenses also add up — brown-bagging can provide substantial ongoing savings. Entertainment costs are another area of concern. Movies, plays and concerts have become real luxuries for most of us. The same level of entertainment — or even more fun — can be had far cheaper by going to public concerts and borrowing books and videos from local lending libraries.

Spending on kids, as everyone knows, is another budget-breaker. As hard as it may be to deny your children anything, you will improve your financial health and their character by teaching them financial responsibility — and the lesson that happiness doesn't mean getting whatever they want. They may discover they can survive without getting the latest athletic shoe, electronic game, etc.

After implementing all these savings solutions, don't forget to periodically review your financial goals and gains — you may be in for some pleasant surprises for a change.

## GETTING AHEAD DURING A RECESSION

The first thing to do in a recession — especially if you're going under — is to eliminate your debt, or pay it down as much as possible. If you're making only minimum payments on house, car, home  equity loans and credit-card balances, you're obviously in trouble.  Here are some key steps to take:

* Start by doing some tough budgeting. Allocate as much as possible toward paying off debt. If necessary, sell assets. If you're in a serious recessionary period, that could include your home. Remember:  The prices you can get will drop as a recession deepens, and 80 cents  on the dollar now beats 60 cents a few months later.

* Cut expenses across the board. Use the same methods outlined in  the previous item and add any others you can think of, such as cleaning and ironing your own shirts instead of sending them out. Look for  free or cheap enter-tainment — museums, picnics, community programs.  Go to a free high-school baseball game instead of the nearest major league park.

* Once you get your head above water, begin building a reserve.  Set aside six months or more of living expenses in a secure bank,  credit union or money market account, or in short-term government  securities. This money needs to be highly liquid and very safe so you  can get at it in the event of an earning interruption. Lots and lots  of compa-nies have been laying off — and, while you may think your job is safe, it's better to be prepared.

* Inventory all your assets — the cash you have in institu-tions,  property, investments, etc. Then get rid of any risky investments.  Make sure all your deposits are in secure institutions, insured by the government. And, during a

recession, if you've got stock in a company that looks to be in financial trouble, you're probably better of selling it. The price isn't likely to improve if you hold on. Do hold on to high-quality stocks.

Once you've got a reserve set up and are generating some extra cash, there are various ways you can use a recession to your advantage. Here are a few:

* **Bargain shopping** — Check out garage sales and Classifieds for real steals, looking for people selling valuable assets at bargain basement prices to raise needed cash. The same goes for retail sales; businesses need cash flow too, so shop around, study ads and wait for sales. In any recession, the deals are out there — if you're savvy and patient.

* **Real estate** — If you have cash in hand, there's no better time than a recession to get into the real estate market. Prices are dropping and sellers are desperate to deal. Make sure, however, that you research the neighborhood thoroughly before buying or offering. Find out what equivalent properties have been going for; check schools, recreational and municipal services, crime rates. Remember: Location is the most important factor in resale value. And don't forget to check into owner financing, which makes possible a much smaller down payment on your part.

* **Start your own business** — Believe it or not, a recessionary period can be favorable for certain start-up businesses — a credit— counseling service, for instance, or a home-published newsletter listing area jobs. Other possibilities: Hang out your shingle as a handyman or provide shopping services for elderly or shut-in neighbors. Or make your hobbies pay. Like to sew, knit or make pottery? Try marketing your wares at local gift shops on a consignment basis.

\* **Check out the stock Market:** Even during down times, some stocks go up — and many others are real bargains. However, don't throw your hard-earned savings into a volatile, risky market. Check with a broker, or look into a mutual fund that has shown steady growth without a lot of volatility.

## GET MORE THAN INVESTMENT POTENTIAL WITH YOUR STOCKS

If you like to see some tangible results from your investments, you might consider buying shares in a company that offers something more than potential price appreciation — free product samples, to be specific. Many companies offer shareholders free gifts — or at least special deals — in addition to dividends. Here are just a few examples:

\* **Disney** (NYSE: DIS) shareholders get about $75 a year in perks, including $15 discounts on Magic Kingdom Club Gold Cards, which provide admission discounts and bargains on other Disney products. Attend the annual shareholders meeting and you and a friend also get a free pass to either Disneyland or Disneyworld in Florida.

\* **Quaker Oats** (NYSE: OAT) sends new shareholders a coupon package worth about $15 — and you get additional coupons for everything from cereals to pet foods with each quarterly dividend check. Those who show up at the annual meeting also get a coupon book valued at $30, about equal to the recent price of a share of the company's stock.

\* **Dial Corp.** (NYSE: DL) sends about $5 worth of coupons for the company's consumer products with each quarterly dividend check.

**\* Wm. Wrigley Co.** (NYSE: WWY) sends out an annual gift pack  including 20 packs of the company's gums (worth $5 to $7).

**\* Santa Anita Realty** (NYSE: SAR) gives new shareholders six free  "Clubhouse" passes to Santa Anita Raceway (horses) in Arcadia, Calif.  The retail value of the tickets is $39 — which gives you an instant 178 percent profit if you buy just a single share of stock at the recent price of around $14 (forgetting about commissions, of course).

**\* Minnesota Mining & Manufacturing** (NYSE: MMM) sends a $20 gift box to  new shareholders, but existing shareholders get giveaways only if the  attend the annual meeting.

**\* Colgate-Palmolive** (NYSE: CL) gives new shareholders coupons for  around $5 in company products — and existing owners get freebies if they attend the annual meeting.

Perhaps the biggest perk available for shareholders in many companies, however, is the right to buy additional shares or to reinvest dividends (through so-called "DRIP" plans) without any commissions or  transfer frees. Roughly 850 companies offer such plans, which can allow you to build your holdings rapidly and inexpensively — and some companies allow commission-free purchases of up to $10,000 worth of  new shares per year. (For more information on DRIPS, see the earlier  item in this Section titled "Buying Stocks With No Commissions.)

---

CHAPTER 8

# A QUICK GUIDE
# TO ESTATE PLANNING

---

## HOW TO KEEP THE FEDS FROM GRABBING YOUR ESTATE

Most folks don't like thinking about death, and estate planning is avoided for the same reason. But, even if you don't have a lot to leave behind, a little planning can make a huge difference in how much goes to your heirs and how much to the IRS — and federal estate taxes can take as much as 55 percent. Here are some tips on better estate planning:

* Consult a professional. This is one area where doing-it-yourself is a false economy. Estate tax rules are extremely technical, and mistakes can be very expensive. Currently, an individual can pass on up to $600,000 of assets to any beneficiary tax free. (A husband and wife, if the bequest is properly planned, can will $1.2 million tax free.) Note: There have been reports of possible congressional action to lower the tax-free limit to $200,000. Fortunately, nothing has yet gone beyond the talk stage, but estate planners all over the country have been keeping an vigilant eye on the legislative horizon. You should too.

* Life insurance can be an important element in your estate. The insurance lobby has so far fought off all attempts at taxing insurance payouts. As a result, life insurance is one of the few remaining shelters against estate taxes. Here's a breakdown of useful policies:

— **Life insurance.** There's a wide a variety of policies to fit specific needs — i.e., to guarantee a family's lifestyle in case of premature death, help maintain a family business or pay estate taxes.

— **Survivorship insurance.** Also known as "second-to-die" insurance, this is usually offered to older couples concerned about preserving their estate for their heirs. Both lives are insured and the death benefit is paid when the second person dies. Even when bought at an advanced age, with the blending of two lives, the policy has a single premium lower than two individual premiums, and is available to people at ages when they would normally be uninsurable. These policies can also be used in combination with trusts to pass on a business to one's children.

— **VAL policies.** One of the most popular insurance tools is the variable appreciable life (VAL) policy, which provides a guaranteed death benefit, but also allows the policyholder to direct cash values into different investment funds. Also, the buyer can pick a premium payment schedule to fit a particular budget and adjust payments as resources change. VALs also offer several death-benefit options. And no matter the investment performance of the policy, the initial death benefit is guaranteed as long as premiums have been paid and there have been no loans or withdrawals. A principal attraction of VALs is their link to higher-yielding investment funds, which allows the own- ers more flexibility in combatting the effects of inflation than do fixed-income instruments.

* Trusts help preserve wealth. Anyone with an estate valued above $600,000 — or a couple with more than $1.2 million — should definitely consider them as they not only protect your excess assets, but assure their flow to the designated beneficiaries according to your wishes. Basically, a trust is a relationship in which a person or institution (trustee) holds legal title to the property of another, which the trustee administers for the benefit of the beneficiaries — either heirs or a charitable institution. Trusts can take many different forms. For example:

— Irrevocable living trusts allow an estate to avoid probate, while also reducing the assets subjected to estate taxes.

— Revocable living trusts allow an estate to avoid probate on certain assets set aside in the trusts, while allowing you to retain control of those assets.

— "Q-TIP" trusts provide all income to the surviving spouse for life. Upon that spouse's death, money is distributed to beneficiaries selected by the first spouse to die.

— Unified credit shelter trusts provide for maximum use of the unified tax credit in the estate of both spouses. It allows them to give $1.2 million tax free to their beneficiaries.

— Marital deduction trusts provide surviving spouses with access to family wealth, while reducing estate taxes payable in the estate of the first spouse to die.

— Standby trusts provide for control and management of a person's assets in the event of physical or mental disability.

— Pourover trusts, in order to avoid probate, provide for the receipt of assets into the trust from other trusts, life insurance or retirement accounts.

— Testamentary trusts transfer the property to the designated heirs upon the death of the benefactor.

— Charitable remainder trusts provide income for life to the grantor or other individual beneficiary, with the remaining property passing to charity on the individual's death. It also provides for a charitable income tax or estate tax deduction.

Do you need a trust? There's no easy answer. It's best to seek professional advice. But consider this: Since a will doesn't take effect until death, and doesn't reduce the bite of estate taxes, there may not be enough cash available to pay those taxes. And remember: Wills mean probate — a time consuming and costly process. Heirs may wait more than a year for their bequests. A trust can handle all of these problems.

Deferred or charitable trusts can be used to accomplish a variety of financial, tax and estate planning objectives. And a deferred gift in the form of a charitable trust confers an immediate tax benefit — a charitable contribution deduction on this year's tax return. Unfortunately, deferred gifts slow the flow of cash to the designated charities, but they are ideal for people with family obligations, as well as for those concerned about providing for their own retirement.

## CHOOSING BETWEEN LIVING TRUSTS AND WILLS

The current popular wisdom seems to be that living trusts are superior in every way to wills, but this is not always the case. Here are some things you need to know about living trusts, what they can do — and what they can't:

Revocable living trusts are the most common type, and can be changed or revoked at any time (testamentary trusts are established by your will, and come into existence only after you die). For tax purposes, in the case of a living trust, the title to the property remains with the grantor, who must declare any income received and pay any associated taxes. However, for state law, the ownership of property in the trust is transferred from the grantor to the trustee, who holds and manages the property for the benefit of the beneficiaries.

Living trusts avoid probate, which can be expensive and time consuming and is a matter of public record. Also, living trusts are harder to overturn or contest than wills, which means they bring more certainty that assets will be distributed the way you want them to be. Unfortunately, they don't solve all estate-planning problems. For instance, if you have minor children, you'll still need a will and probate to appoint a guardian. A trust can look after property for the minor children, but a court-appointed guardian is needed to care for them. Some assets and situations are also unsuited to a living trust, among them:

* Autos. Insurance companies would prefer to cover a person, not a disembodied trust.

* Jewelry. Assigning title is often difficult.

* Where litigation is pending at the time of death, or as a result of death, probate is required.

* Where a tax audit is under way, probate is also necessary.

* Administrative costs of living trusts are on a par with those for probate.

* Living trusts don't save income or estate taxes. For instance, there are estate tax returns that must be filed if assets exceed the filing threshold ($600,000 for federal estate tax purposes). Also, income tax must be paid on income earned up to the time before the distribution of property. Sometimes substantial legal fees are also entailed with living trusts.


Should you have a living trust? Here are some answers to that question, depending on your circumstances:


* Yes, if you own real estate in more than one state. This way you'll avoid ancillary probate — the judicial process that kicks in when the decedent owns real estate in a state other than the one in which he or she lived. This process is costly in time and money and delays distribution of assets to heirs.


* Yes, if you want to avoid family disputes. Living trusts can be effective in providing for distribution of assets with less chance of successful challenge by unhappy relatives.


* No, if you have a small estate. You can provide for passing on your property much more easily and cheaply by simply having jointly owned property. Such property passes outside of probate directly to the surviving joint owner. All you have to do is put the property in the names of both parties, specifying rights of survivorship.

* No if your assets are already in the form of annuities, retirement benefits, IRAs and life insurance. Proceeds from these vehicles do not need to be protected from probate by a living trust since they will pass directly to the named beneficiary.

## THE BASICS OF LIVING TRUSTS

You can legally draw up a revocable living trust any time during your adult life, and you can change it, amend it or revoke it also at any time. You may name yourself trustee in some states, thereby maintaining control over your trust property during your lifetime. Other states require a co-trustee be named. The basic purpose is to arrange for someone you trust to manage your assets if you become incapacitated. For instance, if you suffer a stroke or catastrophic accident, or fall victim to Alzheimer's, you may be suddenly unable to cope with your financial affairs. The simplest transactions may be impossible for you. If that happens, your relatives may be required to petition a court in order to run your business, buy or sell your property or withdraw money from your accounts to pay essential bills.

To head off such a potential problems, you transfer assets to a the living trust, nominating a trustee or co-trustee with power to immediately assume management of the property in the event of your incapacity. Obviously, a co-trustee should be a person in whom you have unreserved trust. Secondly, the person you name should possess not only the willingness but the financial knowledge to serve as trustee. The best advice is that the co-trustee be named unconditionally. If instead you permit the co-trustee to act only when your incapacity is certified by a physician, you may be creating future problems. Doctors are often reluctant to involve themselves that deeply in the financial affairs of their patients. Result: Your trust is gridlocked.

The living trust gives instructions for asset management and distribution after the your death, empowering the trustee to carry out those instructions without need for probate hearings or other court proceedings. In this way, living trusts not only avoid high probate costs, but prevent often disturbing delays. Through a trust, property can be distributed to heirs in short order, whereas the probate distribution process can take months or even years. As noted earlier, probate proceedings are also a matter of public record, whereas trust distributions are completely private.

A final advantage of trusts over wills comes in heading off the possible contesting of your wishes by disgruntled heirs. Bequests in a trust are considerably harder to challenge than those in a will.

From a tax standpoint, a living trust offers few if any benefits. As the owner, you must pay tax during your lifetime on all income derived from the trust. After your death, the trust becomes a separate tax-paying entity. Similarly, all trust assets must be included in the gross estate for estate tax purposes. In fact, a trust has certain tax disadvantages relative to an estate in that estates are allowed a larger exemption and can choose a fiscal year.

Living trusts, like wills, are subject to state laws mandating disposition of certain assets to a surviving spouse. In addition, even if you opt for living trust, you'll probably still need a will, just to cover certain legal contingencies. For example, suppose you die in an accident and a lawsuit is brought on behalf of your estate. You'll need probate to recover the legal proceeds. Likewise, if debts are owed to you — and subsequently to your estate — you will be unable to distribute such collections without a will. Finally, as mentioned earlier, a living trust cannot name a guardian for your minor children — only a will can do that (though a trust can manage property on your children's behalf).

## CONSIDER A DURABLE POWER OF ATTORNEY

A lesser-known alternative to living trusts for purposes of asset management is the durable power of attorney, which may better suit some middle-income people. With such a document, an agent is appointed to oversee financial matters for the person assigning the power. The agent can continue to perform if the principal becomes incapacitated. The durable power of attorney is cheaper to draft than a living trust, but has less flexibility and doesn't deal with what happens to the property when the principal asset holder dies.

## KEEPING INSURANCE PROCEEDS OUT OF YOUR ESTATE

As already noted, insurance can play an important role in estate planning. For example, if your estate is large enough to be subject to estate taxes (currently $600,000 or more), a life insurance policy is a good way to provide funds to pay those taxes, eliminating the possibility that your heirs might have to liquidate family assets. Estate taxes are due nine months following death, and most life insurance claims are settled well within this time frame. There are several ways to handle life insurance policies so that the proceeds are not counted in the estate itself:

* Buy a policy on yourself and give it to someone else as a gift. For gift-tax purposes, life insurance is valued at its cash value at the time of the gift — not at its face value. Since most people buy term insurance for estate planning purposes, it will have no cash value and can thus be given away with no tax consequences. Warning: You must live at least three years after giving away a life insurance policy on yourself. Otherwise, the proceeds of the policy will be counted as part of your estate.

* Have someone else buy the policy and pay the premiums. If one of your children or your spouse is the owner of the policy and makes the premium payments with their own funds, the proceeds of the insurance policy are not considered part of your estate. However, you must surrender all claim to the insurance in order for someone else's ownership to be valid — meaning you cannot borrow against the policy, cancel it or change the beneficiaries.

* Place the insurance policy in a trust. By making a trust the owner of the policy, you can retain control over both beneficiaries and the means by which the proceeds are disbursed, while still having the value excluded from your taxable estate. This is a particularly valuable strategy if you have a surviving spouse or minor children and want to make sure the policy proceeds are distributed according to your wishes. For example, you can set the trust up so that all the insurance is held in an income-generating account for the benefit of your surviving spouse until his or her death, with the remaining proceeds then divided among other surviving heirs.

* Insurance, in combination with a trust, can allow you to make sizable bequests to charity while still providing for your heirs.

* Buy-sell insurance. This is an important tool for small business owners — particularly if partnerships are involved. The insurance is set up to provide the necessary cash for the surviving partner to buy out the deceased partner's interest. In the case of sole proprietorships, insurance can also be used to replace lost income and/or hire professional business managers to keep the firm operating until it can be sold. For best tax results, each owner in a business should be listed as an owner of the others' policies, but not as an owner of his or her own. An alternative is to have the business itself own the policies, although that could subject a portion of the proceeds to taxes on the estate of the deceased.

For more information on how to maximize life insurance benefits  and minimize tax consequences, consult with an estate planning specialist or an attorney whose practice is devoted to trusts.

## MISSING INSURANCE POLICIES

Too many people go to great lengths to hide insurance policies  and other vital documents in safe places — then forget to divulge  those hiding places to their loved ones. The tragic consequence can  be that, when the person dies, the vital document is never located.  If survivors are desperately seeking a lost insurance policy, however, there are specific search strategies they should try:

**1.**  Go through the decedent's check stubs, looking for any premium payments. If they find an insurance company as a payee, they should  contact the company.

**2.**  Contact the decedent's employer and inquire about any company— sponsored insurance.

**3.**  Contact the American Council of Life Insurance and ask for its  free policy search service. Write to ACLI, Policy Search Dept., 1001  Pennsylvania Ave. NW, Washington, DC 20004.

## A HANDBOOK FOR HEIRS

Anguished survivors and heirs can find systematic answers to many  of the issues that trouble them in the "Survival Handbook for Heirs."  You'll find guidance on how to settle an estate, who to contact, what  records are needed, as well as after-inheritance advice, such as how  to locate a good financial advisor. The book can be ordered for just $5 by writing Foord Van Bruggen & Ebersole Financial Services, 2222 Watt Ave., Ste. B12, Sacramento, CA 95825, or calling 1-800-466-BOOK.

## OTHER ESTATE-RELATED TIPS

Here are some final items you might find helpful with regard to planning your estate for maximum protection of family assets:

* The easiest way to reduce your potential estate-tax liability is to reduce size of your taxable estate before you die. One way to do this is by taking advantage of the annual $10,000 gift tax exclusion ($20,000 when gifts are made jointly by a married couple). You can make any number of gifts of this amount to separate recipients each year, thus removing the money from your taxable estate.

* If your estate is considerably larger than your spouse's, a marital deduction will (MDW) will can delay estate tax liabilities. You can leave all or any part of your adjusted gross estate (total taxable estate, less funeral expenses, debts and settlement costs) to your spouse, and the bequest will be free from U.S. estate taxes at your death. However, your spouse's beneficiaries will be taxed on your estate when he or she dies (unless you establish some form of trust).

* If you don't want your spouse remarrying and giving away the family farm or business, create a family trust that specifically limits the secondary transfer or your assets after your death.

\* Second-to-die life insurance helps pay estate taxes because it pays the benefits on the second to die — the husband or the wife. For example, a $600,000 second-to-die policy (which would cost under $6,000 a year) would cover all taxes due on a $2 million estate, thus providing your heirs with a 42 percent increase in their inheritance.

## WRITE A LEGAL WILL YOURSELF — AND SAVE

No one likes to think about it, but we're all going to die sometime. And, since you worked hard for your money, you've earned the right to dictate where it goes when you die. That means you have to have a will — but it doesn't mean you have to have a high-powered attorney. In fact, you can draft a will yourself quite easily and save the legal fees. For a very nominal fee, most legal aid centers now offer a standard will-writing kit that can guide you through the do's and don't's like a pro, as well as telling you where and how to file. A variety of commercial will writing kits are also available at bookstores — and several computer programs are now being marketed to help you create a will. If you have doubts about the result, you can always have your attorney review the will you create, which will cost considerably less than having him or her draft it from scratch.

## HOW TO REVOKE YOUR WILL

Revoking a will sounds easy, but there are pitfalls. Some wills are even revoked against their maker's wishes. For instance:

\* A will may be automatically revoked whenever a testator (person making the will) gets married or divorced, has a child or there is a death of a principal beneficiary.

* After a death, there can be confusion about whether a will was revoked. It may have been destroyed in the presence of a witness who has also died. Or people may be looking for a document that no longer exists.

To avoid these pitfalls, consult a lawyer when any family event could trigger automatic revocation. In addition, write a separate document of revocation and keep it where the will would have been.

## LIVING WILLS AND YOUR RIGHT TO DIE

More and more states have "living will" legislation. This honors an individual's written statement that he or she doesn't wish life artificially prolonged with no hope of recovery. Here are some keys to enforcing a living will:

* Make sure the doctor is aware of a living will and that it's on the patient's medical chart.

* If medical opinion is that the relative will never return to his or her former condition, ask why the hospital is maintaining the patient. The doctor must answer this question.

* Ask that a "do-not-resuscitate order" be put on the chart.

* If the doctor won't do what you want, find out why.

* Talk to the hospital's patient representative.

* Try to get a more cooperative doctor assigned.

* Try to get the person transferred to another hospital.

* Notify the hospital's attorney that your relative did not give consent for whatever procedures you're objecting to. If this is correct and the staff doesn't take the patient off the equipment, you can sue the hospital.

\* Finally, you can take the person home to die. A hospital can't  hold a patient against his or her will. However, you should never  pull the plug yourself, no matter how desperate you feel — that's  homicide. Even though so-called "mercy killers" are seldom convicted in this country, a trial on such charges is a terrible ordeal.

## NOTES

_____

_____

_____

_____

_____

_____

_____

_____

_____

_____

_____

_____

_____

_____

---

## CHAPTER 9
## HAPPY EVER-AFTER
## —A RETIREMENT GUIDE

Once they've taken care of their daily living needs and provided for the education and well-being of their children, the primary savings and investment goal of most Americans is to build a nest egg sufficient to all them a comfortable retirement. This Section will discuss some of the ways to ensure that you achieve that goal — as well as some ideas on enjoying yourself and maintaining an adequate life style once you get there.

## PLANNING FOR RETIREMENT — HOW MUCH DO YOU NEED?

Retirement planning time is a time of evaluation, of reviewing memories and making plans for the future. There are many decisions to be made. For example, where are you going to live? Should you keep your house, or buy a condo on a golf course? How about moving to a retirement community? Or buying a recreational vehicle and heading off for the wide open spaces? What will you do with your free time? Golf and tennis? Travel? Art classes? Community volunteer work? A new free-lance career in architecture or some other area of interest? Maybe you just want to get a sailboat and cruise the Caribbean!

All of these are nice choices — and you want to have the freedom to indulge yourself, picking the most comfortable options. Gaining that freedom will require thinking about some other things as well — things such as:

* Where to invest all the money you've amassed through your savings and investments once you retire.
* How to withdraw the funds from your company pension plan, IRAs, Keoghs and other retirement plans.
* When to file for your Social Security benefits.
* How to structure your finances to cope with the rising costs of health care and medical insurance.

Before we talk about how to manage the money you'll have coming in, though, you need to consider where that money will go — in other words, what your expenses are now and how they will likely change when you do retire. Obviously, there's considerable estimation and speculation involved in this process — but with some careful thought and a little effort, you can come up with pretty good picture of what your "everyday" retirement expenses will be.

The first step in this process is to evaluate your current costs, so we've provided a worksheet to help you out. To begin, simply list the monthly amounts for the "fixed expenses" you have today:

### Calculating Your Current Expenses

_____Mortgage, property taxes and insurance

_____Federal, state and local income taxes

_____Medical, dental (insurance premiums, cash payments)

_____Utilities, groceries (power, phone, heating fuel)

_____Other insurance (car, liability, life)

_____Transportation (fuel, repairs and car payments)

_____Clothing (purchases and upkeep)

_____Recreation and entertainment (club memberships, hobby supplies, theater tickets, dining out, travel, etc.)

_____Consumer loan payments
_____Gifts and donations
_____Other expenses
_____**TOTAL**

These are your basic monthly expenses. When you reach retirement age, some of these will change greatly. For example, your transportation costs will surely fall as you stop commuting to work. Likewise, your clothing budget may drop when you no longer have to buy expensive "work" clothes to impress clients (or the boss). The cost of business lunches and other unreimbursed employee expenses will also disappear. However, some of your out-of-pocket expenses are also likely to rise. For instance, the cost of health insurance — although eased somewhat by Medicare — will be yours alone when your employer quits subsidizing that necessity, as many of them now have done.

Past analysts have estimated post-retirement expenses will run 75 to 80 percent of pre-retirement costs. However, we feel a realistic retirement budget today would be 85 percent to 90 percent of your current outlay — reflecting the appearance of new expenses to replace those that go down. After all, when someone works 40 or 45 years to get there, retirement should be a time of relaxation, a time to enjoy a new "comfort zone" in life. It's no time to be worrying if there's enough in the kitty to pay the electric bill. Your only worry should be about getting that choice tee time or finding the right dress for your new granddaughter. That's why you're reading this Section now — showing the foresight to think about your future, your investments and the process of building wealth.

And, be assured that building a significant level of wealth is key to a worry-free retirement. That's because the only way you can ensure having enough money to keep you comfortable each month — regardless of how long you live and how much costs rise — is to amass a large enough sum that you can live off your interest and dividend payments without having to dip into your underlying principal. With that in mind, let's look at the two main factors that will govern whether you have enough money for retirement — inflation and life expectancy.

The first item you must consider when deciding how much money you will need is the length of time over which it will be needed. According to current actuarial statistics, a 65-year-old man can expect to live to the age of 79, while a 65-year-old woman will typically live about three years longer, to age 82. To find out how long the average person is expected to live at various ages, refer to the table below, which is typical of the life-expectancy charts used in the insurance industry.

## Average Life Expectancies in Years

| Current Age | Male | Female | Current Age | Male | Female |
|---|---|---|---|---|---|
| 50 | 25.35 | 29.53 | 66 | 13.38 | 16.57 |
| 51 | 24.51 | 28.67 | 67 | 12.75 | 15.83 |
| 52 | 23.69 | 27.82 | 68 | 12.13 | 15.10 |
| 53 | 22.88 | 26.98 | 69 | 11.53 | 14.38 |
| 54 | 22.88 | 26.98 | 70 | 10.97 | 13.67 |
| 55 | 21.28 | 23.67 | 71 | 10.40 | 12.97 |
| 56 | 20.50 | 24.49 | 72 | 9.85 | 12.28 |
| 57 | 19.73 | 23.67 | 73 | 9.32 | 11.60 |
| 58 | 18.98 | 22.86 | 74 | 8.81 | 10.95 |
| 59 | 18.23 | 22.05 | 75 | 8.32 | 10.32 |
| 60 | 17.50 | 21.25 | 76 | 7.86 | 9.71 |
| 61 | 16.77 | 20.44 | 77 | 7.41 | 9.12 |
| 62 | 16.07 | 19.65 | 78 | 6.99 | 8.55 |
| 63 | 15.37 | 18.86 | 79 | 6.59 | 8.01 |
| 64 | 14.69 | 18.08 | 80 | 6.20 | 7.48 |
| 65 | 14.03 | 17.32 | | | |

(**Note:** The table covers only the years from age 50 to age 80. However, you can adapt it for your personal planning by merely subtracting your current age from 50 and adding the result to the age 50 life expectancy. This figure will be higher than the actual national averages, but that will simply give you a slight cushion in figuring your needs.) Why, at age 60, can a man expect to live to be 77-1/2, but by the time he reaches age 70, his life expectancy jumps to 81?

**Answer:** Because all the things that might have happened to him in the 10 years between ages 60 and 70 didn't. So, on average, he has 11 more years of life instead of 7-1/2. The complete national tables on life expectancy typically begin with "life expectancy at birth" and adjust with age. By the time you reach age 60, you've already survived teen driving, college parties, early-adulthood heart problems and other diseases. Thus, your life expectancy is way above "at-birth" norms.

Remember, these figures are national averages. In other words, of the million-plus 58-year-old men alive today in the U.S., the average one will live 18.98 more years. However, if you're an active non-smoker, 58 years of age, in good health, and have not already had cancer or heart disease, your chances of living more than 18.98 years are quite good. In fact, for your planning, you may want to consider a life expectancy of 25 to 30 years — meaning that, if you expect to retire at age 65, you will want to have adequate funds to last you for 18 to 23 years minimum.

It's also important to remember that it's not enough to simply have your money last for a given number of years. You also need to have that money continue to grow (something too many retirees fail to do, taking far too conservative a stance with their investments). That's because inflation will be taking a bigger and bigger bite out of your asset base with each passing year. No one can guarantee what future inflation rates will be, but the experts say you should plan for a minimum annual rate of at least 3 percent — and figuring in a cushion wouldn't hurt. After all, you don't have to be very old to remember when a gallon of gas cost 65 cents, a $20 bill bought a cart full of groceries instead of just a bag full, and a movie ticket was $3 instead of $7.50. Besides, those small percentage numbers can be deceiving. For example, an annual inflation rate of only 5 percent will cut your purchasing power nearly in half in just 10 years.

Given that fact, it should be painfully clear inflation can't be ignored when calculating your future retirement needs, both in terms of the investments you make now and the choices you make once you retire to keep the money flowing in.

So, having seen how to calculate your probable life expectancy and the potential impact of inflation on your purchasing power both before and after you retire, how do you figure out the actual amount of cash you'll need when you do retire? For starters, go back to the current-expenses worksheet and, if you haven't filled it out yet, do so now. Take the time needed to be as accurate as possible; remember, this is the rest of your life we're talking about. Once you have an accurate total for the cost of your current lifestyle, decide on the life expectancies you want to use for you and your spouse, based on the table just provided — plus at least a couple of years to be on the safe side (if you're in good health and take care of yourself, a minimum of five extra years would be better). Finally, estimate the average future inflation rate you expect, using a minimum annual rate of 3 percent — with 4 percent being even better for those desiring a cushion.

Now comes the tricky part. As we said earlier, your post-retirement expenses will probably be 85 to 90 percent of your monthly pre-retirement costs — or even 100 percent if you plan a fairly lavish retirement lifestyle. However, assuming you still have a number of years remaining until you retire, it's likely that both your standard of living and your expenses will increase in the years ahead. Thus, you don't want to base your retirement cost estimates on today's expense numbers. Rather, you must factor in expected increases between now and your retirement date. To do this, subtract your current age from the age at which you plan to retire. Then take your current expense numbers and multiply them by 1 plus your anticipated inflation rate for each year you have remaining until retirement. For example, if you are now 55, have monthly expenses of $2,500, expect a future annual inflation rate of 4 percent and want to retire at age 65, your monthly expenses will likely be at least $3,700.61 when you reach retirement age, calculated as follows:

$2,500 x 1.04 x 1.04 x 1.04 x 1.04 x 1.04 x 1.04 x 1.04 x 1.04 x 1.04 x 1.04 = $3,700.61

(**Note:** For those with a good mathematical or scientific calculator this procedure can be done in just a couple of steps. Simply enter your inflation factor (1.04), press the "y to the x" key, enter the number of years (10), press the "equals" key, and multiply the resulting number by your current expenses figure ($2,500) to get the same result. This will work with any combination of years, inflation factors or expense numbers. Or, if you don't want to use a calculator, you can also look up the compounded inflation factor on any good interest-rate table and multiply it by your initial cost figure.)

Factoring in an expected improvement in your standard of living is a little more difficult since it must be based on your best estimate of your improved earnings, investment returns, etc. In addition, if you have a longer period remaining until retirement, there may be other lifestyle and expense considerations. For example, if you currently have children living at home (or away at college), your standard of living could improve while your costs actually fall once they  go out on their own. Thus, this factor is, at best, a "guesstimate."  However, an annual lifestyle improvement of 1 percent is probably  justifiable for most individuals.

The quickest way to include this factor is to simply add it to your inflation number before you perform the above calculations — i.e., in our example, "1.04" would become "1.05." However, if you  have a calculator, you can be more precise by multiplying "1.04"  times "1.01" (or whatever your chosen numbers are), then pressing the  "y to the x" key and following the rest of the procedure as out-lined  above. In this case, adding in the lifestyle improve-ment factor would increase your projected monthly expense number at the time of retirement to $4,087.78 (1.04 x 1.01 = 1.0504, press "y to the x," enter 10  = 1.6351106 x $2,500 = $4,087.7765). (Note: Had you simply done the  calculation with 1.05, you would have come up with $4,072.2366 — not  much of a difference.)

Once you have an estimated monthly income figure for your date of  retirement, your next step is to calculate how much you'll need once you actually do retire. As we noted earlier, some expenses (such as  clothing, lunches and commuting costs) will clearly fall, but others  (such as travel, hobby expenses or health insurance) will probably rise. Any cost differences related to planned changes in your housing  situation and city (or country) of residence should also be factored in. Unless you had really high unre-imbursed work expenses or a big  house payment that you'll be shedding, you'll probably find you will  need an income equal to at least 85 percent of the net after-tax pay you were getting before you retired, and 90 percent might be a safer  estimate.

To translate that into dollar terms, simply multiply the estimated monthly income figure you arrived at above by the percentage on which you decide. For example, if you were our 55-year-old with an estimated pre-retirement income of $4,087 a month and you expected to need 90 percent of that amount in retirement, you'd multiply $4,087 by 0.90 to get $4,541 a month. Obviously, your number will be different — but the actual number is not that important. The key question, whatever the number, is: Will your Social Security benefits, pension  proceeds, retirement plan pay-outs and other investments yield that  much? And, more importantly, will they continue to yield enough to last through your full post-retirement life expectancy — keeping pace with inflation along the way? And, that's what the rest of this Section will help you determine.

## SAFEGUARDING YOUR PENSION

Is there a fatal flaw in America's pensions system — or are the  well-publicized pension failures of bankrupt companies merely unfortunate exceptions in an otherwise efficient system? The answer seems to be somewhere in between. Most private plans are well managed, and  covered employees will receive all promised benefits. But, if you  have what is called a defined-benefit plan — based on a formula that  takes into account years of service and salary, there are at least  three possible ways your retirement funds could be lost:

**1.** Your company goes out of business or is taken over. If adequately funded, pension plans can survive company shutdowns, even  bankruptcies. However, although your money is protected by law from creditors, that doesn't mean you can get at it immediately. You may  have to wait in line with other creditors.

**2.** The pension funds are mismanaged or misappropriated. Fraud or incompetence rarely threaten large company pension plans since they  are usually run by professional money managers. Pensions of smaller  companies tend to be more vulnerable to mismanagement or fraud — or simply may make unwise investment decisions, jeopardizing the funds. The U.S. Labor Department's Pension and Welfare Benefits Administration (PWBA) is charged with monitoring the 90,000 private pension plans and protecting against such events, but it's a formidable task — and some say an impossible one.

**3.** Your company simply elects to shut down its plan in order to gets its hands on so-called "surplus" assets. In the 1980s, with a bull market driving up investment portfolios, employers grabbed more than $20 billion in pension funds through what is termed "reversion of surplus assets." In other words, the companies shut down their plans, paid off their obligations to employees, then kept what was left over.

Another possible problem arises when an employer buys annuities to cover the plan's promise to pensioners. There have been several cases in which the insurance company offering the annuities became insolvent, then ended up cutting annuity payments.

So, what steps can you take to protect your pension? Here are some guidelines:

* Check out the rules of the Pension Benefit Guaranty Corp. — the federal agency that insures pension plans. You will probably find you're covered, but that's not always the case, so you should definitely check it out.

* Read your plan summary. The Summary Annual Report (SAR) lists administrative costs, how much money is in the plan, and exactly how it's doing investment-wise. Be on the lookout for any unusual financial deals, such as loans being made to company executives. If you spot something, have your employee benefits officer ask the fund managers for an explanation.

* If you do suspect company mismanagement of your plan, request a copy of the full annual report, known as Form 550, from your plan administrator or from the Department of Labor.

For basic information on pensions rights, send for a free copy of "A Guide to Understanding Your Pension Plan" (document D13533)," from the American Association of Retired Persons, AARP Fulfillment, 601 E. St. NW, Washington, DC 20049.

## MORE ON THE PENSION BENEFIT GUARANTY CORP.

The Pension Benefit Guaranty Corp. is a federal agency that protects the pensions of nearly 41 million Americans in 66,000 private defined-benefit pension plans. PBGC's operations are financed by premiums set by Congress and paid by sponsors of defined-benefit plans, proceeds from investment income, assets from pension plans it has taken over and recoveries from the companies formerly responsible for those failed plans. PBGC has a big job: It pays, or will pay (since some people's pension funds fail even before they retire) pension benefits to about 364,000 Americans. That's 158,000 checks going out monthly, plus 188,000 more that will go to people due to receive benefits when they retire in the future. PBGC paid out $722 million in benefits in 1993, and was trustee for 1,858 plans. The maximum guarantee per pensioner in 1994 was a little over $30,000 yearly — or around $2,500 a month.

Given those numbers, underfunding of pension plans is obviously a big problem in the United States. Accordingly, PBGC has instituted an early warning program under which it monitors plans that are under funded. Currently, the agency is looking at about 300 company plans. The enforcement program has teeth — General Motors recently agreed to contribute about $10 billion in cash and stock to its U.S. Hourly Pension Fund. However, even with that huge payment, GM pension plans were estimated to be underfunded by about $12 billion worldwide. Congress is considering reforms in legislation that governs the PBGC. Among them are tougher requirements to ensure the solvency of pension plans, an increase in premiums for plans causing the greatest risk to the system, notification of workers when their plans are low on cash and more authority for the PBGC to enforce pension-funding rules. If you feel you have reason to be concerned about you plan, you can contact your representative or senator and urge support for these reforms.

## REVIEWING OTHER PENSION PLAN CHOICES

In addition to defined-benefit pensions, many companies offer their employees the opportunity to participate in other types of plans. These include:

* Defined-contribution plans, in which the employer contributes a variable amount each year and you also make contributions and determine (at least in part) how you want your money invested. These plans don't offer a fixed retirement benefit, instead basing your payments on the amount of money accumulated in your individual account.

* Money-purchase plans, in which your employer puts a percentage of your salary into a personal account and you decide how it should be invested. Again, benefit payouts vary, based your account size.

* Employee stock ownership plans (ESOPs), in which contributions (both yours and the employer's) are invested in the company's stock.

* Combination plans, in which the company provides more than one option — such as a money-purchase plan with a fixed annual employer contribution, coupled with a defined-contribution plan with variable added contributions based on company profits.

* 401(k) plans, in which you make voluntary contributions to a personal retirement account (usually getting some matching funds from the employer), and the company manages the money for you, based on your instructions as to type of investment. These are frequently offered in addition to other plans. (More on these later.)

If you have the chance to participate in one of these plans, your next step is to determine how well your company's plan (or combination of plans) will meet your personal needs. Obviously, these needs will vary depending on your age, job status, income and eventual retirement objectives, so there are no hard and fast rules on what to look for. However, here are some suggested questions you may want to ask about a given plan:

* Can I decide where the money in my retirement account is invested? If so, what are my choices — and how often can I move my money from one sector to another?
* Can I increase the value of my account by making additional contributions? If so, how much extra can I put in, and how do I go about it?
* Who manages the pension funds, how long have they been handling the investments and what is their performance record?
* Is this particular plan backed by the Pension Benefit Guaranty Corp. or some other insuring agency?
* Can I borrow money from my account — and, if so, what are the repayment terms and interest rates?
* Based on my expected contributions, what do you estimate my account will be worth when I retire — and how will that translate into monthly benefit payments?

* Will I have the option of taking a lump-sum payout — and what are the advantages and disadvantages of such a strategy?
* Are there restrictions or penalties for early withdrawal?
* What happens to my pension account if I change jobs or leave the company?
* Can I receive early benefit payments if I become disabled?
* What happens to my money if I die? Do the monthly benefit payments continue going to my spouse — or, if I have no spouse, does the remaining money in my account go to my other heirs?
* What happens to my benefits if the corporation goes out of business or is bought out by another company?

Once these questions have been answered to your satisfaction, you are ready to sign up — and, if you have the option, decide how you want your money invested. We recommend taking a diversified approach, particularly if your pension plan offers a variety of options or, in some cases, mutual funds from which to choose. For example, you might choose to split your funds four ways, putting 40 percent in a growth fund, 25 percent in an income fund, 25 percent in a foreign fund and 10 percent in your company's own stock. Such an allocation gives you a solid base, with a quarter of your money in low-risk, income-producing investments. However, it also leaves 60 percent of your funds working in the markets — which should be enough to compensate for the effects of inflation. The 25 percent global component spreads your risk beyond the borders of the United States — reducing the chances you'll be badly hurt should your retirement date come during an economic downturn, as well as giving you a cushion against fluctuations in the value of the dollar (important for those who plan to travel abroad after retirement). Putting the final 10 percent in your corporation's own stock takes advantage of a special situation in that most companies contribute extra matching funds when employees buy a designated amount of stock. This provides an automatic and instant boost in your return — often by as much as 50 percent. And who can afford to pass up a deal like that?

## YOUR RIGHTS REGARDING "VESTING"

Under federal law, you must gain a permanent right to the funds your employer contributes to your pension plan once you become "vested" — in other words, after you have put in a certain period of service with a given employer. Once you are vested in a plan, you have a legal right to those benefits — even if you quit before retirement age. There are two common methods of vesting — "cliff" and "graded." Rules on the maximum vesting periods allowed by law are fairly standard among major U.S. corporations (although some firms accelerate the vesting period, allowing you to qualify with fewer years of service):

* Under cliff vesting with a single-employer plan, you must be fully vested by the time you have five years of service. In a multi-employer plan, full vesting must come after 10 years. Until you complete this service, you have NO vested rights. After you do, however, you have "fallen off the cliff" and are 100 percent vested.

* Graded vesting is phased in over a period of years. You must receive at least 20 percent after three years of service and an additional 20 percent each of the next four years, with full vesting coming no later than at the end of seven years.

**Bonus:** Employees who reach normal retirement age automatically become vested — no matter how many years of service they have under the plan. Note: Contributions that YOU make to a pension plan are always fully vested.

## 401(k)s — BETTER THAN A GOLD WATCH

The hottest — and best — thing going these days in the pension and retirement savings field is the so-called 401(k) plan. Why have plans of this type become so popular? The reasons are simple. Employers prefer them because they reduce company pension costs, encouraging workers to save more for themselves. They also cut down on administrative expenses since management of the pension monies must be handled by outside advisors (usually brokers, registered investment companies, bank trust departments or insurance companies), and the funds are almost always turned over to the employee — via a lump-sum payout — at the time of retirement. You should like them for even more reasons, including:

* Contributions are made with pre-tax dollars — i.e., they are deducted from your salary before withholding and Social Security tax liabilities are calculated, thus reducing the tax bite the IRS takes out of your earnings. For example, if you earn $50,000 a year and put $6,000 into a 401(k), you will owe current-year income and Social Security taxes on just $44,000 — with taxes on the rest being deferred until you take the money out of the plan after you retire. (For this reason, these plans also often called salary-reduction plans.) Most states also allow the full salary reductions for purposes of their income taxes.

* Contribution limits are higher than for IRAs and most other pension plans — up to 15 percent of your net salary or a limit of about $9,000, whichever is less (the actual limit is adjusted annually for inflation).

* Most companies offer generous matching contributions, sometimes as much as 50 cents for each dollar you contribute up to a certain percentage of your salary (usually 5 to 7 percent, although it can be higher).

* Taxes are deferred on all plan earnings until the money is withdrawn after retirement, thus providing much faster growth than in taxable savings plans.

* You have a significant say in how your retirement funds are invested, yet you retain the benefits of professional management hired either by the outside pension advisor or by mutual funds the plans offer as investment options (or both).

* Under many 401(k) plans, you can borrow from your account, up to a maximum of 50 percent of assets or $50,000, whichever is less. Interest is charged on these loans, but rates are typically lower than for secured bank loans. However, repayments must be made at least quarterly and the entire loan must be repaid within five years (unless the money is used for purchase of a principal residence).

* Money can be withdrawn without penalty after age 59-1/2 — even if you don't retire — (or after age 55 if you lose your job with the company sponsoring the plan). Withdrawals before age 59-1/2 are subject to taxes and a 10 percent penalty. However, money can be taken out of the plan early under certain hardship conditions — including disability, catastrophic illness and some financial problems, such as preventing foreclosure on a home — without incurring the penalty.

* Once you retire, you have full control over how the money is paid out (subject to limitations imposed by federal law) — and money not withdrawn continues to grow free of taxes.

* If the money is withdrawn in a lump sum after age 59-1/2, you can take advantage of five-year averaging — another tax break.

## 401(k)s OFFER MAXIMUM GROWTH POTENTIAL

With their tax-free compounding, a 401(k) plans are unmatched for  accumulating a retirement nest egg. Here's an example: Suppose, at  age 25, your annual salary is $25,000, with a typical annual raise of  4 percent. Now let's say you put 6 percent of your pay into a 401(k),  with a 50 percent employer match (a common percentage). Result: Assuming a 9 percent annual return, by age 65, before taxes, you'll have  $1,315,944. Even if your employer doesn't contribute, you'll still  pile up $877,296. However, if you saved at the same interest outside  a 401(k), you'd end up with  less  than  $500,000 — $472,778, to be exact. The spread  between  $1,315,944  and  $472,778  comes  to $843,166 — and that's a nice little retirement present.

## IRAs, KEOGHs AND SEPs

As just noted, the 401(k) plan is rapidly becoming the retirement-savings vehicle of choice for most employed Americans — from  those who work for smaller local companies  to  those  with  major  international  corporations. However, they  aren't  the  only  vehicles  available. All Americans who earn money by working — i.e., who have what are known as earned incomes, as opposed to interest or dividend  earnings — are also eligible to contribute up to $2,000 ($2,250 for  married  couples)  annually  to  an Individual Retirement Account, or  IRA. This includes young children and people who are already retired  and collecting other types of pensions (until they reach 70-1/2). In  addition, self-employed people can set up Keogh plans or simplified  employee pension (SEP) plans to provide for their retirement needs.

Since there  is  ample  information  available  about these plans, we won't go into a great deal of detail here. However, we  will  note  that  you should take maximum advantage of these retirement-savings plans — particularly if you are self-employed, which means you have access to no other type of pension (except for Social Security). The tax  savings are substantial during your working years — and the tax-deferred growth potential is an essential element in amassing substantial wealth. (Note: Determining the structure and contribution levels  for Keogh and SEP plans can be complicated, so you may need professional help in setting up your plan. If so, consult with your banker or broker for advice, or employ the services of an attorney, accountant or Certified Financial Planner who specializes in these areas.)

We do want to offer a little more information on IRAs since they play an integral role in how you handle your 401(k) holdings when you  change jobs, as well as how you take out your money when you retire.  Here are the IRA basics:

* You are allowed an annual contribution of $2,000 — or $2,250  if you have a non-working spouse. (This joint contribution can be split in any proportion between two accounts, so long as neither account receives more than $2,000.)

* Your contribution is deductible from your pre-tax earnings so  long as neither you nor your spouse is covered by a pension plan at  work. If you are covered by another plan — including a 401(k), Keogh  or SEP — you can still make the full IRA contribution, but the money  is not deductible for tax purposes. However, it's still a good idea  to fully fund your IRA if you can afford it, simply because taxes are deferred on all earnings produced by the funds in the account.

* IRA contributions must be invested with an IRS-approved custodian. These include banks, insurance companies, brokers and (most commonly used) mutual funds. However, you can open as many IRAs as you  want, using

a different custodian and choosing a different investment each year in order to reduce your risk. From a practical standpoint, it's probably a good idea to limit yourself to no more than four or five separate accounts, simply because the paperwork and bookkeeping can become onerous. Besides, if you make good investment choices, you want to maximize your results by having larger sums build up in those accounts.

* You can begin withdrawing money from your IRA at age 59-1/2 — and you must begin withdrawing money at age 70-1/2. As was the case with 401(k)s, there is a 10 percent penalty for early withdrawals and such withdrawals are also taxed. However, the penalty can be avoided if withdrawals are taken in equal annual payments over your remaining life expectancy. There is also a penalty if you fail to begin withdrawals at age 70-1/2.

* All money withdrawn from IRAs funded with deductible (pre-tax) contributions is taxed as ordinary income. However, only the earnings from IRAs funded with nondeductible (after-tax) contributions are taxable when withdrawn, the original contribution being considered a return of principal.

## STANDARD 401(k) AND IRA WITHDRAWAL RULES

IRA withdrawal provisions are extremely important because, in virtually every case, you will be both managing and withdrawing your much larger 401(k) account funds through the IRA structure once you actually retire. That's because, whenever you leave an employer with whom you have one of these plans, you are required to take your money with you — either accepting it outright and paying the taxes and penalties or, more appropriately, moving it into what is known as a tax deferred "IRA rollover account," a change that results in no taxes or penalties.

Here's a breakdown of the typical exit rules (many of them mandated by federal law) for these pension plans:

* If you take your 401(k) money directly, you will owe taxes on everything but any returned after-tax contributions you made.

* If you are under age 55, you will also owe a 10 percent penalty on the taxable funds received.

* If you are moving to another company, your current employer may be able to make a direct transfer of your funds to the new employer's 401(k) plan.

* If that option is not available, you can roll the money into an IRA account without paying taxes or penalties. However, you must be sure to have the funds transferred directly to the IRA custodian, not paid to you and then placed in an IRA. If your account proceeds come directly to you, your employer is required to withhold 20 percent of the payout money for taxes. While you can reclaim this money from the IRS when you file your tax returns, you must make up the money from your own pocket when you fund the IRA or it will be considered a permanent taxable withdrawal and penalties may apply.

* When you roll your 401(k) money into an IRA, keep the funds separate from any other IRA money you have and don't make additional contributions to that account. Otherwise, you won't be able to move the funds into any new employer's 401(k) plan.

## KEEP THE IRS AWAY FROM YOUR 401(k)

The new IRA and 401(k) withholding rules, effective as of Jan. 1, 1993, represent a particularly onerous trap for retirement savers. If you change jobs and want to take your pension money with you, your employer is required to withhold 20 percent of your total assets. To make things worse, you still have to roll 100 percent of those funds — including the 20 percent you didn't get — into another retirement account within 60 days, or suffer early withdrawal penalties.

For example, say you had $250,000 accumulated in your 401(k) when you decided to switch to a new employer. You'd get a check for 80 percent — $200,000. The only way to get the rest back would be to put that $200,000, plus another $50,000 you'd have to raise yourself somehow, into a retirement account within 60 days. Then you could ask the IRS for a $50,000 refund on your tax return. However, if you only put $200,000 into an IRA, then other $50,000 would be subject to a 31 percent tax ($15,500), plus a 10 percent penalty ($5,000) for early withdrawal (if you're under 59 1/2), plus state taxes (say 5 percent, or $2,500). That comes to $23,000 the government got instead of you.

As nasty as this tax trap is, it only works to raise taxes from the ignorant — from people who don't know any better. You can easily sidestep it, as long as you know it's there. All you have to do to avoid the 20 percent withholding is ask your employer — before you walk out the door — to switch the money DIRECTLY into an IRA, without you withdrawing any of it.

You should also investigate where to tell them to switch your 401(k) funds, instead of just accepting whatever IRA your company may choose for you. Here are your three basic options:

* Switch the funds to your new employer's plan. This won't work, of course, if you don't have a new employer, or your new employer has a waiting period for 401(k) participation.

* Switch the funds directly to a "conduit IRA." This is an IRA you set up especially for this purpose, with the idea of rolling it later into another employer's plan. A bank or brokerage can help you get it going. (Again, if you merge the funds with your other retirement accounts, you lose the option to roll them into another employer's plan later on.)

* Leave the funds where they are. Even if you quit, you can still leave your 401(k) account with your ex-employer in many cases. Just make sure you know the rules for getting it out later — some plans won't allow distribution until 60 days after your 65th birthday.

## HOW SOCIAL SECURITY WORKS FOR YOU

You see it on every check stub and wonder if you'll ever see it  again: FICA. It stands for Federal Insurance Contributions Act, and  the tax amounted to 6.2 percent of the first $57,600 of your income in 1994. Your employer paid an additional 6.2 percent, making your maximum "contribution" $7,142.40 that year. What did you get for this money? You helped to pay Social Security benefits to Americans who  are currently retired, widowed, orphaned or disabled. That's the way  the program works — today's workers are taxed to support the previous generation of workers. When you hit retirement age and it's your turn to collect, you'll be supported by Social Security taxes paid by the next generation.

Payments are made to retirees, their spouses and, in many cases  their surviving dependents, according to how well paid they were when  they worked and contributed to the plan. To receive the maximum payment, you must have paid the maximum amount in at least 10 of your employment years. Also, you must be fully "insured" to receive benefits — meaning you must have paid the FICA tax for 40 calendar quarters, or 10 years. How much will return will you get? The current rate for new retirees who are 65 and receive the maximum payment is $1,128 a month (this amount rises each year, based on inflation). If you have a spouse who is 65 and has no Social Security benefits of his or her own, the spouse is entitled to 50 percent of your benefit — or an additional $564. That's a total annual benefit of $20,304.

It's your responsibility to find out what the Social Security Administration's records say about you. To do that, you can call 1-800-772-1213 (or visit your local SSA office) and ask for a Form SSA-7004, "Request for Social Security Earnings and Benefit Statement." Fill out the form and mail it in. In a few weeks, you'll get a year-by-year printout of all earnings credited to your account in the last 10 years. If there are errors, you'll need to show backup documentation to get them corrected, so be prepared with old paycheck stubs, W-2 forms, employer's name and address, and dates of employment. Your employer can provide copies of old W-2's that you may have discarded. It's a good idea to check this statement every few years whether you are near retirement age or not. Better to uncover and fix any mistakes now, rather than three months before you retire.

You become eligible for Social Security upon reaching age 62, but at a reduced rate. For full benefits, you have to wait until age 65 — and this age will rise in the future, as shown in the top portion of the table below. The U.S. government has re-evaluated its actuarial tables and decided that the way to stretch its Social Security funds is to avoid paying them until later in the recipients' lives. Lower benefits will still be available at age 62 under the new rules, though the reduction will be bigger. There is also a delayed retirement credit, which was 4 percent a year for workers reaching age 65 in 1994. It will gradually rise to 8 percent a year by 2008. This benefit may be accrued if you don't retire, or if you simply choose not to file for benefits. The full benefits schedule, with ages for reduced benefits and credits, is shown in the bottom portion of the  table below:

## Eligibility Ages for Full Future Social Security Benefits

| Birth Date* | Age for Full Benefits | Date |
|---|---|---|
| Jan. 1, 1938 | 65 years, 2 months | March 1, 2003 |
| Jan. 1, 1939 | 65 years, 4 months | May 1, 2004 |
| Jan. 1, 1940 | 65 years, 6 months | July 1, 2005 |
| Jan. 1, 1941 | 65 years, 8 months | Sept. 1, 2006 |
| Jan. 1, 1942 | 65 years, 10 months | Nov. 1, 2007 |
| Jan. 1, 1943-54 | 66 years | Jan. 1, 2009-20 |
| Jan. 1, 1955 | 66 years, 2 months | March 1, 2021 |
| Jan. 1, 1956 | 66 years, 4 months | May 1, 2022 |
| Jan. 1, 1957 | 66 years, 6 months | July 1, 2023 |
| Jan. 1, 1958 | 66 years, 8 months | Sept. 1, 2024 |
| Jan. 1, 1959 | 66 years, 10 months | Nov. 1, 2025 |
| Jan. 1, 1960 | 67 years | Jan. 1, 2027 |

* — A Jan. 1 birthdate was used for illustration only. Individuals born on other dates in the stated year would have to reach the same  age listed in Column 2 in order to qualify for the full benefit.

## Current Social Security Benefits Structure

| Retirement age | Monthly benefit |
|---|---|
| 62 | 80 percent |
| 63 | 85 percent |
| 65 | Full benefit |
| 68 | Full benefit, plus 12 percent |
| 70 | Full benefit, plus 20 percent |

## YOU DO HAVE TO FILE FOR BENEFITS

Social Security isn't automatic — you have to file for benefits. About three months before your scheduled retirement date, call the SSA at 1-800-772-1213. Unless there is something unusual about your application, the phone call is all it takes to get the ball rolling.

## SOME OTHER SOCIAL SECURITY DETAILS

Here are some additional facts regarding Social Security benefits and adjustments that you may find helpful:

* If you are 62 and will continue working, it usually doesn't pay to file for SSA benefits. Why? Because the SSA reduces your benefits by the amount you earn that is above $7,440 a year. They cut it by $1 for every $2 you make above that amount. Assuming you'd normally get $12,000 a year in Social Security benefits and you earn $20,000, your benefit is cut to $5,740 a year. That's still a fair benefit since it still represents more than 25 percent of your earned income. However, your monthly checks will remain at a smaller percentage throughout the rest of your life, so it may not be worthwhile later. If you earn more than $31,440, your benefit disappears altogether until age 65, so you're better off waiting. It gets easier between ages 65 and 69. Then earnings of more than $10,200 will reduce benefits, and the cut drops to just $1 for every $3 you earn above that amount. With the same $12,000 annual payout, it would take an income of $46,200 to totally eliminate your SSA benefit. Once you turn 70, you can earn as much as you want without reducing benefits.

* A spouse who pays Social Security tax accumulates her or his own benefits. A non-working spouse qualifies for a retirement benefit half the size of what their retired spouse receives. This drops to 37.5 percent if you start taking benefits at age 62.

* Self-employed individuals are also covered under Social Security if they pay the yearly self-employment tax, which the law says they must. However, since there's no matching employer contribution, this tax is double the normal employee FICA tax — amounting to 12.4 percent of earned income up to the maximum of $57,600 (in 1994). Benefit payouts and schedules are the same for formerly self-employed retirees as for other recipients.

* Half your annual SSA benefit may be taxable if you have other income (from any source) that totals $25,000 if you are single, or $32,000 for married couples filing joint returns. Your gross income includes interest from tax-exempt municipal bonds. The taxable amount is the lesser of: (a) half of your total benefit, or (b) half of the amount by which your gross income, PLUS half your SSA benefit exceeds the limit. These taxes apply even if you are over 70 years of age.

* Your spouse and other dependents — whether children, grandchildren or parents — are entitled to a share of your benefits if you die. Your children could receive benefits until they reach age 22 if they are full-time students, or age 18 if they forgo higher education. Disabled children can continue receiving benefits for life. And, benefits for other dependents are calculated based on individual circumstances.

* Investment income is not taxed for Social Security purposes. You pay FICA taxes only on income earned from employment.

## ANOTHER REASON TO DELAY BENEFITS

Perhaps the best argument against taking early Social Security benefits is the steadily growing life expectancy of retirees — i.e., the actuarial odds are you will live long enough to collect the money you passed up between ages 62 and 65. The break-even point arrives at 77, after 12 years of higher benefits. The average 65-year-old woman can expect to live to 84, collecting seven more years of the higher benefit. The average man at age 65 has more than 15 years of life remaining, so he'll get an extra three years of higher payments. As the "official" retirement age creeps up, the incentive to wait will be even greater because the age-62 benefit will be smaller. Instead of 80 percent of the full benefit, it will drop to just 70 percent.

## MEDICARE AND POST-RETIREMENT HEALTH INSURANCE

The topic of the year in 1994 was national health insurance, but the United States already has national health insurance for retirees — and it has since 1966. It's called Medicare. There are really two programs under Medicare — acute care or "hospital insurance," which covers everyone who also gets SSA payments, and medical insurance, for which you pay a monthly premium. There is no "early" retirement under Medicare; you must be 65 to qualify. To have coverage begin on your 65th birthday, you have to apply in the three months before the month you turn 65.

Medicare is a strong support program for retirees, as far as it goes — but it has its problems. A major one is that it is intended to cover the cost of a hospital stay and does not provide "extended" or "custodial" care after the patient is well enough to go home, but still needs help doing the shopping, fixing meals or just getting out of bed in the morning. Another is that maximum Medicare payments for certain medical procedures are far less than doctors and hospitals actually charge. As a result of these and other problems, you should not count on Medicare to deal with your health-care costs after retirement. If it's at all possible, plan to stay with your employer's coverage — remaining in that lower-cost (at least in terms of insurance premiums) pool of individuals as long as you can.

If you can't stay in your employer's group plan, consider purchasing a private Medicare supplement policy. You may also want to consider private insurance for longer-term care. The maximum Medicare covers is 100 days a year in a skilled nursing-care facility. And if, in Medicare's opinion, the nursing home can't provide skilled care, it won't pay.

## GETTING OUT OF YOUR MUTUAL FUNDS AT RETIREMENT

Just as crucial as buying and holding an equity is the decision to get out of the market. In the case of mutual fund shares, many investors choose to switch these over to bond funds on retirement. One trouble with this strategy is it sacrifices growth over the remaining years of the investor's life — which can be substantial. An alternative offered by most mutual fund companies is systematic withdrawal — basically dollar-cost averaging in reverse.

Instead of reinvesting distributions, have your fund switch them to its money market fund. Then instruct the money fund to write you a check for a specified amount each month. Some months the fund distributions will more than cover the check; in other months the investment fund will have to liquidate some of your shares. However, your investment fund shares will keep working for you, and only be drawn down gradually as you need them.

Systematic withdrawal plans have been around forever, but not many people know about them — the Investment Company Institute, the industry's largest trade association, reports that only about 250,000 plans are presently in effect among the more than 50 million mutual fund accounts currently open nationwide. One reason, of course, is that these plans don't offer much benefit for younger people still earning money in the job force — for them, the variable withdrawals can be a bear at tax time, with lots of extra paperwork involved.

## TAKE THE RETIREMENT MONEY AND RUN

An attractive option for many older Americans is retiring overseas. The lure is to find a place in the foreign sun where the cost of living is still low and the Yankee dollar still strong. However, if you're thinking of joining this outgoing tide, you should bear in mind the following:

* U.S. citizens living abroad are still subject to federal income tax — though, to avoid double taxation, taxes paid to a foreign government are credited. However, some foreign countries tax U.S. Social Security income of resident American retirees.

* Renouncing U.S. citizenship isn't a foolproof way to escape the IRS. They'll take their bite out of any investment income, such as dividends, before it gets sent to you. And you may still be taxed as a U.S. citizen if Uncle Sam suspects you've recently renounced your citizenship simply to escape income taxes.

* You must live (or be) outside the U.S. for a full calendar year — or for 12 of 13 consecutive months — to qualify as a foreign resident for U.S. income-tax purposes. You will also be exempt from U.S. local and state taxes.

* You qualify for a U.S. tax exemption for the first $70,000 of earned income if you earn income while legally living abroad. You also qualify for a living allowance exclusion — a windfall if the foreign country doesn't impose an income tax.

\* While retiring abroad, you may wish to maintain a U.S. residence as a rental investment you can depreciate. For tax purposes, it won't be considered a principal place of residence if used as a permanent abode fewer than 183 days a year.

\* After selling a principal residence in the U.S., a person moving abroad has four years (instead of two as in the U.S.) to buy a home of equivalent value and qualify for tax deferral on the gain.

\* You may wish to rent rather than buy a home abroad. The reason: Rules on currency restrictions and capital gains vary from country to country, but some foreign countries have restrictions on how much money you can take out of the country after the sale of a house.

A popular choice for Americans retiring abroad is Costa Rica, because it welcomes U.S. retirees so long as they have a guaranteed after-tax annual income of $18,000 or more. For those who aren't familiar with the Central American country, the capital city of San Jose is very cosmopolitan, with fine restaurants, entertainment ranging from the national opera company to American TV via cable, superb international transportation and communications links and a climate similar to that of Los Angeles.

For other ideas on low-cost retirement meccas — both here and abroad — look for the latest edition of a book called "Paradise Found: How to Live in North America's Best Climate for Under $500 a Month," published by Ross Paron. Paron's favorite hideaway is a 60—mile-long lake in the mountains of Mexico, offering low prices, clean air, good medical services and U.S.-style shopping. According to Paron, the place is ideal for Americans on Social Security and small pensions. To order, send $12.95, plus $3 postage and handling, to: United Research Publishers, 249 S. Hwy. 101, Solana Beach, CA 92075. The book carries a 30-day money-back guarantee of satisfaction.

## BABY-BOOMER BIND — CARING FOR KIDS AND PARENTS

Many adults who put off starting a family until mid-career are finding they can't retire themselves because they're in a double financial squeeze — not only are they faced with the formidable task of still raising their kids, but their aging parents now need looking after. For many in this Baby-Boomer trap, the double demand on their time and financial resources is more than they can cope with and still contemplate retirement.

If this dilemma is yours, what can you do? The best advice is to get help — and, fortunately, there's a growing number of resource groups and community services are out there to assist you. There are roughly 700 "Area Agencies on Aging" across the country, coordinating and funding more than 20,000 local organizations. Call the national Eldercare Locator at 1-800-677-1116 to find the number of an agency near you. The Area Agencies will also help you track down community services such as Meals on Wheels and others that can help the elderly shop, clean house, cook or commute to a nearby adult day-care center. They will also put you in touch with nearby volunteer programs from churches, synagogues or public agencies that offer daily drop-ins and other services.

Resources for the aging are also listed in Nora Jean Levin's "How to Care for Your Parents: A Handbook for Adult Children." Send $5.95, plus $1.25 shipping, to Storm King Press, Box 2089, Friday Harbor, WA 98250. A more widely distributed book is Dr. Michael T. Levy's "Parenting Mom and Dad" (Prentice Hall, 1990).

Additional help is available from geriatric or gerontological counselors. These professionals will meet with your family, provide advice and counseling, and can also put you in touch with resources. Ask a doctor, hospital, nursing home or senior citizens' center to recommend one.

If an aging parent lives at an inconvenient distance and your budget can handle it, you might consider hiring a geriatric social worker in that vicinity to make a comprehensive assessment. You can ask for recommendations on local doctors, lawyers, accountants, housekeepers, etc. You can also hire a care manager to arrange for services and be on call for emergencies. A list of recommended care managers by state is available from Children of Aging Parents or the National Association of Private Geriatric Care Managers, 655 N. Alvernon, Ste. 108, Tucson AZ 85711, 602-881-8008.

You also should take care of yourself and your own needs during these difficult times. You can benefit from support groups of other people who've dealt with all these same generational problems. A list of such groups from Children of Aging Parents, 1609 Woodbourne Road, Suite 302A, Levittown, PA 19057, or call 215-945-6900. These groups can help you deal with the range of emotions common to adult caregivers as they experience sudden parent-child role reversal. These feelings include denial, grief, anger and guilt.

Geriatric counselors agree that aging parents and their children should set up their own personal resource directories, preferably in large-print. These should include the names and phone numbers of family members, friends, neighbors, doctors, hospitals, ambulance companies, pharmacies and other area support and delivery services.

General advice for adult caregivers is offered in two free brochures from the American Association of Retired Persons, "A Path for Caregivers" (D12957) and "Miles Away and Still Caring" (D12748). Mail a postcard requesting these by title and stock number to AARP Fulfillment, 601 East Street NW, Washington, DC 20049. For legal information on aging parents, you might send for another free booklet: "Questions & Answers When Looking for an

Elder Law Attorney," from the National Academy of Elder Law Attorneys, 655 N. Alvernon, Suite 108, Tucson, AZ 85711. Include a stamped, self-addressed envelope.

Naturally, to the extent that elder parents are capable, they should be included in all family planning discussions. In addition, middle-aged parents caring for elderly parents should not overlook one other valuable resource — their own children. If the kids are old enough, willing enough and can handle responsibility, they should be enlisted in caring for their grandparents.

## COMPUTER HELP IN PLANNING YOUR RETIREMENT

If you've tried the mathematical estimating we discussed earlier in this Section and find you still need help working out retirement planning scenarios (or want to use different assumptions), T. Rowe Price, the big mutual fund company, offers a user-friendly IBM-PC compatible computer program that does "what-if" analyses based on your assumptions, then displays the results graphically in seconds. Change an assumption, and the program quickly recalculates the probable outcome. The kit costs $15, plus local sales taxes, and can be ordered by sending a check to T. Rowe Price, P.O. Box 15098, Worces- ter, MA 01615, or with a credit card by calling 1-800-541-3022.

## FINDING EXTRA MONEY FOR RETIREMENT SAVINGS

If your calculations show you need to put more money into retirement savings plans than you currently have available, consider these two ideas for getting more funds for that purpose:

* Drop your life insurance policy. Many couples maintain life insurance policies with premiums that gobble up sizable chunks of their after-tax incomes. To free up that income for other — and better — investments, buy only sufficient term insurance to replace your lost income — taking into account reduced taxes and living costs after death. With lower-cost insurance in effect, you may be able to drop the previous policy (though it means accepting the loss of all those premiums paid over the years) and add its cash value to your savings.

* Calculate your monthly tax savings from your tax-deferred savings plans and IRA contributions and invest that sum each month in another retirement account. This is money you'd be giving to Uncle Sam anyway, so it shouldn't be factored into your budget. Why not compound your own retirement savings by putting it to work in some other type of investment that provides diversification from the investments you have in your tax-deferred plans?

**NOTES**

_____

_____

_____

_____

_____

_____

_____

## CHAPTER 10
# LEGAL SURVIVAL GUIDE

It's a strange world out there — and one of the strangest things about it these days is the legal system. Over the past three decades or so, federal, state and local legislative bodies have decided that it is the duty of government to protect people against every possible contingency — and they've attempted to pass laws to do just that. As a result, Americans have had less and less cause to take responsibility for their own actions, or their own safety. They rush blithely forward in all their affairs — and frequently wind up running smack dab into either a confrontation or a physical mishap. And, when they do, suffering any kind of real (or perceived) injury — be it physical, emotional or financial — their first reaction is to sue. And, what's even worse — they all too often win! It makes no sense that this should happen — but, as one best-selling author on the subject recently said, "the America system of laws has completely wiped out basic common sense." So, how do you protect yourself from the growing number of legal pitfalls in our society — making sure both your assets and your rights are secure from assault? The information in this Section will provide some guidelines. Read on.

## PROTECT YOURSELF AGAINST LAWSUIT FEVER

As just noted, lawsuits or threats of lawsuits are flying everywhere these days — and, as ridiculous as it may seem, courts and juries are handing down tremendous (and potentially crippling) monetary award for even the smallest of injuries or the most ludicrous of claims. Here are just two recent examples:

* An elderly woman orders a cup of coffee from a McDonald's drive-through window, removes the cover, sets the cup between her legs and is then burned when the driver of the car in which she's riding takes off too fast, spilling the coffee in her lap. She sues McDonald's for serving coffee that's too hot — and win's $3.2 million in damages! (The award was later reduced, but was still over a million dollars.)

* Two New York business partners are confronted by a would-be robber armed with a knife. They take the knife away and hold the man for the police, who arrest him. He's later convicted and sentenced to prison. However, because his arm was broken when the businessmen subdued — and because he can no longer ply his trade due to his resulting prison sentence — he sues the businessmen for personal injury and loss of future income. Amazingly, the jury agrees with his claim and awards a judgment so large the partners are forced to sell their business to pay the damages.

Both of those cases are almost impossible to believe — but they are true. Thus, even though you may think you couldn't possibly pose a risk to anyone, it's still essential for you to take precautions to protect yourself and your assets against both legitimate and spurious claims. Failure to do so could be catastrophic — and there's no good reason not to since it's really not that hard. Here are some ideas on how to avoid against being targeted by lawsuits, as well as some tips on putting your assets out of reach of anyone lucky enough to win one of them:

**1.** Always put things in writing. Before doing work for some-one — or employing someone to work for you — have a written agreement that  details what each of you expects the other to do, and how and when  payment will be made. You don't need a fancy contract full of legalese — just a sin-gle sheet spelling out responsibilities and terms.  Do, how-ever, include clauses stating that all disputes will be han-dled in the courts of your state and that legal costs will be paid by the losing party. These prevent having to fight a costly out-of-state  legal battle and guarantee any mone-tary award you might win won't be  wiped out by attorney's fees.

**2.** Don't be afraid to sue. The high cost, in both money and time,  of pushing a claim through our legal system prevents many people from seeking legal redress. However, if you develop a reputation as someone who's not afraid to sue — and counter-sue — people will think  twice before trying to take advantage of you.

**3.** Buy an excess liability insurance policy. Most insurance companies will sell you a $1 million to $2 million "umbrella" policy covering most any liability for which you might be sued (except malpractice or libel) in excess of your home-owners' or auto policies. The  cost is quite reasonable — usually less than $200 a year, though the  insurer may demand that you also give him your home and auto insur-ance business. Be sure the policy specifies that the duty to defend  against lawsuits rests with the insurer, not with you. That way, if  you are sued, you just turn the case over to the insurer to handle.

**4.** If you are in a high-risk profession or see problems with creditors or the tax collector arising in the future, consider transferring assets to your wife or children. Remember, however, this can be  a double-edged sword — getting you off the hook, but exposing your  family members. If you do transfer assets, do it now. Transfers made  after a suit has been filed or within a year before debt or tax problems arise will generally be invalidated — and you could be charged with trying to defraud your creditors.

**5.** Your home is probably your biggest asset — and one you can't stuff into a Bahamian bank vault. Most states have homestead laws to protect your home from creditors, but some are quite weak — and nobody can protect you from the IRS. As a result, you're highly vulnerable if you hold your home as individual property — and joint ownership or community property designations aren't much better. However, there are some alternatives that provide more protection:

* Limited partnerships — These are usually comprised of the immediate family — i.e., spouse and children only. It's very hard for creditors to reach a limited partner's interest if you set things up properly (which provides added protection for your children). Here's how it works: You create one general-partnership share and 99 limited—partnership shares. Initial title to the shares rests in the name of the partnership. You serve as general partnership, and therefore have control, but other family members hold all of the limited partnership shares. (Note: Some of the shares can be transferred to your children annually as a gift, thereby qualifying for the $10,000 gift-tax exclusion and avoiding any transfer tax.)

* Family corporations — Put your assets in a family owned corporation, with someone else (other than a closed family member) named as chief corporate officer. You are protected since that person cannot act without approval of the shareholders (your family), but because his or her name is listed as head of the corporation, your creditors won't know — or will have trouble proving — that you are the owner. (**Note:** Nevada has made this into an art form, and many Nevada lawyers specialize in asset-protection corporations. And, you don't have to live in Nevada to have a Nevada corporation.)

* "Spindthrift" trusts — Put your assets in an irrevocable trust with a non-family member as trustee. Income from the trust is payable to you for life, then the trust property passes to a named beneficiary. Illinois makes it very difficult for creditors to touch a "spendthrift" trust, and you don't have to live there to set one up. (Note: Don't rely on a "living trust" — these protect you from probate, but do nothing to protect your assets while you are alive.)

**6.** Perhaps the ultimate in personal asset protection involves a combination of a limited partnership and a trust based in an offshore locale with strong asset-protection laws (such as the Cayman Islands or Bahamas). Once again, you create a limited partnership with yourself as general partner, which means you keep control of the assets. However, you retain only a 1 percent interest in the partnership — transferring the rest of the shares to the offshore trust. As a result, 99 percent of the assets become untouchable — by both you and your creditors. However, you get to specify when the assets again become free — say, perhaps, after your retirement.

One problem is that such arrangements must be put in place well in advance of any action (or anticipated action) by your creditors, who have two years to challenge a trust as a fraudulent conveyance — i.e., a phony way of placing assets out of reach. You also are prohibited from putting so many assets into the trust that you are left insolvent (the legal limit is about two-thirds of your net worth). Obviously, you'll need professional help to set up this type of arranment. One expert is Jerome Schneider of San Francisco, who has over 20 years experience in the offshore financial field and has authored several books on the subject. He offers free telephone consultations, which you can arrange by calling 1-800-421-4177.

**7.** To protect your business assets, you should always incorporate. This way creditors can only get to the corporation's assets, so you lose only what you've invested. If you don't incorporate, creditors can take everything you have. To be doubly safe, set up a separate corporation for each of your businesses. (Note: You can keep patents or other business assets as your sole property. You merely license or lease these assets to your company for its use.)

**8.** As an added protection, be sure you have ample disability insurance. Most people get life insurance, but few get disability coverage, even though the latter is a far more likely catastrophe. For example, if you're age 42, you're four times more likely to be disabled  than to die before age 65 — and the costs of caring for such a disability can wipe you out financially just as surely as a lawsuit.

## HOW TO SUE AND WIN

Given the time and expense it takes, it makes very little sense  to sue someone unless you're pretty sure you can win — but how can  you guarantee that. You can't, of course, although a great attorney  will certainly help — as will the following five things you can do  to strengthen your case:

**1.** Get your facts straight. Be precise on meeting dates, times of  phone calls and details of conversations. Get the names of witnesses  or people you speak with. Write down addresses, times of day, order  of occurrence, etc.

**2.** Be specific about how you were wronged — and what you want in  return.

**3.** Ask your attorney a lot of questions and tell him everything.  The more information he has, the stronger the case he can build.

**4.** Be businesslike in your attitude, both in and out of court. Make it clear you expect satisfaction, recount the facts and calmly  and firmly  state  your  demand  for  compensation. Communication works;  hysteria works against you.

**5.** Be willing to negotiate in good faith. If a reasonable offer for an out-of-court settlement is proposed, be open to at least considering it. In terms of time and expense, it might work out to your advantage to take it.

## DON'T GET PECKED TO DEATH BY THE LEGAL EAGLES

Everyone complains about lawyers and lawyers' fees. But, unlike the weather, there IS something you can do about it. There are firms that audit legal bills to help you avoid rip-offs. Of course, they charge, too. However, you can do your own auditing — and also take other steps to watch your wallet. Here are three strategies:

**1. Demand a monthly statement.** Do this even if you intend to pay at the conclusion of the attorney's services. It will let you know right away if you're getting in over your head budgetwise — plus, you'll be able to review the bill while the services provided (or not provided) are still fresh in your mind. If you find what you think are overcharges, don't hesitate to complain. Request copies of any documents prepared for you, and compare the likely difficulty or preparation against what you're being charged. A brief boilerplate letter shouldn't cost you an hour's prime billing. Many law firms will remove specific charges if questioned. If yours won't — and you're not satisfied — your local bar association can arrange a fee-dispute hearing.

**2. Beware of phony issues.** Some lawyers will take on more than you asked them to do, then charge you extra. Example: Suppose, in a divorce case, you're satisfied with the child support, but not the property settlement. Your lawyer may try and convince you he can reduce the settlement — but even if he succeeds, you may end up being charged more for his efforts than he saved you.

**3. Get the specifics up front.** Get a clarification at your initial consultation regarding the level of fees and how they're
assessed. Find out what the hourly rate will be, who will
work on your case, and what each person's function will be.
You don't want to hire one lawyer, then be billed for two or
three, plus several paralegals.   Your client agreement
should stipulate that clerical work be handled  by clerks and
mundane work by paralegals — at appropriate rates.

**4. Ask for a better deal.** Think attorneys won't bargain?
You're  wrong — there's a glut of attorneys out there and a
shortage of clients. In other words, it's a buyers' market, so
take advantage of it  — bargain (or shop around) and save!

## WANT A LOWER ATTORNEY'S FEE — JUST ASK

If you need a lawyer, you may think just finding one
who'll take your case on a contingency basis is the best you
can do — but you're  wrong. Don't go for either the first
lawyer you see — or for the  first contingency percentage
they quote. Many attorneys will agree to  lower a 40 or 50
percent contingency fee to 30 percent — or even 20  percent — if they think your case is a strong one. If the attorney  refuses to negotiate, shop around for one who will —
and who may be hungry enough to work harder for that percentage. Note: Your initial consultation should be free —
which is when you should ask what kind  of contingency fee
the attorney charges, and if he or she is willing  to negotiate (especially if that fee is 35 percent or more).

## WINNING — OR AVOIDING — THE DIVORCE WARS

Whatever your reasons for seeking a divorce, there
are things you need to consider — and consider hard —
before legally undoing your marriage vows:

**1. Trying to save the marriage.** It's almost always better to work out your problems and preserve the marriage — and the best way to do  that is through third-party counseling. You can't know it won't work if you don't try it. A good marriage counselor can't decide whether your marriage is over; no one but the husband and wife can say that.  He or she can only assist them in making that determination. Both  parties need to be willing to attend counseling. The more the couple talks, the more they can clarify problems — and possible solutions.  If one spouse won't agree to counseling — or the differences prove  irreconcilable — you'll need to brace yourself for divorce. Before  picking a counselor, be sure he or she is qualified in marriage counseling or family therapy. For a free list of qualified therapists,  send a stamped, self-addressed envelope to The American Association  of Marriage and Family Therapy, 1717 K St. NW, Ste. 407, Washington,  DC 20026.

**2. Finding a divorce lawyer.** Once you've made the decision to  divorce, don't wait on this — you need one right away. And, never use your spouse's lawyer. Ask other attorneys for recommendations.  Interview several candidates. Ask how many years they've practiced law and divorce work, and what their retainers and fees are (expect  a range from $1,000 to $7,500, then $100 to $1000 an hour afterward),  and if they'll work to settle out of court. Remember: You need an  attorney with answers — and a personality and legal style — that  you can be completely comfortable with. Caution: Never use a company  lawyer or a general-purpose attorney.

**3. Settling out of court.** This will not only save court costs, but enable the couple to come to their own agreement rather than relying on some judge make custody decisions and divide their assets.  To prepare for this, begin tracking your daily expenses, checking receipts and records, going over your tax returns, etc. Then ask your  lawyer to help you figure how much you want from the divorce. Make  the figure realistic. If you've been living on $2,000 a month, you're unlikely to get $4,000. Note: Women should tell their attorney about all their non-financial contributions to the marriage, such as homemaking and child rearing. These can and should be given a dollar value in the final settlement. Other guidelines: Whether you're trying for an out-of-court settlement or heading for the courtroom, be sure your lawyer keeps you continuously informed of all the legal maneuvering. Also include your spouse's attorney in any agreement between you and your spouse — and get the specifics of any financial compromises or agreements in writing.

**4. Know your state laws.** Divorce laws vary by state. If you file for divorce in one of the eight community property states, the state will view all assets and debts acquired during the marriage as being equally shared. The remaining states practice common law, where the name on the title or bank account solely determines ownership. If yours is a common-law state and your name does NOT appear jointly with your spouse's on titles, credit cards and accounts, consider establishing your own line of credit and bank accounts BEFORE the divorce. This will strengthen you in the divorce settlement and help you establish yourself as a single person AFTER the divorce. Remember, these days it's property — not alimony — that constitutes the major portion in divorce awards.

**5. Final thoughts.** While contemplating divorce, a wife — working or non-working — needs especially to revaluate her job skills and marketability. Alimony and child support may not provide for all her needs. So, if you're a women facing divorce, update your resume, sign up for vocational skills classes, talk with career counselors or take other actions to prepare yourself for re-entering the job market. If you're already employed, try for a promotion or consider switching to a higher-paying job.

Remember: Negative emotions — anger, frustration, even rage — are almost inevitable in traumatic divorce proceedings. Try and channel these into constructive areas. The more you prepare for divorce and its aftermath, the better shape you'll be in when its done.

## DON'T LET DIVORCE DESTROY YOUR BUSINESS

Many people work for years to build a successful business, only to be wiped out from within their own family — by a divorce. At the least, a divorce when a business is involved will blow up into a battle between accountants and appraisers, and you could even be forced to sell or liquidate the business just to satisfy a settlement. Here are some suggestions for covering yourself before it goes that far:

* Keep your spouse informed about your firm's financial affairs. An unrealistic sense of value may lead to an ex who feels cheated.

* Craft a good shareholders' agreement for your company. Provide for buyouts in case of divorce, and spell out the process for establishing the company's value.

* Request a prenuptial agreement. These can be invaluable — even in first marriages — when one of the marriage partners is involved in a prosperous family business. However, if you want the agreement to stand up in court, make sure your betrothed has his or her own attorney, that the agreement is signed before the wedding, that all assets of both parties are disclosed and that the agreement is consistent — i.e., that others who have or will marry into the family are required to sign a similar agreement.

## GETTING THE BEST DIVORCE SETTLEMENT

Under modern no-fault laws, divorce is simply the dissolution of an economic partnership. In most states, community property laws and 50-50 splits have been replaced by an indefinable standard called "equitable distribution." Here are some effects of this:

* Since nobody knows what equitable or fair means, distribution proceedings can be drawn out and costly.

* Women generally get less under "equitable distribution," and receive alimony only for a limited time.

* A working wife may get no alimony, even though she may have earned much less than her husband.

* If a business is involved, the court will likely demand a professional evaluation before making a decision on distribution of family assets. Work with qualified accountants and property appraisers to provide as clear a picture as possible of the values involved.

Here's some vital information on other issues that may come into play in a divorce:

* **Mediation.** This is recommended over a legal battle if large sums of money aren't involved. However, you should check out the mediation firm carefully. Does it have a proven record of equitable rulings? How about business expertise and access to qualified counseling? Some poorly qualified people have hung out their shingle as mediators.

* **Custody agreements.** Joint custody is the trend, but judges usually only award it where spouses can agree amicably. Keep financial issues separate from custody

issues — and work to spare the kids as much trauma as possible.

* **Negotiation tactics.** Revenge will cost you emotionally and financially. Make a genuine attempt to resolve emotional conflicts, and negotiate based on facts and genuine needs rather than emotions.

* **Settlement offers.** Consider these carefully — and, if you make one, try to ensure that it's fair. A little generosity may keep the IRS or a spouse's lawyers from intruding in your financial affairs.

## TAKE MINOR GRIEVANCES TO SMALL-CLAIMS COURT

There's a time to walk away and a time to sue. Unfortunately, it is not always easy to know which solution fits a specific grievance. However, there is an in-between path — small-claims court. These forums are ideally tailored for resolving minor grievances and settling minor financial disputes. Most states limit the dollar claims to $1,000, although some go up to $2,500 and a couple up to $10,000. However, regardless of how small, if the sum involved is important to you, it's worth taking action. In addition, if it's a case where the "principle of the thing" is more important than the actual money involved, small-claims court provides an inexpensive way to make your point — i.e., most of these don't allow lawyers; you act as the "prosecutor" yourself. Cautions: Unfortunately, the small-claims process isn't much faster than the regular court system — you should be prepared to wait a month or more for your suit to be heard. Small— claims proceedings are also a matter of record, so you have to be willing to air your grievances in public. Finally, just winning a judgment doesn't mean you can automatically collect. You may still have to hire a marshal or enforcement officer, which could wind up costing you as much as you won in the judgment.

## RECOURSE FOR CONSUMER RIP-OFFS

Too many of us get stuck with defective or unsatisfactory merchandise because we don't have a fight-back attitude and don't want to go through the hassle. But getting consumer satisfaction doesn't have to involve a nasty battle, if you understand your rights. Here's a rundown of consumer rights and obligations in various situations:

* Retail merchandise. Legally, stores must post return policies in full view at the check-out counter. If a retailer fails to adequately compensate you, notify a consumer agency. State offices are generally listed under the attorney general's office. The Better Business Bureau also has offices nationwide with upwards of 100 consumer hotlines. Hotline listings are available from Call for Action, Inc., 575 Lexington Avenue, New York, NY 10022. Many local TV and radio stations and newspapers also sponsor consumer advocate watchdogs.

* Professional associations or trade groups may be effective in dealing with your problems if the company is a member organization. Or, if you can assign a reasonable dollar value to your loss, you may be able to win a small-claims judgment.

* In-home purchases. The Federal Trade Commission allows consumers three business days to change their mind on purchases of $25 or more. This grace period also applies to "party" sales at hotels and other locations, but not to mail-order or telephone purchases. Nor does the FTC provision apply to sales of real estate, insurance, securities or emergency home repairs. To get refunds or resolve disputes related to purchases you make at home, adhere to the following guidelines:

**1.** Along with your sales receipt, ask for two copies of a dated cancellation form showing date of sale and dated contract with seller's name and address. Make sure the contract also specifies your right to cancel.

**2.** To cancel the sale within the FTC three-day limit, sign and date the form and retain the second copy. Send the cancellation notice to the company by registered mail (receipt requested).

**3.** Within 10 days, the seller must respond, returning any signed papers, down payment or trade-in and arrange to pick up any goods, or pay for the return shipping. You must make the goods available for pickup — but if no attempt is made by the seller within 20 days of your dated notice, you may keep the items.

**Caution:** Should you fail to comply with the conditions for return of the goods, you can be held responsible for the original contract.

## NOTES

_____

_____

_____

_____

_____

_____

---

## CHAPTER 11
# DOLLAR-WISE GUIDE TO
# HIGHER EDUCATION

Not so long ago, it seemed as if a college education was within reach of almost any American youngster who wanted one. Today, however, the cost of getting a four-year degree at many leading universities is equal to — if not higher than — the cost of buying a new house in most middle-class neighborhoods. And, unlike a house, you don't get 30 years to pay for it. Instead, you have to plan well in advance to ensure you'll be able to afford a college education for your child, combining both savings and the pursuit of scholarship opportunities. And, you also have to work with the child to ensure he or she will be able to get into the college or university of his or her choice. In this section, we'll provide some information to help you with all three areas — college savings, scholarships and qualification — as well as providing some tips on choosing the right school.

## PIGGY-BANKING YOUR CHILD'S COLLEGE EDUCATION

The old "only pennies-a-day" claim actually applies quite nicely to those who want to start at birth and save for a child's college career. Putting away less than a dollar a day — only $21 a month — in an 8 percent interest account will net more than $10,000 by the child's 18th birthday. More realistically, with current savings interest hovering around 4 percent, $32 a month would be required to reach that same plateau. For the improvident, however — those who wait until the child is 16 to start saving — the monthly cost will rise to $401 every month (at 4 percent) to reach $10,000 in just two years.

According to recent surveys, the average cost for a four-year public college is $5,400, and for a state university, it's $6,043. For a four-year private college, the figure zooms to $13,061 — and a four-year university costs $17,638. You get a break at public two-year colleges, with the cost dipping to $3,728. Of course, all those figures go right out the window if your kid has his eyes on Harvard, Stanford or one of the other high-prestige, high-cost universities — some of which can cost upwards of $100,000 for a four-year degree.

And, since you're planning for the future, you'd better bank on all those figures growing even fatter. One projection, made by T. Rowe Price Associates Inc., is for the four-year costs of a public college to be $138,669 by the year 2012 (see table below). Yet, even that inflated amount would be reachable in 18 years by parents of a newborn who managed to save $251 a month.

The following table shows how much you need to set aside and for how long to meet total costs at a variety of four-year institutions. The costs are based on the College Board's Annual Survey of Colleges for the 1993-94 school year, and include tuition, room & board, transportation, books and other expenses. For public schools, in-state residency is assumed. An annual increase in college costs of 7 percent is also assumed, with an 8 percent after-tax annual return on investment, and investments made at the beginning of each year.

## PROJECTED COSTS AND MONTHLY SAVINGS NEEDED TO PAY FOR COLLEGE

| Years Till Savings Needed College | Four-Year Total Cost | | Monthly | |
|---|---|---|---|---|
| | Public | Private | Public | Private |
| 1 | $ 38,343 | $ 80,891 | $3,059 | $6,454 |
| 2 | $ 41,027 | $ 86,553 | $1,527 | $3,315 |
| 3 | $ 43,899 | $ 92,612 | $1,076 | $2,270 |
| 4 | $ 46,972 | $ 99,095 | $ 828 | $1,747 |
| 5 | $ 50,260 | $106,031 | $ 679 | $1,434 |
| 6 | $ 53,778 | $113,454 | $ 581 | $1,225 |
| 7 | $ 57,543 | $121,395 | $ 510 | $1,076 |
| 8 | $ 61,571 | $129,893 | $ 457 | $ 964 |
| 9 | $ 65,881 | $138,986 | $ 416 | $ 877 |
| 10 | $ 70,492 | $148,714 | $ 383 | $ 808 |
| 11 | $ 75,427 | $159,125 | $ 356 | $ 751 |
| 12 | $ 80,707 | $170,263 | $ 333 | $ 703 |
| 13 | $ 86,356 | $182,182 | $ 314 | $ 663 |
| 14 | $ 92,401 | $194,943 | $ 298 | $ 629 |
| 15 | $ 98,869 | $208,580 | $ 284 | $ 599 |
| 16 | $105,790 | $223,180 | $ 271 | $ 573 |
| 17 | $113,195 | $238,803 | $ 260 | $ 549 |
| 18 | $121,119 | $255,519 | $ 251 | $ 529 |
| 19 | $129,597 | $273,406 | $ 242 | $ 510 |
| 20 | $138,669 | $292,544 | $ 234 | $ 493 |

Most advisors suggest parents spread their investments among several financial instruments, including savings accounts. Here is a short list of options to consider:

* Money-market mutual funds or bank money-market accounts (savings accounts that pay a higher rate of interest than regular passbook accounts, but that typically require a high minimum balance).

* Tuition-keyed certificates of deposit. The College Savings Bank  of Princeton, N.J., has a unique CD targeting the funding of higher  education. It pays annual interest equal to the rate of inflation in  average college costs.

* U.S. EE Savings Bonds pay variable interest (with a guaranteed  minimum), and are guaranteed by the U.S. Treasury at the bond's face value if held to maturity. However, they pay the full guaranteed rate  of interest if held six months. Interest is also exempt from state and local taxes, and federal tax liability is deferred till the bonds mature. If EEs are in your name instead of the child's, and used exclusively for tuition, the interest may be entirely tax free.  For more details, ask your bank or credit union for a copy of the free Treasury pamphlet titled: "EE Savings Bonds: Now Tax-Free for  Education." Note: One advantage of college-tuition and savings-bond  programs is that they can be structured to exhaust themselves when  the money is no longer needed.

* U.S. government securities can be chosen to mature within in a  specific time frame for college savings. Of particular value are  so-called "zero-coupon" government bonds. These can be purchased at  steep discounts, maturing whenever you need them in the future at  full face value — and they're guaranteed by the government. One drawback: Even though you receive no annual interest payments, you still  have to pay taxes on the imputed interest (i.e., the increasing value  of the bonds), just as if you had received it in cash. Another caution: Any interest above $550 annually earned by "zeros" held in the  name of a child under age 14 will be taxed at your rate, not that of  the child.

* Corporate bonds involve variable risk, but promise to return  face value plus a fixed rate of interest at some future date.

* Equity mutual funds are suitable in the early years of a long— term savings program. However, you should look to shift your funds (into securities guaranteeing a full return of principal) at least two or three years in advance of needing the money — just to ensure you don't have to cash in during a major market downturn.

A bad college-savings option: Whole-life insurance. Insurers like to advertise these policies as terrific long-term investments, which can be borrowed against to finance a college education. However, nearly all financial advisers (who are not employed by insurers) say life insurance is a lousy investment. You get only 3 or 4 percent a year, with part of your investment being siphoned off into commissions.

## PRE-PAID TUITION AND COLLEGE BONDS

College-assistance programs in Florida and dozens of other states may point the way to affordable financing of higher education. Florida's successful pre-paid college trust fund program works like this: For only $47 a month — or a single payment as high as $5,412 — state residents with a newborn are guaranteed tuition funds adequate for any state college or university 18 years in the future. Florida also offers a pre-paid tuition scholarship. This promises a college education to disadvantaged students who remain in school, out of jail and off drugs. Funding for the scholarships comes from the state lottery and private matching grants.

A similar savings bond program in Connecticut is available to residents and non-residents alike. Twice a year, the state sells $1,000 bonds with 5 to 20 year maturities. Prices and interest rates vary with changing market conditions, but recently ranged from as little as $289 to as much as $791 at rates of 4.75 to 6.30 percent.

Other tuition-assistance programs are offered by Alabama, Alaska, Arkansas, California, Delaware, Hawaii, Illinois, Indiana, Iowa, Kentucky, Louisiana, Michigan, Missouri, New Hampshire, North Carolina, North and South Carolina, North and South Dakota, Oklahoma, Ohio, Oregon, Rhode Island, Tennessee, Texas, Virginia and Wisconsin.

**Warning:** Before buying into any plan limiting tuition guarantees to state-specific schools, you'd better be pretty sure your kid will go along with the deal. If he or she refuses to attend any of the state institutions, you'll recoup your original investment, but lose all interest earned.

## GET YOUR DEGREE IN COLLEGE AID

By January of your child's junior year in high school, it's time to start filling out the Free Application for Federal Student Aid and other forms for financial help. As a rule, income is weighted more heavily than assets in deciding if an applicant qualifies for financial help. That's why it's good to save as much as you can for your child's college expenses (starting as early as you can), rather than waiting to finance costs out of current earnings. The federal rules also shelter a certain portion of family assets. The amount varies with the number of parents in the household, the age of the older parent and the number of other children in the family. Here are some strategies you can use to improve your chances of getting the maximum amount of federal aid:

* Shift assets. Certain assets aren't figured into the federal formula for deciding if an applicant qualifies for financial help. For instance, tax-deferred retirement plans, cash-value life insurance, annuities and home and farm equity are all disregarded. Any assets you can convert into these hidden areas can increase your federal aid. (Note: These

moves should not be made if they don't also make sound financial sense, especially since parents' assets have the least bearing on how much aid you qualify for.)

* Defer income. Income from parents gets hit hardest after the student's assets and income. Thus, if you anticipate large capital gains, try to schedule them before January of your child's junior year in high school, or after the junior year of college. That will keep the income out of the financial-aid picture. Ditto for bonuses and other any lump sum payouts you can schedule.

* Spend your student's savings first. Conventional advice is to invest in the child's name so earnings are taxed at the child's rate. However, 35 percent of such savings will be figured into your family's contribution toward college costs, while parents contribute only 5.6 percent of savings in their own names. So, spend the student's savings on college costs early in order to qualify for more aid in later years. Put last-minute savings in your own name if you expect to qualify for more than token aid.

There is a little-used way around this trap, known as the "Crummy Trust." This allows you to transfer assets to a minor, shelter those assets so they don't disqualify a child for financial aid, and yet limit the amount your child can withdraw to only the trust income, not the principal (which is why the trust's assets don't count in college aid formulas). You can set the age for final distribution of those trust assets at any age beyond 21 (unlike the Uniform Gift to Minors Act Trust). Another nice feature for parents: You can link income distribution from the trust to the child's college attendance, so dropouts will have their income from the trust cut off. Other dispersion of trust moneys can be at the discretion of your child's trustee. (This shouldn't be you, by the way, or you won't be legally deemed to have yielded control of the funds, in which case the assets will be considered part of your estate should you die before distribution.) Caution: The Crummy Trust is a sophisticated instrument, with  lots of variables and features, so you should definitely have it drawn up by a good estate or tax attorney.

* Don't rule out private colleges. Yes, they're expensive, but some will meet 100 percent of your need, with a mixture of student  loans, work-study programs and even grants, which don't have to be  repaid. Research the private colleges and universities. Schools with  large endowments will obviously have more money to give away than  schools with less, and may be more generous with grants. If your child is especially desirable to that school, you have even qualify  for a "preferential" aid package that replaces loans with grants.

* Start a business that allows you to deduct business losses and expenses from income. This may increase the amount of federal aid you  can get. You can also consider refinancing your home and rolling the money into your business, which will reduce the family assets that  can be tapped for college bills and take advantage of the allowance  for small-business assets.

## SCHOLARSHIPS AND OTHER COLLEGE FINANCIAL AID SOURCES

Is there an antidote to poisonous college costs? Yes. Just don't swallow them. Take advantage of all available financing sources, some  of which include:

* **Scholarships.** Your high school's college counselor — or financial-aid counselor, as they're increasingly known — can best advise  you on up-to-date scholarship information — and do it for free. You  don't need to pay $50 or $100 to some outfit offering to do a computer search and printout of obscure scholarships. By the end of your  kid's junior year in high school, you should have compiled a target list of sources for scholarships, grants and other awards programs.

Of course, full scholarships sound fantastic, but they're becoming almost an endangered species, seldom seen on the campus landscape — outside of star quarterbacks or slam-dunking centers. However, partial scholarships remain plentiful. Here's a short list of the kinds of organizations that may offer partial aid packages:

— Major corporations or other employers.
— Military or veteran's associations.
— Local businesses or trade organizations.
— Ethnic, ancestral or minority organizations.
— Athletic booster groups.
— Community civic groups or fraternal organizations.
— Religious organizations or church scholarship funds.
— Labor unions.

The bulk of these private-sector financial aid programs aren't based on academic performance or need. Some, in fact, have downright bizarre qualifying criteria. For instance, Arizona State once had a scholarship for a person with one blue eye and one brown eye — which was never used; Duracell once offered $10,000 for a student coming up with the most innovative battery-operated device; and Pennsylvania's Juniata College still offers a $2,600 grant for left-handed students. Some encouraging news: One study discovered that 94 percent of the $7 billion made available by corporations for education each year goes unclaimed. But read the instructions carefully: 82 percent of applications for college funding are rejected simply because they're filled out incorrectly or submitted late.

Private scholarships that don't reduce other financial-aid awards are best — but many don't, so be sure you are aware of the particular requirements and deadlines for each source. Most scholarships of this type permit application without specifying a particular college. Also note: Scholarship cash used for room, board or personal expenses is taxable to your child, so receipts must be kept. Only money used for tuition is exempt. A valuable sourcebook for scholarships of this kind is Debra Kirby's "Fund Your Way Through College" ($19.95), available at most book stores.

**\* Pell grants.** One of the broadest of the federal aid sources is the Pell Grants program, which gives awards ranging from around $200 to $2,300 per student. The appeal is simple: Students don't have to pay them back. The catch is they're designed to help only the neediest young people — and the more money the parents earn, the less a qualifying student receives. The same rules as discussed earlier for federal aid programs generally apply in setting eligibility and aid.

**\* Academic grants.** Encouraging your child to achieve excellence in school can obviously have all kinds of payoffs in later life. However, one benefit you might overlook is that top grades may qualify them for academic scholarships from even the most expensive private colleges and universities. To counteract the perception that they are only havens for rich kids, Harvard and Radcliffe-type institutions are on the lookout for needy and deserving scholars. Besides grades, however, university admission offices examine the applicant's entire resume, noting such extracurricular pluses as service clubs, volunteer work, community programs and summer internships that develop experience in an employment field.

**\* Declaration of independence.** Your college-bound child may also qualify for financial aid by declaring (and proving) himself or herself financially independent. Many colleges set aside substantial amounts for such students as part of programs intended originally for children without parents. To qualify as an independent, your child:

— Must not have lived in your home for more than a month and a half during the three preceding years.

— Must not have appeared as a deduction on your income tax return for those three years.

— Must not have received more than $750 support from you in each of those years.

Even though a child may not be deemed independent at the start of college, perhaps by the senior year the status will have changed — and, there are other ways to qualify. A young person meeting even one of the following criteria is considered independent:

— Being an orphan or ward of the court.

— Being at least 24 years old.

— Being a military veteran.

— Having legal dependents other than a husband or wife.

## INFO ON SCHOLARSHIPS AND FINANCING SOURCES

To give you a head start on finding student aid, here's a list of sources providing information on scholarships and college financing:

* The College Financial Aid Emergency Kit. Sun Features Inc., Box 368, Cardiff, CA 92007; $4.95 each, plus 55 cents postage.

* The Ultimate College Shopper's Guide: 327 Lists of Insider Rankings and Comparative Data on Hundreds of Schools, by Heather Evenas & Deidre Sullivan. Available from Addison-Wesley, One Jacob Way, Reading, MA 01867; $12.95.

* Cooperative Education Undergraduate Program Directory. National Commission for Cooperative Education, P.O. Box 999, Boston, MA 02115; updated annually; free.

* Directory of Internships. National Society for Experiential Education, 3509 Hayworth Drive, Suite 207, Raleigh, NC 27609; updated biannually; $24 (prepaid).

* CASHE: College Aid Sources for Higher Education. National College Services, Ltd., 600 S. Frederick Ave., 2nd floor, Gaithersburg,  MD 20877; call 1-800-288-NCSL or 301-258-0717.

* B. Wellman & Daughter Financial Aid/Educational Resource Center, 14  Parker St., Suite E, Southborough, MA 01772; 508-485-6704.

## NEGOTIATING FINANCIAL AID

A little-known fact about colleges is that many are willing to  negotiate on student-aid packages in order to attract students in   certain favored categories. Of course, everyone knows about universities competing for top football prospects, with each offering all   kinds of incentives. However, the same bargaining process can occur  in nonathletic areas.

The specific areas are not always predictable. One institution could be looking for students with a particular musical or  artistic skill; another one for those with scientific prowess. The goal of the  college admissions office is to get a broad range of interests among  an entering class. This kind of academic negotiation has been going  on for years — and seems to be on the increase. An average amount by which colleges may improve their offer is $2,000 to $3,000 — but  more is possible. So, if there's something that distinguishes your  child from other applicants, you might reap large dividends by testing its value on the competitive market.

How do you dicker with a college? First, when you receive a specific student-aid offer from a college, Xerox it, then enclose the copy when you write to another school. You should also attach proof of the particular expertise or skill. Remember, it won't help your leverage to let a particular institution know it's your first choice. You want them to up their ante in order to keep you from going elsewhere. Surprisingly, many will.

## PICKING THE RIGHT COLLEGE

Picking a college or a university can be both an enjoyable and an agonizing process. It's also one of the more complex decisions a person will ever face — and one with profound effects on the rest of your life. If you're standing at this pre-collegiate crossroads, here are a handful of key questions to steer you into the right choice:

**1.** How far do you want to go? Or how far do you want to be from home? A majority of students stay within a few hundred miles. Deciding this up front can give narrow your search radius dramatically.

**2.** Big school or small school? Small campuses can offer a greater feeling of community and more intimate student-professor ratios. With big universities you get a more impersonal landscape and atmosphere, but have the choice of more courses, majors and cultural resources.

**3.** Is social life an important factor? If so, you need to decide what kind of campus or college will provide what you want or will be comfortable with.

**4.** What about climate or surroundings? This may have no bearing on academics, yet can be very important to some students. For example, a serious skier needs to have access to nearby slopes. Ability to attend big-city ballet performances may be a decisive factor to a serious student of classical dance.

**5.** What about specific degree programs? A student interested in a nursing degree must obviously narrow his or her choices to universities that offer such a program. Ditto for an engineering degree.

## CREAM OF THE CROP COLLEGES — HOW TO RISE TO THE TOP

Most parents want their child to have a college education — and receiving a degree from a prestigious college is a top priority in households earning over $50,000. However, preparing your children for college — both financially and educationally — can take years. Even going to a top-notch high school is no guarantee of acceptance — and straight A's alone may not be enough to ensure your child entrance. In other words, if you want to get your child into the best college, you probably need help — so we'll give you some. Here's a look at the key areas colleges consider when looking at candidates for admission:

**\* High school records.** Good grades are still your best weapon, but college advisors say getting a good grade in an easy subject is not the way to go. Students should focus on higher-level classes. Also keep in mind that some colleges look at class ranking — meaning your child is competing against his or her classmates.

**\* Test scores.** The Scholastic Assessment Tests (formally called Scholastic Aptitude Tests) are essential. The basic test is called SAT I, while the subject tests are SAT II. Leading schools usually want top SAT II scores in math, English and another subject of the applicant's choice.

Although most experts agree that test scores are a poor determiner of a student's overall ability, high SAT scores still count greatly at most universities.

* **Extracurricular activities.** Most schools want to know that your child didn't just sit in his or her room and study for four years. Encourage your child to become involved in those things that interest them. However, don't go overboard — a couple of quality extracurricular activities will do.

* **Recommendations.** Just as with prospective employers, universities like to see some references. Recommendations by the high school (prepared by the college counselor), and a teacher's assessment of the student should be adequate. Note: It's not advisable to use celebrity recommendations.

* **The essay.** Over and above the SAT, the essay gives the school an opportunity to find out how introspective the candidate is and how well he or she expresses themselves. Essays that are natural and reveal the student as a person are often the most effective.

* **The interview.** Many colleges don't bother with the interview any more, but it can be a powerful tool for a marginal candidate who is able to shine in this area. It's worthwhile asking for one if your child is in this category.

* **Finally,** a note on **mailing the application**. Include a self-addressed, stamped postcard and ask the admissions office to send it back to you as proof it received the application. Keep a record of the postcards you receive. If you haven't gotten a card from a particular institution as the application deadline approaches, call the school for verification.

## SCORING HIGH ON SATs

SAT tests have often been criticized from several standpoints, with detractors claiming they don't accurately measure intelligence, aptitude or even academic potential. These criticisms are probably all true. What SATs do measure — and measure accurately — is an aptitude at taking this particular test — and, so long as SAT scores continue to be criteria in college admissions, it's obviously critical to learn to do well at them. Here are some pointers:

* Make sure the college you want to attend requires SAT scores. If it does, you should begin to prepare yourself at least two months ahead of the test date.

* Buy or borrow an SAT prep book such as "Ten SAT's," which is available from The College Board, 45 Columbus Avenue, New York, NY 10023. This lets you study sample exams from the last few years.

* Take an SAT prep course, concentrating on areas where you need to improve. A regular course teacher will not be as effective a tutor as an SAT specialist.

How you take the test is equally important in getting good results. Here are some tips:

* Don't rush. Haste causes carelessness.

* Don't get bogged down on questions that completely throw you. Move on. If you're stuck in a whole section that puzzles you, skip ahead to an area you're strong in. All questions get equal weight.

* If you don't know an answer, eliminate all the obvious wrong responses, then take a guess.

* Don't bother erasing any mistakes you've made in math calculation. Better yet, do your calculations on the scratch paper provided.

* Give the answer you feel is expected, even if you disagree or have a better answer.

* Be on the lookout for suspiciously easy questions, especially in a harder section. The right answer may be trickier than you think at first glance.

* Do the reading section last. Because reading long passages is involved, you could lose precious time.

## STRETCHING COLLEGE DOLLARS

Meeting tuition costs is only half the battle. Your collegian will encounter expenses at every academic turn — living, housing, books, entertainment. You're going to need more dollars — and you're going to need to stretch those dollars as much possible. Here are some practical suggestions on both counts:

* **Pension plan loans.** Because your contributions to a company pension plan are taken out before taxation is assessed, you're already ahead around 30 percent or so. With employer-matching plans, you're even further ahead. If you need an extra financial boost for college costs, consider borrowing from your retirement plan. This is usually at the current bank prime rate. Caution: As soon as possible, pay back the loan. You don't want your retirement to suffer.

* **Home equity loans.** This makes a lot more sense than a personal loan to pay for educational expenses. A personal loan won't be tax deductible; mortgage interest is. And personal loans carry higher interest charges.

**\* Buy rental property.** More and more parents of college students are availing themselves of this financial strategy. Again it allows you to deduct mortgage interest, while you accumulate tax deferred equity that is convertable into college money if you decide to remortgage the property. There are a couple variations on this property theme:

— You can hire your teen-age child to manage a rental property near your home, and the salary can go toward college while you take the deduction.

— When a college-ager goes off to school, you can swap the local rental for one near your child's campus. The new property should be of equal value in order to sidestep capital gains. Again, hire your collegian as manager, maintaining and renting out apartments or rooms to fellow students.

Now tote up all the dollar advantages: Your student gets a free room (like most apartment managers), plus a small salary, while you take a tax deduction. Final payoff: After graduation, you sell the property — probably for a profit since many college-town properties have outperformed the sluggish national real estate market.

## MORE WAYS TO SHRINK COLLEGE COSTS

One obvious way to reduce the cost of a college education is to reduce the time it takes to get one. Contrary to what you might assume, your child doesn't have to be an Einstein to finish a four-year curriculum in three years. Here are three possible shortcuts:

**1. Life-experience credits.** College credits in such classes as political science, sociology and theater arts can be earned through what are termed "life-experience credits"

— by participating in local political campaigns, charity work or community theater. Before getting involved, however, the student should request a "life-experience credit special assessment" from a college counselor.

**2. Correspondence courses.** Some very respected "independent study programs" are offered by some of the nation's most prestigious institutions. By taking one or more such courses, a student can attend college part-time while working to earn money. Here are details on a few such correspondence programs:

\* University of Wisconsin, Independent Study, 209 Extension Bldg., 432 N. Lake Street, Madison, WI 53706, 1-800-442-6460 or 608-263-2055. It offers almost 500 courses; $150 for a three-credit course, plus $15 charge per course. No degree program.

\* University of Minnesota, Independent Study, 45 Wesbrook Hall, 77 Pleasant Street S.E., Minneapolis, MN 55455, 1-800-234-6564 or 612-624-0000. It offers 300 courses; $182.25 for a three-credit course. No degree program.

\* Indiana University, Independent Study Program, Owen Hall, Bloomington, IN 47405, 1-800-457-4434 or 812-855-3694. It offers 250 courses; $213 for a three-credit course. A degree in general studies is possible.

\* Ohio University, Independent Studies, 302 Tupper Hall, Athens, OH 45701-2979, 1-800-444-2910 or 614-593-2910. It offers 250 courses, $151 for a three-credit course. A degree is possible through the External Degree Department.

\* University of North Carolina-Chapel Hill, Independent Study by Correspondence, CB #1020, The Friday Center, Chapel Hill, NC 27599, 919-962-1106. Offers 150 courses; $165 for a three-credit course. No degree program.

\* Oklahoma State University, Independent & Correspondence Study Department, 001 Classroom Bldg., Stillwater, OK 74078, 405-744-6390. Offers 200 courses; $150 for three-credit course. No degree program.

**3. Proficiency exams.** Another cost-effective means to cut college degree expenses is for a student to earn credits by passing a single proficiency examination. The exams — available for courses in business, education, language, humanities, science, social issues, math and medicine — are not free, but are much cheaper than class time. Have your child ask his or her high school or college counselor about all available proficiency tests.

**4. Two-year junior and community colleges.** Willing to swap prestige and snob appeal for major bucks? Then talk your child into doing the first two years at a two-year community college — for a fraction of the cost of a four-year institution. What kind of fraction? How about $100 instead of $12,000 or $15,000 a year (tuition, fees, room and board at some private universities). And, because the first two years usually emphasize required classes, the coursework at the local JC is likely to be just what you'd find at State U. In fact, it may be better, since class size will probably be smaller, and large universities often rely on teaching assistants and grad students to handle first- and second-year courses. By the way: There's no loss of status if your child goes on to get a sheepskin at a well-known university. The degree is the same. Only your bank account will know the difference.

**5. Attend your state schools** — or move! Out-of-state students at state schools pay far higher tuition and assorted fees. For instance, UCLA charges California students less than $2,000 a year, while out— of-staters get socked for around $8,000. If your state doesn't have what you feel is a high-quality institution, you might consider re-establishing your family's residency in a state that does.

**6. Cheapest off-campus living** — at home. On-campus or off-campus living runs thousands of dollars more than living at home and commuting to school. Have a serious money talk with your would-be collegian. Explain the fiscal realities and how he or she can have a first class college education without bankrupting the family.

**7. Let Uncle Sam pay the bill.** All the military service academies are free, and that includes tuition, room, board, books and supplies. Of course, your child must qualify academically, be accepted — and agree to mandatory service after graduation. Similar deals are available through Reserve Officers Training Corps programs at more than 600 colleges and universities. Here, too, a military service commitment goes along with the ROTC subsidies.

Uncle Sam will also forgive up to $20,000 a year of student loans if you attend medical school and agree to practice afterward for two years in a designated health-shortage area. Call the National Health Service Corps Loan Repayment Program at 301-443-0963. The government also waives student loans for teachers agreeing to work in certain teacher-shortage areas. Those who agree to Peace Corps service can also qualify to have federal student loans forgiven. A portion of students loans will be canceled for those who join VISTA (Volunteers in Service to America). Applications for all of these are available by calling 202-606-4902.

**8. Add kids and save bucks.** By sending two of your kids to the same school or university system, you may qualify for a major tuition discount for the second child. Other schools may offer a discounted package deal. Of course, you can increase the savings by persuading your kids to room together.

**9. Alumni benefits.** If your child attends your alma mater, don't forget to investigate any perks he or she might qualify for. There may be a special discounts, low-interest loans or a grant or credit programs for children of alumni.

## FINANCING TIP FOR THOSE WITH CREDENTIALS

There's one other way to put your child through college. If you  have skills — academic or otherwise — that might make you suitable  for employment by the college of your child's choice, you should try  getting a job there and then moving to the campus area. Reason: Many  universities offer employees free tuition for family members.

**NOTES**

_____

_____

_____

_____

_____

_____

_____

_____

_____

_____

---

## CHAPTER 12

# MAKE THE MOST OF YOUR JOB

Although we said earlier that making your money work for you is the most important element of wealth building, simply making money is still highly important. After all, few people — particularly in the early years of life — can generate enough money from investments to meet daily living expenses and support a growing family. Thus, for most of us, making money means employment — either working for someone else, or as the hardest worker in our own businesses. And, since work takes up at least a third (and most likely more) of our lives, it's important to know how to both make the most of it and enjoy it. This Section will give you some guidelines on doing both.

## THREE KEYS FOR OPENING EMPLOYERS' DOORS

With many companies downsizing and others actually laying off, job seekers face some tough obstacles — but an applicant convinced of his or her abilities, and who can communicate that confidence to management, will find doors opening. The secret is to work hard — and smart — at getting hired. Here are three steps for selling yourself to a prospective employer:

**1.** Look for employment that makes the most of your abilities. This requires realism in assessing your strengths and targeting related job categories. For instance: A would-be actor who knocked on  studio casting doors for years with minimal success happened to have a wonderful head for numbers. He now works for one of the biggest  studios — but in the accounting department.

**2.** Research your target companies. A wealth of information on any  employer can be had at the public library. Check your company out in  Standard & Poor's, Value Line, Dun & Bradstreet, annual reports, business magazines, etc. If possible, speak to customers of the company, as  well as managers of key departments. You shouldn't go to an interview  spouting off information, but at some point you'll have an  appropriate opportunity to show the extent of your knowledge about — and  interest in — the company.

**3.** Offer solutions. Doing your background research, you likely  came across some problems facing the target company. One way to set  your application apart from others is to propose a solution to such a  problem or suggest an area for operating improvement. To make this tactic effective, however, direct your letter to a specific departmental manager, not the personnel department, which will likely bury it. Whether or not your specific idea is ever implemented, it could  get you a job — or at least send your resume to the top of the pile.  Even failing that, you may make a contact that will pay off later on.

## MONEY-SAVING PERKS AND FRINGE BENEFITS

More and more employers are offering flexible benefits plan. By  opting for one of the lower-cost health insurance plans (with a higher deductible), you can save hundreds of dollars a year in lower premiums. Another plan being adopted by employers are health-care reimbursement accounts. These allow you to take pre-tax dollars and set them aside in an account you draw on to pay medical bills. This money comes off the top of your salary, so you're not taxed on it — saving you money both on federal and state taxes. A major drawback: If the money isn't used within the year, it's forfeited. As a result, when Hospital Corp. of America offered a health-care reimbursement plan to its 49,000 employees, only 8.5 percent signed up. A similar reimbursement account allowing employees tax-free dollars to pay for child day care drew less than 2 percent participation. However, those who signed up for either plan had few regrets. The average participant in the HCA health care account set aside $600, used all but $24 of that and saved nearly $250 in taxes. Day care prepayment participants averaged around $1,000 in savings.

## KEEPING THE JOB ONCE YOU'VE GOT IT

Once you've landed a job, you not only have to think about getting ahead, you also have to be cognizant of situations that might cause you to lose it. Here are some steps to make sure you never have to hearing the words, "You're fired!":

* When you suspect you might be in danger of being fired, go directly to your boss and talk things over. Be direct.

* If there's a problem with your work, ask why he or she isn't pleased with your performance and what you can do to improve it.

* Show your boss a self-made personnel file that summarizes your successes on the job. Include any commendations, favorable reviews or memos praising your work. Inform your boss that this is what you've done for the company so far, but will eagerly do more if needed.

\* Offer to work overtime or even weekends if that's what it will  take to get the job done.

\* Ask your supervisor for any suggestions he or she might have  about you or your performance — and pledge to follow them.

Your boss should be impressed with both your candor and  your  desire  to  make  improvements  or  increased efforts. However, if you discover your supervisor is set on firing you, go to his or her boss and plead your case there.


## WHEN YOU'RE CONSIDERING LEAVING A JOB

Of course, the decision to leave a position doesn't always rest  with your boss or your company — sometimes you have to make it. So,  how can you tell if you should quit your job, or perhaps even change  careers entirely? Mere job dissatisfaction probably isn't enough —  everybody experiences that at one time or another. Job switching is one thing — applying for a new position while holding on to the old  one. However, some bold career moves require a gigantic leap of faith  — walking away from temporary security and fringe benefits. Can that  even be considered during sluggish economic times, when layoffs and  cutbacks are happening all around you? To answer these questions, you  need to ask yourself a few more:

**1.** Are you on an upward track in your present job? How have you  done compared to others hired at the same time? This can be a painful  thing to assess, but if you've been left behind while others have advanced, you may be poorly positioned — and could be vulnerable.

**2.** Are you increasing your marketable skills, or just vegetating?   How  many  new  career  skills  did  you  gain  or improve in the last year? Are you working on a first or advanced degree? Honing your computer expertise? Making strides in a second language?

**3.** Are you working in an area you find rewarding? Were a good percentage of your projects enjoyable? Or, do you find yourself chronically complaining?

If you get resounding "nos" to these questions — and a "yes" to the last one — you should certainly consider changing either your job or your career. Which — job or career — depends on several factors — working conditions, values and geography. If you like your current career field, try changing some of the present conditions — say, by arranging transfer to a new department or a new plant site. If you do this, and your complaints fade away, then your career may get right back on track.

## BE A STAR, BE A STAR!

The best way to set yourself up for a raise or a promotion is to become a star. Study your company's top performers, and do what they do. Take the initiative and go beyond what is standard job performance. Build strong technical skills and contacts. Learn to manage your time more effectively and work more efficiently. Be open to new ideas and listen to others. Demonstrate your leadership abilities while showing that you are a team player.

Many leaders become managers because they have problem-solving skills. They repeatedly find ways to balance the everyday problems, inconsistencies and dilemmas of the workplace. They see office problems as career opportunities. Realize that 90 percent of most jobs involves handling difficult situations, people and tasks. Instead of complaining about your woes, look for and implement solutions. Keep a positive, cheery outlook toward people and exercise good judgment.

## DEALING WITH OFFICE POLITICS

Sometimes, getting a raise or promotion is much more a factor or office politics than your job performance. Here are some tips on how to play the office political games in order to get ahead:

* Be aware of the "official" chain of command. Before you go off and follow someone's orders, check things out with your boss first.

* Be aware of the "unofficial" office chain of command. A secretary or long-standing assistant can wield more power than the title would suggest.

* Don't be secretive with information. Keep people informed of what's going on with issues that could affect them. You will earn a reputation as someone who is trustworthy and willing to face issues head on.

* Communicate in writing. There is nothing clearer than the written word. Use this to protect your ideas and to demonstrate to others that you are a team player.

* Avoid criticizing others, especially your boss. People sometimes come up with crazy ideas. Diplomatically steer your boss away from anything that could prove embarrassing.

* If you must take on a difficult co-worker, don't attack them personally. Stick to the issues and stay calm. Always keep your emotional control. Make sure your facts are straight — and, if it turns out you were wrong, apologize. Remember to respect subordinates — even the difficult ones — and always confront issues, not people.

* Don't spread gossip or rumors. It's fine to keep abreast of what's going on, but don't be an instigator. It's good to be known as someone who's impartial and can keep a secret.

* Be aware of how things seem. It's normal to socialize with co-workers — but too much can cause you to lose your ability to manage them. Be aware of how things might look to others. Repeated lunches with a single co-worker of the opposite sex could be misconstrued as a possible romantic liaison.

## BEAT JOB BURNOUT AND GET COOKING AGAIN

Burnout — marked by feelings of frustration, disillusionment, futility and fatigue — is the employment plague of the '90s. It's really just prolonged stress, but it can impact both your job performance and your health. Many small business owners and entrepreneurs also fall prey to burnout because of their idealistic, overly committed, perfectionist, workaholic attitudes — in other words, the belief that who they are is defined by what they do for a living.

In the past, many workers beat burnout by taking a vacation, cutting back on their work load, changing jobs or even careers. Given today's weaker economy, however, those solutions aren't as viable. Still, it is possible to beat burnout — just follow these steps:

* Take time for non-work related endeavors like exercise, laughter and meditation.
* Change your perception. Instead of seeing the economy gorging on your business, see it as a new economy with new challenges.
* Set positive goals and attitudes.
* Change your pace.
* Get creative with your business and your personal life.

\* Do something for others — this often takes your mind off your own woes.

\* Read anything and everything — not just trade magazines or journals.

\* Develop diverse friendships that are not work related.

## STARTING YOUR OWN BUSINESS

Owning a business — and being one's own boss — is a dream of countless Americans, and with good reason. Not only does a business of your own let you reap the full rewards of your own efforts, but it also offers tremendous satisfaction, the potential for large profits and, not to be overlooked, absolutely the best tax benefits available anywhere. Of course, there are also risks; roughly half the new businesses started fail within the first five years — and costs associated with such a venture may be high. However, with some careful planning, reasonable expectations and lots of hard work, you can succeed, even if you begin operations out of your home with only a shoestring budget.

Before you start, though, there's one thing you should be aware of: Most successful entrepreneurs started their businesses NOT because they were unsatisfied with their previous employment, but instead because they had a great idea they just HAD to pursue. In other words, it's extremely important that you truly believe in the venture you are planning to start, not just viewing it as an escape from your present situation.

## SELF-EMPLOYMENT PLANNING — AND KEY FACTS TO CONSIDER

When you start a business from your home, you should approach it the same way you would a new job. Be professional, organized and manage your time effectively. Be sure you have enough money. Remember, you'll need to purchase office supplies and possibly equipment, you will likely have to advertise, and you may have to buy raw materials or products for resale. You must also be certain you have a cushion in case of an emergency — or just to tide you over while you get things going.

It's a good idea not to start a home business that will be your sole source of income unless you're sure you can exist on only 50 percent of your anticipated sales. To determine how much money you need to start, work out a detailed one-month, cost-of-living budget and multiply it by four, then add in the estimated expense of starting the business, including initial operating capital. The result is approximately how much cash you should have to carry you through the start-up period. You will also need to make a careful projection of your monthly cash needs for the first three to six years, and compare that to your revenue estimates, adjusted for any seasonal sales fluctuations and expense factors such as insurance or tax payments. This should help you identify potential low points, and give you an idea of how large a reserve you'll need to carry you through. Get a copy of the Small Business Administration cost worksheet if you need help getting organized.

Here are some additional points to consider before you make your final decision about going out on your own:

* Is the money you are planning to invest in the business money that you need to survive? Think this over carefully.

* Will you be capable of getting another job as good as the one you're leaving should this venture not pan out?

* What about your employer-supplied health insurance? You need coverage for both yourself and your family, so be sure you can replace it without too much additional cost. Look into group coverage for the self-employed.

* You're basing this business on your idea, your hobby or your current sideline business — but do you really know everything about it? Explore the field thoroughly and learn the nuts and bolts of pricing, suppliers, product quality, inventory, cash cycles, the legal pitfalls, even just your basic day-to-day operating procedures. Make sure, too, that you know the ins and outs of your market, as well as trends in popular taste if they may have an impact on your business.

* To that end, evaluate who your customers will be and how you can effectively reach them. Figure out how much you can competitively charge for your product or service — and whether you can live on the profits generated by supplying it at that price. Determine if the field you select has a future — or if it could be made obsolete by technology. If you're looking at an operation with technical aspects, be sure to calculate the cost of periodic retraining for yourself as well as initial training for any employees you might take on. Your local Chamber of Commerce or the U.S. Small Business Administration can help you with answers to many of these questions.

* Make sure you have a place from which to run your business. Find a spot in your home that can be yours — and keep it that way. Don't end up sharing the second bedroom or a corner of the kitchen. Besides cutting down on distractions, you'll feel more like you're "at the office."

* Rather than spending lots of scarce money on new stuff, scour garage sales, estate sales, auctions, bankruptcy sales, equipment supply houses, classified ads and trade journals for equipment or usable objects you can get for practically nothing. What you can't find there, lease — it's much cheaper than buying. Negotiate with suppliers to whittle down your start-up costs. Then, keep all your business supplies and equipment separate from the ones your family uses.

warranty to your credit card issuer with receipts from the credit card and store. American Express also offers a one-year extension on warranties of less than five years — if you register the purchase with in 30 days.

## 10 TIPS TO SUPERMARKET SAVINGS

Food costs make up a significant portion of most family budgets, but there are a number of ways to cut them. Here are 10:

**1.** Make a list. Don't go wandering aisles, shopping on impulse — unless you want to empty your wallet. A thoughtful list will limit your purchases to what you need. You can always make in-store adjustments — adding sale items, deleting overpriced articles. Another tip: Comparison shop local markets. Buying some items at one store, others at a second store, takes extra time, but can net substantial savings.

**2.** Shop when you're stuffed. Entering a supermarket with an empty stomach is the easiest way to overbuy — adding around 10 percent to your bill. You'll buy junk you don't need, and in larger quantities.

**3.** Avoid name brands. "No name," off-brand or plain-wrap products can be 10 percent to 15 percent cheaper than famous-brand counter- parts, since they don't have to charge you for expensive ad costs. And most of the time you can't tell or taste the difference.

**4.** Buy king-size. Giant economy items — larger containers, four-packs and so on — can be real bargains. Warehouse membership stores specialize in this kind of volume discounting. Of course, you have to be able to store unused quantities and be aware of spoilage.

**5.** Save coupons. Stop throwing away all those discount coupons from your Sunday paper and daily junk mail. With a little effort and organization, you can reap big savings on items you need. By joining a club, you can also swap unwanted coupons for ones you do use.

**6.** Shop in season. Produce and fruit are a lot cheaper during the height of the harvest season. That's when to shop, even if you have to can or freeze what you don't use right away.

**7.** Look for weekly markets. Many communities have produce and fruit markets offering home grown food. Fruits and vegetables are better than supermarket quality and can cost 30 percent less than supermarket prices. Or look for those summer roadside stands, which crop up all year in Western and Sun Belt states.

**8.** Keep highly prepared and packaged items out of your basket. A bag of rice or potatoes is a much better value than packaged rice dishes, or mashed-potato mixes — not to mention potato chips. Most processed and junk food items are extremely costly per unit volume. Frozen TV dinners also fall into this overpriced category. Basic buying will benefit your health as well as your pocketbook.

**9.** Don't use your market as a convenience store. You can usually find non-grocery items cheaper elsewhere — stationery, picnic supplies, drugstore items.

**10.** Shop by the week. In other words, plan a weekly menu and budget it. This will also help you buy larger quantities, use them wisely and avoid wasting food.

## USE YOUR COUPONS BETTER — AND CUT YOUR GROCERY BILL

Most people clip coupons, tuck them in a drawer — and let them expire. But it doesn't have to be that way. Here are eight tips on maximizing coupon savings:

**1.** Organizing your coupons. Collect newspaper inserts and junk mail offers and other sources. Clip likely coupons, put them into a shoe box or large envelope. Sort by category. Before heading to the supermarket, select the coupons that match your shopping list. Then, as you shop, sort the coupons actually used, so you won't need to do that under pressure at the checkout line.

**2.** Shop supermarkets that honor coupons — with a smile. Even better, look for markets that give double face value.

**3.** Check your market for coupon-exchange bins. These allow customers to swap coupons they don't want for those they do.

**4.** Avoid clipping coupons for stuff you don't need. Your savings will go out the window if you're lured into buying products you have no use for. Also, your brand loyalty should definitely be replaced by coupon-brand loyalty. Remember, you're trying to save money!

**5.** Coupons, coupons everywhere — get as many as you can. Check product labels, cartons, market ads, Sunday newspaper inserts, junk mail and supermarket displays.

**6.** Join a coupon-exchange club. Members mail coupons they don't need to the club, and the club mails back coupons they do.

**7.** Watch for coupon-plus savings. Some supermarket ads offer items discounted by both coupons and special sale prices. Or, one better, an item on sale, coupon discounted with a mail-in rebate offer. Hint: to track refund offers (there are thousands at any one time), subscribe to the Refundle Bundle, Box 141, Centuck Station, Yonkers, NY 10710. Price: $9 for six issues.

**8.** Open a coupon savings account. It's too easy to spend the few dollars saved from one visit to the market. For a real reward, start a savings account for some item you've always wanted, and make faithful deposits to it.

## DON'T FORGET FUN AND LEISURE

You're obviously going to want to have some fun with all the cash you save by using your new coupon skills — and you may even want to reward yourself by dining out in style. However, dining in style need not mean paying ultra-high prices. Many major restaurants advertise 2-for-1 specials, and many others participate in discount programs in conjunction with major credit-card issuers such as American Express and Visa. However, for consistent value all across America (and in Canada too), its difficult to beat the program of ENTERTAINMENT Inc., P.O. Box 1014, Trumbull, CT 06611. ENTERTAINMENT publishes value books — each containing hundreds of 2-for-1 and discount coupons — for more than 100 cities or areas around the country. Each book has a section on fine dining, featuring 30 to 40 of the city's best restaurants, as well as coupons on casual dining, fast food outlets, movies, theaters, sporting events, tourist attractions, car rentals and hotel and resort savings in nearby areas. In larger cities, such as Baltimore, Boston, Chicago, Long Island, Los Angeles, north New Jersey, New York, Philadelphia, Seattle and Washington, there are even books for different areas of the city. The books are generally sold for $30 to $40 as part of fund-raising drives by local charitable and civic organizations. However, you can purchase up to four different books (only one per city) directly from the publisher for only $25, plus $3.50 shipping and handling. Just call 1-800-374-4464 and use your Visa or MasterCard to order.


## PAIN-FREE SAVINGS ON PRESCRIPTION DRUGS

Drugstores used to be considered almost like the "five and dime." Not any more. For some needy Americans, pharmacy bills have become so prohibitive they're even forced to do without essential prescribed medicines. If you're worried about this happening to you, or you just want to avoid those big pharmacy markups, you should definitely check out these mail-order sources for discount drugs:

* Pharmail, 87 Main Street, P.O. Box 1466, Champlain, NY 12919, (1-800-237-8927 or 518-298-4922). Ask for their price list, which includes an index of equivalent generic drugs. Minimum prescription price is $4.99, so it may pay to buy larger quantities. Visa and MasterCard are accepted.

* Action Mail Order Drugs, P.O. Box 787, Watersville, ME 04903 (1-800-452-1976 or 207-873-6226). You can get a quote over the phone, with prices guaranteed for 30 days, and their catalog comes with a $5 coupon good for the first order. Accepts all major credit cards.

* Family Pharmaceutical, P.O. Box 1288, Mt. Pleasant, SC 29465 (1-800-922-3444). Phone for current prices. Free medical ID tag given with new orders. Accepts Visa and MasterCard.

The following comparison shows several common prescription drugs with available prices at various sources:

| Drugs | Retail | Pharmail | Action | Family |
|---|---|---|---|---|
| **Premarin** | | | | |
| (100), .625mg | $45.54 | $31.99 | $32.99 | $31.59 |
| **Amoxicillin** | | | | |
| (40), 250mg | $13.64 | $ 4.99 | $11.99 | $ 7.13 |
| **Zantac** | | | | |
| (100), 150mg | $165.09 | $132.00 | $123.39 | $137.40 |
| **Xanax** | | | | |
| (100), .5mg | $76.90 | $57.99 | $56.39 | $59.91 |
| **Lanoxin** | | | | |
| (100), .125mg | $14.82. | $ 7.99 | $ 6.99 | $10.29 |

## GET BARGAINS ON YOUR DOCTOR BILLS, TOO

Contrary to popular belief, many physicians are willing to reduce their fees or work out special pricing arrangements in certain instances — particularly if you are paying your own way rather than billing an insurance company. If you think your bills are too high, just ask for a reduction. Here are some other ideas for cutting medical costs:

* Agree to schedule your surgery or medical treatment during a slack period or off-peak time in exchange for a reduced fee. Doctors, especially surgeons, have slow periods (such as right before holidays) and may be willing to charge less rather than sitting idle.

* Be on call for the doctor. Rather than calling your physician for an appointment, offer to make yourself available whenever he or she has an opening and can give you 30 minutes notice to show up. The same can apply with elective surgery, though you'll obviously need more notice.

* Use a younger or newer doctor. Many beginning practitioners charge much less than established physicians who have built up a reputation. The fee will usually be less and, in most cases the treatment just as good (if not better, because the newer doctor will be freshly trained and up to date on the latest procedures.)

* Bunch your appointments. For routine check-ups or preventative care, many doctors will charge substantially less if you bring the entire family in at once.

* For a chronic illness, suggest phone visits with your doctor instead of regular, more expensive, office visits.

## NEVER FORGET THE OUTLET STORES

Conscious of the growing price awareness of consumers, more and more manufacturers are opening factory outlet stores, You won't get fancy displays or a lot of personal attention, but you could save 25 to 75 percent over standard retail prices on quality name-brand merchandise — particularly women's shoes and clothing. Here are some guidelines to help you get the best bargains when shopping outlets:

* Pick the outlet store of a manufacturer whose products you know and like.

* The best savings at a manufacturer's outlet will be on its own line. At a Liz Claiborne outlet, for example, don't expect the same discount on other label clothing.

* Irregulars are fine if the defects are minor or easily repaired. Be wary of packaged items that can't be opened for inspection.

* Always inspect products for defects. If buying clothing, check material for flaws, look at stitching, make sure plaids are matched across seams.

* Many larger outlet stores carry goods from a variety of manufacturers or designers, so comparison shop here just as you would at a retail outlet.

* If you need a particular item and want to ensure getting the best quality, check the department stores or specialty shops first, then look for the same item at an outlet shop to get a better price.

## DON'T BE AFRAID TO BARGAIN IN REGULAR SHOPS

If you don't feel comfortable shopping at outlet stores, it's also possible to save money at specialty stores, but you'll probably have to ask. These stores depend on big mark-ups — always at least 100 percent and sometimes as much as 150 percent — to make up for high overhead and fairly low sales volume, and most have very few sales. However, if you shop during off-peak times, when the store isn't busy, and aren't afraid to ask the owner or manager for a personal discount, you can usually get a better price. Explain that you really like an item, and would like to buy it, but it's a bit much for your budget. Say you will, however, take it if you can get a markdown of, say, 25 to 40 percent off the listed price. In most cases, with a store empty of customers and a mark-up sufficient to still provide a nice profit, the owner or manager will say yes. And, if they don't, it didn't cost you anything to ask. Here are some other tips on getting better prices on specialty — and even luxury — items:

* Check out new specialty stores as soon as they open. Most set initial prices at reduced levels to draw as many

potential customers into the store as possible. Then, once they've built up traffic levels, they'll gradually raise their prices to the levels they want to maintain over the long term.

* A luxury item is still a luxury item even if it's not new. Resale shops have become extremely popular in recent years by offering big savings on designer suits and dresses that have been well maintained. These stores are especially good sources for party clothes and high-fashion items, which may have been worn only once or twice. It helps to know something about brand names — and always check each item carefully for damages.

* Consider smaller clothing stores where the owner is the buyer, perhaps selecting better quality and more distinctive fashions at lower prices than department stores.

* Before shopping for appliances, electronics or other big-ticket items, establish what you want — make, model, options, colors, ball- park prices — and then look for the best deal on precisely that. Don't let yourself be switched to a higher-priced or lower-quality item. Ask about discounts for paying cash, buying a floor model or taking immediate delivery.

* Don't overlook department stores. According to a recent survey, the major department stores sell only 35 to 40 percent of their merchandise at full price. The rest goes at sale or, eventually, at clearance prices.

## PROSPECTING FOR UNCLAIMED GOLD

Can you imagine forgetting about stock certificates worth tends of thousands of dollars, or savings accounts with a five or six-figure balance? Impossible? No, it happens all the time. Since 1989 the value of unclaimed property in state-administered repositories has reached into the billions — around $4 billion for New York State alone! How could it happen? Well, elderly people sometimes misplace stock certificates or bank books. Or perhaps dividend checks have been sent to a wrong address and keep being returned to the sender. Other stockpiled goodies are intended for estate beneficiaries who can't be located.

Under state laws, banks, insurance companies, brokerage houses and others holding unclaimed valuables must attempt to track down the rightful owners. Usually, after a five-year "abandonment period," a final warning must be sent to an owner's last known address. If there's no response, the unclaimed valuables revert to the state's abandoned property division. In all but two states, owners can recover property whenever they learn about it — no matter how long it's been in the fund. But Wyoming bars claims beyond five years, and New Hampshire after only two years. Half the states pay interest on money in the accounts.

Think you might have something coming? Well, instead of waiting to be contacted, write to the likely state's unclaimed property office using the addresses below. You can even request property on behalf of deceased relatives, if you legally inherit from them — and can prove it. When writing or calling, give your name (maiden or former, if necessary), Social Security number, current address, plus all previous addresses while you lived in that state. Expect to wait two or three weeks to hear back. If there's something for you, you'll receive an abandoned property claim form.

Send back the form with proof that the property belongs to you — such as current ID and any document linking you to the property. You will have to provide proof you resided at a previous address. If your claim is approved, expect to get a check in around two months.

Beware of firms promising to locate unclaimed money for a 10 percent finder's fee — and some want half. If you're so contacted, call or write the state fund yourself — and keep whatever they've got all for yourself. How to contact state unclaimed property divisions:

* Alabama,

P.O. Box 327580, Montgomery 36132
(no phone).

* Alaska,

Department of Revenue,
Room 106, 1111 W. Eighth St., Juneau 99801
(907-465-4653).

* Arizona,

Department of Revenue,
1600 W. Monroe, Phoenix 85007
(no phone).

* Arkansas,

Auditor of State,
230 State Capitol, Little Rock 72201
(501-324-9670).

* California,

P.O. Box 942850, Sacramento 94250
(1-800-992-4647)

* Colorado,

1560 Broadway, Ste. 630, Denver 80202
(303-894-2433).

* Connecticut,

55 Elm St., Hartford 06106
(no phone).

* Delaware, Delaware State Escheator,

P.O. Box 1039, Boston 02103
(302-577-3349).

* District of Columbia,

300 Indiana Ave. N.W., Room 5008, 20001
(202-727-0063).

\* Florida,

State Capitol,
Tallahassee 32399
(1-800-848-3792)

\* Georgia,

270 Washington St., S.W., Room 404, Atlanta 30334
(404-656-4244).

\* Hawaii,

P.O. Box 150, Honolulu 96810
(808-586-1589).

\* Idaho,

State Tax Commission,
P.O. Box 36, Boise 83722
(208-334-7623).

\* Illinois,

Department of Financial Institutions,
P.O. Box 19495,  Springfield 62794
(no phone).

\* Indiana,

Attorney General,
219 State House, Indianapolis 46204
(1-800-447-5598).

\* Iowa,

Hoover Bldg., Des Moines 50319
(515-281-5366).

\* Kansas,

900 S.W. Jackson, Suite 201 North, Topeka 66612
(1-800-432-0386).

\* Kentucky,

Revenue Cabinet,
Station 62, Frankfort 40620
(502-564-6142).

\* Louisiana,

P.O. Box 91010, Baton Rouge 70821
(504-925-7425).

\* Maine,
Treasury Department,
State House, Station 39, Augusta  04333
(207-287-2771).

\* Maryland,
301 W. Preston St., Room 310, Baltimore 21201
(1-800-492-1751).

\* Massachusetts,
State Treasury,
1 Ashburton Place, 12th Floor,  Boston 02108
(617-367-0400).

\* Michigan,
Escheats Division,
Lansing 48922
(no phone).

\* Minnesota,
Commerce Department,
133 E. Seventh St., St. Paul  55101
(1-800-925-5668).

\* Mississippi,
P.O. Box 138, Jackson 39205
(no phone).

\* Missouri,
P.O. Box 1272, Jefferson City 65102
(314-751-0123).

\* Montana,
Department of Revenue,
P.O. Box 5805, Helena 59620
(406-444-2425).

\* Nebraska,
Office of the State Treasurer,
P.O. Box 94788,  Lincoln 68509
(402-471-2455).

* Nevada,
State Mail Room,
Las Vegas 89158
(1-800-521-0019).

* New Hampshire,
Treasury Department,
25 Capitol St., Room 121, Concord 03301
(603-271-2649).

* New Jersey,
Department of the Treasury,
CN-214, Trenton 08646
(no phone).

* New Mexico,
Taxation Revenue Department,
P.O. Box 25123, Santa Fe 87504
(505-827-0767).

* New York,
Alfred E. Smith Bldg., Ninth Floor, Albany 12236
(1-800-221-9311).

* North Carolina,
325 N. Salisbury St., Raleigh 27603
(919-733-6876).

* North Dakota,
P.O. Box 5523, Bismarck 58502
(701-224-2805).

* Ohio,
77 S. High St., Columbus 43266
(no phone).

* Oklahoma,
Business Tax Division,
2501 Lincoln Blvd., Oklahoma City 73194
(405-521-4273).

* Oregon,
Division of State Lands,
775 Summer St. N.E., Salem 97310
(no phone).

* Pennsylvania,

2850 Turnpike Industrial Dr., Middletown 17057
(1-800-222-2046).

* Rhode Island,

P.O. Box 1435, Providence 02901
(401-277-6505).

* South Carolina,

P.O. Box 125, Columbia 29214
(803-737-4771).

* South Dakota,

State Treasurer's Office,
500 E. Capitol, Pierre  57501
(605-773-3378).

* Tennessee,

Andrew Jackson Bldg., 11th Floor, Nashville 37243
(615-741-6499).

* Texas,

Texas Treasury,
P.O. Box 12019, Austin 78711
(1-800-654-3463).

* Utah,
341 S. Main, Fifth Floor, Salt Lake City 84111
(801-533-4101).

* Vermont,
133 State St., Montpelier 05633
(1-800-642-3191).

* Virginia,
P.O. Box 3-R, Richmond 23207
(no phone).

* Washington,

1101 S. Eastside St., P.O. Box 448, Olympia 98507
(206-586-2736).

* West Virginia,

Department of the Treasury,
Capitol Complex,  Charleston 25305
(304-343-4000).

* Wisconsin,

Treasurer's Office,
P.O. Box 2114, Madison 53701
(no phone).

* Wyoming,

State Treasurer's Office,
State Capitol, Cheyenne 82002
(307-777-7408).

## FINDING GOLD UNDER THE DUST

For many of us, collecting is a nostalgic ticket back to childhood, a way to recover favorite things you once had and lost, or always coveted. There's nothing wrong with this impulse. But while you're recovering those misplaced treasures, keep an adult open for collectibles that may also provide a hedge against inflation. Surprisingly, the right stuff from the attic can outperform investments such as precious metals, not to mention the increasingly risky stock and bond market. Things to be on the lookout for:

* World War II posters and memorabilia. These items will be in continuing demand at least through the 1990's, the 50 anniversary period.
* Cap guns.
* Cereal premiums. You know, those little trinkets unearthed at the bottom of Lucky Charms, Corn Flakes and other boxes.
* 1950's Haywood Wakefield furniture.
* Monster collectibles, such as items from the Munsters and the Addams Family.

Things everybody thinks are hot, but aren't anymore:
* Baseball cards and souvenirs. The markets are glutted.
* Disney collectibles. Again, there's just too much of it around.

* Bakelite and rhinestone jewelry. Don't buy these —
  unless you  really want to wear them on.
* Lunch boxes. The market has rusted out.
* Pedal cars. Prices have gone down hill.

How can you find out what a given item is worth? Your
bookstore  or library should have "Warman's Americana &
Collectibles" price guide. Or you can have your item
appraised. Accredited appraisers can be  located via the
American Society of Appraisers (1-800-ASA-VALU).
They'll also send a free directory.


## BIDDING FOR BARGAINS

Some great bargains are going under the gavel these
days, as  luxury items from the go-go '80s are being auc-
tioned off to raise  much needed cash. Also, dozens of government agencies use auctions to  sell off foreclosed property, unclaimed merchandise, seized or surplus goods.
Avoid IRS auctions and look for private estate sales. The
tax agents or auctioneers will usually require immediate
cash in full  for most items. Here's how to get into the auction game, and how to  play it to save big.

Some Government Auctions That Pay Off:

**1. Department of Defense.** For pennies on the dollar, the
DOD  regularly auctions off items bought by the Pentagon.
Since you  finance these boondoggles with your taxes, you
might as well get in  one the sell-off savings. Contact your
local military base's Defense  Reutilization Marketing Office
for auction information.

**2. RTC.** The Resolution Trust Corporation "FF&E" and Real
Estate Auctions  offer some great buys on real estate, as
well as "furniture, fixtures  and equipment."

**3. U.S. Trustees Bankruptcy Auctions.** Check the classified ads in your local newspaper to spot these. Not only are good bargains available. If not enough bidders show up, you could walk away with some real steals.

Some Federal Auctions to Avoid:

**1. U.S. Marshals Service Auctions.** If you've heard about these, you're not alone. Bidders show up in droves, often bidding up merchandise beyond retail value. Stay away.

**2. U.S. Customs Auctions.** These folks confiscate some pricey items, including so-called "drug bust" goodies. As a result, some heavy bidders frequent these, and bargains are rare.

**3. GSA Public Auctions.** The General Services Administration sells off some luxury vehicles, and usually at luxury prices. You might, however, want to investigate their sealed-bid sales, conducted entirely through the mail.

General tips of shopping and saving at auctions:

* Attend a few auctions as a spectator to get the "feel" before showing up to make your first bid.

* Watch out for "auction fever." Getting swept up into a bidding war is the easiest way to overpay — and heavily. And auctioneers are paid to spread this fever.

* Decide what you want before you go to the auction — and your top bid. Study the catalogue, limit your interest, then research or talk to appraisers to assess actual value.

* Inspect the item carefully before bidding. Bring along an expert if possible.

* Make sure you know the "conditions of sale" — cash in advance, financing requirements, terms available — before attending the auction. Then bring the necessary wherewithal.

* Be ready to take your purchase home. If you plan to buy a car, bring along a driver or a towbar. Call ahead to find out removal requirements for large items.

## DON'T BE FOOLED BY GOLD

Gold jewelry seems never to go out of fashion. But how can you be sure that gold chain is actually 18K, as advertised, instead of, say, 14K or 10K? (Note: most U.S. stores sell 14-karat gold jewelry — 14 parts gold and 10 parts base metal. 18-karat gold is more common in Europe.) Answer: When it comes to gold content, even an expert eye can be deceived. Most jewelers don't even bother checking, but rely on the reputation of the manufacturers or wholesalers they buy from. But if they want to test, here are the ways:

1. Fire assay, which destroys the piece by melting down a part until the gold separates from the alloy.
2. X-ray fluorescence, which is costly, hard to find and not necessarily conclusive.

What you should check: Look for the karat content mark on the item, and the manufacturer's registered trademark. These are usually reliable guarantees. Hint: a 14K mark on the clasp of a bracelet or necklace doesn't mean the rest of the piece is also 14K. Look for the karat mark on a loop or tab attached to the chain. If you can't find markings on the jewelry, shop elsewhere. Also check the workmanship on all surfaces. Is the gold color consistent. Is the detail work good (especially in a pin or charm)? Does the piece seem flimsy? On chains, check for flaws in the end caps, connecting rings and clasp. Is the clasp soldered or only pressed close? Is the soldering clean or gloppy? Don't hesitate to ask to use the jeweler's loupe. Or carry your own. Best deals: Flea markets often offer the best buys, but price may not be the key factor. Other criteria: Availability of repair or refunds.

Mail-order catalogs and TV shopping channels offer hard-to-beat convenience, but refunds and replacements will involve shipping costs and delays. Beware: TV and catalogues also offer gold electroplate as well as karat gold. Make sure what you're buying. Note: gold electroplate consists of a thin layer of gold, 10K or more, over base metal.

Is gold jewelry a good investment? No. Gold chains or earrings or pins are not a very convertible asset. Jewelry stores will typically offer you less than a fifth of what you paid — basically the meltdown value. If an item has artistic or antique value, you might get close to its wholesale value on resale. If you want to invest in gold, go instead for newly minted bullion coins, such as American Eagles, Canadian Maple Leafs or Kruggerands. However, shop even the reputable coin dealers carefully as prices vary substantially.

## FINDING AND NEGOTIATING BARGAINS

Bargaining for merchandise has been around forever. But surprisingly, most of us are afraid to question price tags. The result: We pass on an item we'd like to buy and the merchant loses a sale.

Guess what: Price tags are not Holy Writ. Most merchants are perfectly willing to negotiate prices, taking a somewhat smaller profit on an item if it means they can reduce their inventory. So, give the seller — and yourself — a chance. You don't have to be rude or confrontational.

Ask, in a perfectly friendly manner, "Can you do any better on this price?" A merchant may knock 20 percent to 40 percent off the ticket price.

## ARE WARRANTY CARDS WORTHLESS?

What happens if you forget to send in the warranty card for some big-ticket item — home computer, stereo, refrigerator and so forth? Do you lose out? If you don't need to send them in to be protected, what's the point of the cards? Most of us wonder about these things. In fact, if you keep a dated purchase receipt, you don't have to fill out that little card and send it in to qualify for the manufacturer's warranty. So why do it? Probably the only reason is to register your name and address with the manufacturer, in order to receive updates on new products (or recalls).

Caution: If that registration or warranty card asks for a lot of seemingly extraneous data — income, marital status, hobbies, age, so on — it's probably destined to be added onto a mailing list and sold to or exchanged with other companies. If you don't want this to happen, but elect to send in the card, write on the card that all information is strictly for the use of the manufacturer. And skip any questions that seem irrelevant.

**NOTES**

_____

_____

_____

_____

---

CHAPTER 15

# TAX FACTS
# AND SAVINGS GUIDE

A mericans have had to deal with three new sets of tax laws in the past decade — and all of them have contained provisions that make it harder and harder to keep your hard-earned dollars in your own pocket. However, that doesn't mean you're at the complete mercy of the Internal Revenue Service. There are still a number of ways to reduce your tax bill, even with the new higher brackets and the tougher restrictions on deductions. Here are the three major areas where you can still act to cut your tax bite:

**1.** Make maximum use of the remaining tax-free and tax-deferred investments. This means making the full contribution to your IRA, Keogh plan, SEP (Simplified Employee Pension) account or your employer's 401(k) plan. These accounts, which let you deduct your full contribution directly from pre-tax income — and then grow on a tax— free basis until retirement (minimum age 59-1/2) are still the best legal tax shelters you can find. You can also invest in tax-exempt bonds, such as those issued by state or municipal governments; permanent life insurance, which builds cash value tax free; deferred annuities, which allow tax-free growth; and certain other tax-advantaged vehicles such as equipment-leasing funds.

**2.** Take advantage of remaining pure tax shelters. These include self-managed rental real estate, low-income housing, historic properties that you intend to restore, and certain oil and gas drilling projects or partnerships. Each of these provide either deductions or direct tax credits.

**3.** Maximize your deductions — and be sure not to overlook any to which you're entitled. For example, if your state assesses personal property taxes on cars, boats or other equipment, this tax can be deducted on your federal return. This deduction is often overlooked, especially when the state tax is collected through a licensing or registration fee. You may also be able to deduct such items as hobby expenses, home office expenses, home computer expenses, even your child's allowance if you own your own business or structure your part-time endeavors properly.

All of these strategies can significantly lower your tax bill, even under the new laws, but they require some knowledge and planning. The remainder of this Section will give you some specific tips on other areas in which you may turn the tax laws to your advantage — or, at least, keep them from hurting you too much.

## MAKE SURE YOUR WITHHOLDING IS CORRECT

The biggest change in recent tax laws is the increase in tax rates. With the top tax rate at 36 percent (plus a high-income surchange), as opposed to 31 percent prior to 1993, your tax bill could be substantially bigger than the amount withheld from your paycheck. Taxpayers with income over $140,000 on a joint return, over $115,000 on a single return or over $127,500 on a single head-of-household return will pay 36 percent on the amounts over those levels. A 10 percent surtax will boost this rate to 39.6 percent on income over $250,000 on all three types of returns. As a result of these higher rates, you should take some time now to calculate how much tax you'll owe next year and adjust your withholding or estimated payments accordingly. Don't, however, just guess the amount — the tax system is too complex, so do the math. You don't want to either pay to much withholding, thus giving the government an interest-free loan from you, nor do you want to have to little withheld, as this could subject you to a stiff non-deductible penalty. Be sure to check, as well, to ensure you won't be subject to the alternative minimum tax (AMT). There are a tremendous number of variables in these calculations, and errors can be very costly.

## SMART CHARITY IS SWEET CHARITY

When it's time to make your annual charitable contributions, make a smart distinction between straight cash donations or the gift of tangible assets. Do it the "tax smart" way. If an asset has gained in value, give the charity the asset outright. This way you avoid the capital gains tax and can deduct a larger charitable contribution. If an asset has lost value, sell it, use the loss to offset any other capital gains, then give a cash contribution and take the charitable deduction.

## DEDUCT NOW, PAY LATER

It's perfectly legal to take tax deductions this year for things you won't pay for until next year. Here's are two ways:

\* Pay by check. It's not sufficient to date a check in the current year. Payment is legally deemed to have been made when a check is delivered by hand or mailed — even if the check isn't cashed until next year. So you'll need proof of the delivery or mailing date, such as a certified mail receipt.

* Pay by credit card. Business expenses, medical expenses, charitable contributions — these items are deductible when they are made, even if the charges won't actually be paid off until the following year. Exception: This applies only to credit cards that function as a third party when you make charges. Charges made on department store cards are not deductible until paid.

## CHANGE INVESTMENT TACTICS TO SAVE TAXES

The current tax laws make the investment arena one of the richest areas when mining for tax breaks. Here are some ways your investments can help you save on taxes as well as making you money:

* The tax rates now favor long-term capital gains over regular income by 8 percentage points, as opposed to the former 3 percentage points — and capital gains are not included in income subject to the 10 percent surtax that could raise rates to 39.6 percent. Thus, you should structure your investments to produce more tax-favored capital gains and less high-tax income.

* Don't take a capital gain or loss on just one security. Net out all your capital gains against your losses on paper, and then decided which gains and losses you should actually realize. If you have excess losses, you can use $3,000 annually to offset ordinary earned income. You can also carry forward unused losses to future tax years.

* Investment interest is deductible only to the extent that you have investment income. As a result, removing the long-term gains from such income may reduce your available interest deduction. However, the law does allow you to include long-term gains in your "investment income" and deduct investment interest against it if you elect to have such gains taxed at ordinary tax rates. Thus, if you have a

lot of investment interest expense in a particular year, you might do better to forfeit the lower capital gain rate in order to  take all of your deductions.

* Now, more than ever, it's important to seek out tax-exempt income. Consider shifting investments from taxable stocks, bonds or mutual funds into tax-exempt municipal bonds or tax-exempt bond funds.

* Carefully look over your mutual fund investments. Many people  report too little income because they don't include the gains they  realized on investment switches made within a fund group during the year. This applies when fund shares are sold and the proceeds are  switched to a money fund, even if no money is taken from the fund.  The fund managers usually send statements disclosing these transactions. Likewise, some people report too much income by counting reinvested dividends from tax-deferred funds. And never forget that the cost basis in mutual fund shares includes the sales fee. Keep track  of this for IRS reporting.

* "Sell short against the box" to lock in capital gains now while  deferring taxes into next year. This works by selling stocks that are  borrowed from you broker, locking in today's price. After year-end,  you pay the broker with the shares that you own. This way you can fix  your gain now, although it won't be taxed until next year when the  deal closes.

* Passive activity gains can be realized to produce a double benefit. When you sell a passive investment, the undeducted passive losses — along with the capital losses from other investments — can offset passive capital gains. Consider this before year end.

* Consider exercising outstanding non-qualified stock options to  capture the long-term capital gains. When you exercise a non-qualified stock option to buy shares of stock at less than their market value, the amount of the discount

you receive is deemed ordinary income. That income can be taxed up to 39.6 percent. However, appreciation that occurs in the shares after you purchase them is capital gains, which is taxed at 28 percent if the shares are held for more than a year. So, if you think the underlying stock will increase in value, exercise the options now to assure that future appreciation will be taxed as capital gains instead of ordinary income.

* Buy real estate. Trade up to a bigger home, or purchase a vacation home. A boat can even qualify as a second home as long as it has sleeping quarters, a toilet and cooking facilities. With higher tax rates and interest rates still near their recent lows, owning a home becomes more attractive than renting — and real estate also becomes a better investment.

* Don't forget to adjust your real estate deductions. The new law increases the depreciation period on non-residential real estate from 31.5 years to 39 years for properties that went into service after Dec. 31, 1993.

* Take the money from a taxable savings account and buy a certificate of deposit or Treasury bill that matures in the following year. This will push your tax liability ahead by one year.

## BEWARE OF "TAX-FREE" INVESTING TAX TRAPS

Whether it's a bull market or a bear market, look out for the traps set for the investor in tax-free bond funds. Here are just a few:

* Don't get snared in the "ordinary dividends" trap. Form 1099 calls for "ordinary dividends" to be reported on tax-free bond funds. Many people think these should equal the total dividends paid by the fund in that year, but they don't.

Dividends marked on statements cover only a fund's income, while the Form 1099 category includes any short-term capital gains — of which bond funds may have a lot in years when interest rates fall. Thus, you should always be sure to separate short-term capital gains from ordinary dividends for tax purposes. Note: Any long-term capital gains should also be reported separately.

* Retirees receiving Social Security benefits while relying on muni bonds for tax-free income can get a bite taken out of them in another IRS trap. Fifty percent of Social Security benefits become taxable when tax-free income, plus half of Social Security benefits, plus other income, exceeds $25,000 for singles and $32,000 for couples. Eighty-five percent of Social Security benefits are taxable when income exceeds $34,000 for singles and $44,000 for couples.

* Don't forget to claim your credits for foreign taxes paid by your international funds (many people think such credits aren't allowed on overseas funds). If you invested in a foreign fund last year, expect to receive a Form 1099 reporting foreign taxes paid by the fund on income from foreign securities. If you elect to file a special form, you can receive a dollar-for-dollar offset against those taxes — or you can simply choose to deduct the amount on Schedule A of your Form 1040.

* Many investors fall into the trap of believing that if they have owned a fund for a year or less, they can claim no long-term capital gains. In point of fact, the holding period isn't based on the amount of time you've held shares, but on the amount of time the fund has owned the securities.

* If you think income paid by national muni funds is free of only federal taxes, the IRS has sprung another trap! Exactly how your fund buys national funds should be reported to you in its tax information letter. But, any way the fund handles it, income paid by each state's issue is free of state and local taxes for residents of that state.

* Switching from one fund to another stock, money market or bond fund in the same "family" of funds does not shield you from taxes. That's another IRS trap. Unfortunately, those wonderfully easy telephone transfers are considered taxable sales according to the Tax Code. IRS rationale: If you sold shares in one fund, then reinvested in another in a different family, taxes would be owed on the gain, so the same applies to switches within a single family.

* Another IRS trap is leading you to believe that dividends paid by Treasury funds are fully taxable. They are subject to federal taxes, but not state and local taxes. Additional trap in California, New York, New Jersey, and Connecticut: These states will only offer a tax break if a fixed percentage of the fund is in Treasury securities.

* Don't get trapped into thinking that tax-free bond funds are only for the rich. They aren't. With tax brackets creeping up, more and more investors can benefit from tax-free muni bond funds. Trick: To find out if tax-free bonds are for you, simply figure the equivalent taxable yield of the fund. To do this, divide the fund's tax-free yield by 1 minus your bracket. For example, if the tax-free yield on a fund was 4.67 percent and you were in the 31 percent tax bracket, the equivalent taxable yield would be 6.768 percent (4.67 / [1.00 - 0.31 = 0.69] = 6.7681).

* Probably the easiest trap you can fall into is not keeping adequate records. This is highly important with reinvested dividends. Taxes are owed in the year paid, even if you didn't get any cash from the fund in that year. Not keeping thorough records could have you paying the IRS twice, first in the year the dividend is paid — and then again when the shares are sold!

## OTHER PLACES TO LOOK FOR TAX SAVINGS

Income taxes can eat up as much as 50 percent of your income if you live in a high-tax state and also pay local income taxes. However, many people pay $500 or $600 a year in extra taxes, simply because they overlook certain key rules or deductions. Here are a few places to look for possible additional tax savings:

* File the long form, even if you don't itemize. Filing the IRS short Form 1040EZ not only eliminates itemizing, it also prevents you from taking your IRA deduction (even if you're qualified) — which can cost you as much as $720 in extra taxes each year.

* Claim every exemption. Each one is worth $2,450 (at 1994 levels) — which will save you between $368 and $970, depending on your tax brackets. Most commonly overlooked exemptions are for parents or children who don't live with you.

* If you do plan on claiming a parent as a deduction, be sure the parent's gross income doesn't exceed $2,450 per year. (Gross income for this purpose means earned income plus investment income. It does not include Social Security, welfare benefits, insurance proceeds, inheritances or gifts). If it does, you lose the $2,450 deduction — which could again cost you up to $970. Thus, if your parent has earned $2,440 and needs more money, just give it to them — but don't let them work for it.

* Remember your medical insurance deduction if you're self-employed. You may be allowed to deduct 25 percent of the premiums, depending on your overall income level.

* If you're self-employed and failed to get a Keogh retirement account set up by the end of the year, you can still set up a Simplified Employee Pension (SEP) until April 15

and make a contribution  equal to 15 percent of your compensation or $30,000, whichever is  less. This reduces your
gross income dollar for dollar, which will  save you big dollars on last year's tax bill.

* Don't overlook credits for child-care expenses. If you
hired  someone to watch your kids so you could work, you
may be eligible for  the Child and Dependent Care Credit
on Form 2441.

* Get full credit for mortgage interest paid. If you made a
house  payment late in December, it may not be reflected
on the Form 1098  you receive from your lender. If it isn't,
deduct the interest anyway  and attach a note with your
return explaining the discrepancy.

* Alimony payments are deductible; child support isn't. If
you're  getting a divorce, try to have as much of the monthly payment to your  ex-spouse designated as alimony as
possible.

* If you get lucky in Las Vegas, and have to report your winnings  (casinos must tell the IRS any time you win a jack-
pot or wager of  $1,200 or more), don't forget that you can
also deduct your verifiable losses against those winnings.
Most gamblers have more downs than ups, so it pays to
keep a small book with your gambling  winnings and losses — just so you'll be able to prove your losses  should you
need to offset part or all of a big win.

## CUT YOUR PROPERTY TAX

If you think your property tax bill is too high you can
always  appeal it . Get a list of property tax exemptions for
your area from  your tax assessor, plus information on filing
deadlines and forms to   fill out. But to get your thinking

going in the right direction, here are a half-dozen exemptions that apply in many areas — and which too many homeowners don't know about:

**1.** Veterans exemption. This could get you $50 off, if you're a veteran, a veteran's spouse, or the child of a veteran.

**2.** Home business exemption. This is better known, and allows a tax write-off for any part of the house used for business.

**3.** Senior citizens exemption. This gives a property tax break to those 65 and older.

**4.** "Homestead exemption." This provides a full 25 percent off your property tax bill.

**5.** Solar or wind-powered energy deduction. These offer a nice tax reduction for folks who install certain energy-saving devices in their home.

**6.** Personal property tax exemption. This unusual exemption actually allows deductions for necessary household items like washers, dryers and ovens.

## SOME TAX FILING TRICKS TO INCREASE AND HASTEN REFUNDS

Hidden in the 2,000-page Tax Code are little-used deductions waiting to be discovered by folks (or their accountants) who are willing to search aggressively. That doesn't mean you need to break the law, or even fool the IRS. It does mean going to the limit of the law. Usually, according to aggressive tax accountants, what arouses IRS suspicions are familiar deductions that are overused and unsubstantiated. For instance, overly large charitable deductions often raise a red flag. Here are a few tax-preparation tips:

* Be sure to deduct all expenses for books, magazines subscriptions and phone calls related to your job (deductible over 2 percent of adjusted gross income) or business (100 percent deductible).

* To speed up a refund, ask your accountant to file electronically. He or she may charge you an extra $15 to $25 for the service.

* If self-employed, prior to April 15 change your Keogh plan to a defined-benefit plan. You can increase the amount sheltered as you get older — up to an amount of $108,000. This can convert a taxable profit into a loss.

* Use your own mailing label, not the ones supplied by the IRS, which are sometimes coded to trigger an audit. Note: Using your own labels may delay a refund several weeks.

* Don't blindly accept the wage or withholding figures listed on your W2 forms. Go over your pay stubs and add up the amounts. Mistakes can be made — and not always in your favor. And the best time to correct them is when you file, not later.

* Consultants should make sure their tax form matches the figures reported on Form 1099. The tiniest discrepancy can trigger a computer generated IRS audit.

If you want to stay up to date on the tax laws and IRS rulings, you can subscribe to the "Tax Hotline" newsletter. It tells you how to beat the IRS and keeps you abreast of all the tax news from Congress, the White House and your state legislature. A yearly subscription is $39 and can be ordered by calling 1-800-288-1051.

## TAKE THIS JOB AND MOVE IT

We're hearing a lot these days about the mobile work force, and how a new worker should expect frequent job changes in his or her lifetime. With these trends, it's only fair that moving expenses should be deductible. And yet, many relocated workers neglect these deductions, or don't write off as much as they should (usually around one-third of total moving costs). You can deduct your move if your new job is at least 35 miles from your old residence. If you're self— employed and work at home, of course, your new job location will simply be your new residence. Armed service personnel can always deduct the cost of moving their family to a new base, near or far, in the U.S. or abroad. Note: The IRS says you must continue to be employed full-time in the new area for 39 weeks (78 weeks if self-employed). Exceptions: if your employer transfers you, or you're laid off, this test isn't applicable. By the way, either spouse in a marriage can qualify by working the 39 weeks. Following are the rules.

* Direct moving expenses are deductible with no specific dollar limit — including travel costs for you and family members, and the costs of professional movers, including packing and storage fees.

* Indirect moving expenses are deductible up to $3,000 — including hotel or motel charges and 80 percent of meals at new location while waiting to move into new residence.

The cost of selling your old residence — i.e., real estate brokerage commissions, transfer fees, etc. — is also deductible. Note: Moving expenses are deducted on tax form 3903. If your employer reimburses any of your moving expenses, you must report it as income on your Form 1040 — even if it doesn't show up on your W-2.

## HOW TO PAY NO STATE INCOME TAXES — FOREVER

There's only one sure way to avoid paying state income taxes entirely — and that's to move to one of the seven states in the U.S. that impose no income taxes. Alaska, Florida, Nevada, South Dakota, Texas, Washington and Wyoming are the states that have no personal income taxes (although Texans are currently debating an income-tax proposal). Other state income taxes vary from light to heavy.

If moving isn't practical, there are other ways to reduce your state tax burden, though the specifics will obviously vary from state to state. Here are a few ideas:

* If your state has a number of disadvantages when it comes to taxes, you might consider maintaining a residence there, but moving your legal domicile elsewhere. (For legal purposes, domicile is determined by where you vote, have your driver's license and motor vehicle registration, where your will is executed and, most important, where you pay taxes.)

* Probate laws differ significantly from state to state. In states that haven't adopted the uniform probate code, heirs may pay much higher probate costs.

* State sales taxes are also a significant factor, ranging from 3.5 percent to 11.0 percent (including add-ons for city sales taxes). If your state has high tax rates, consider making major purchases — autos, boats, jewelry, etc. — in a neighboring state with lower rates.

* Local taxes also vary substantially across county and municipal lines. If you're thinking of buying a new home in a different area, be sure to check out any tax differentials

for the new shopping areas you'll be patronizing. The same applies to business licensing fees and operating permit costs if you are thinking about moving your  business.

* Some states don't allow an unlimited exemption for transfers to  a surviving spouse. If this could affect you, consider moving your  legal domicile to a state that does as you get up in years and begin  thinking in terms of passing on your estate.

* Before moving, consider factors such as intangible property  taxes, which are imposed by almost half the states and can be particularly heavy for people with large holdings. The tax basis for  capital gains on tangible property sales also vary according to each state's rules. Consider this if you're planning a move, and may need  to sell financial assets to help finance the transfer.

An additional tip related to states: Before moving across state  lines, make sure your will, living will, health-care directives,  pre-nuptial agreement and other legal documents conform to the new  state's requirements.

## NOTES

_____

_____

_____

_____

_____

## CHAPTER SIXTEEN
# PASSPORT TO TRAVEL SAVINGS

As we said back in Section Fifteen, if you're like most people, you're going to want to take at a least some of the money you save by putting everything you've learned to use and celebrate a bit. And, one of the favorite ways to celebrate is to take a trip — perhaps even going first class. Fortunately, as with dining out, there are a number of ways to go first class without having to pay first-class prices — or, in some cases, without paying anything at all. Keep reading this section, and you'll learn some of the best ways to get travel bargains — and even completely free travel.

## FREEBIE GETAWAYS

Got a travel itch you think you can't afford to scratch? Well, think again. With a little planning and ingenuity, you can travel almost anywhere for nothing — or next to it. You just need to take advantage of the opportunities that for too long have been known only to a lucky few. Here are five freebie tickets to exotic adventure:

**1. Air couriers.** Since customs law can require someone to accompany some types of cargo, many firms will pay you to chaperone one of their shipments. Don't worry — you won't have to lug crates, only carry forms with cargo information, hand the goods over to a contact at your destination — then take off for your own vacation. Upside: Using this little-known method, you can usually get in your trip for 50 to 70 percent off a normal fare. Downside: You probably won't be able to check baggage since most shipping companies use your baggage allowance as part of the shipment. For more information, order: "Air Courier Bargains — How to Travel World-Wide for Next to Nothing," by Kelly Monaghan ($14.95); call 1-800-356-9315.

**2. Tour escort or planner.** If you can round up enough family or friends for a vacation on the same plane, you can fly free — depending on the airline. Some require a group of 10, others 15. This can also work for ski trips and cruises. To organize such trips, you should make a deal with a good travel agent — and get a percentage of the agency commissions (10 to 15 percent of airfare, hotels and tours you arrange). Bonus: Once you're in the travel business, all your trip expenses are deductible.

**3. RV delivery.** How about delivering a brand-new recreational vehicle to its new owners somewhere in America or Canada — and getting a vacation en route. Naturally, you'll sleep for free right in the RV. And, as long as you reach your destination in a week or so, the route is up to you. Also, with a little planning, you can get back home again, picking up more money with a return vehicle. These jobs are ideal for college students on summer break, or retired couples who can share the driving. In fact, some people regard this as a "retirement career." To qualify you need only be between 18 and 88 with a driver's license. No special training is required. RV's aren't trucks; they drive pretty much like large cars. Also, some companies prefer retirees because of their maturity.

How much will it pay? Believe it or not, some people earn as much as $50,000 a year. Two companies that hire drivers (for other dealers, check your local Yellow Pages under Motor Homes or Recreational Vehicles):

> * Transfer Drivers, Inc.,
> 10920 East McKinley Hwy., Osceola, IN 46561.
> * TOMCO,
> P.O. Box 384, Forest City, IA 50436.

**4. Travel industry jobs.** Airlines may be going through tough times, but there are opportunities in other travel-related businesses — car rental, hotels, cruise ships, many others. And most of them carry fringe benefits of travel bargains. Cruise ships, by the way, are always looking for employees with experience in everything from food service to entertainment. Another way to enjoy free or deeply discounted travel is to start your own travel agency. This isn't as difficult as it may sound. Start-up help is available from the Independent Travel Agencies of America Association (ITAA) in Rochester, NY. Call: 1-800-947-4822.

You might consider a home travel agency organization, rather than a full-service office. For a home agency start-up costs are around $3,000 for initial certification and stationery. For more information, call 1-800-929-7447, and order "Jobs for People Who Love To Travel" ($12.95), or "The Complete Guide to International Jobs & Ca-reers" ($13.95), both by Ronald and Caryl Krannich.

**5. Small-item importer.** This can be like an extended hobby, and it's not nearly as complicated as you might think. You'll simply buy stuff overseas at outdoor bazaars and bring it back in empty suitcases. Surprise: The U.S. charges no duty on artwork or handicrafts. Back home, you sell the items on consignment to local gift shops or sell them right out of your house, a la Tupperware. The profit will  at least help pay for your trip, and all travel costs will be tax-deductible. For help, consult The Learning Annex's "Guide to Starting Your Own Import-Export Business" (Carol Publishing, $8.95).

## FAMILY VACATIONS ON THE CHEAP

As most parents know, taking the kids on the road to a resort or  theme park can bust any vacation budget — but the alternative isn't  just staying at home and staring at the back yard. In fact, some of  the most rewarding family trips can also be the least expensive. Here  are eight valuable suggestions:

**1. Budget hotels.** Don't hit the road without a list of motel or hotel chains that offer special rates to families.

**2. Hostels.** These are now open to families, and offer hotel-style  lodging at a fraction of the cost.

**3. Fairs and festivals.** With a little research, you can come up with a long list of regional or city celebrations that provide load  of family fun with no ticket price. They range from biggies like New  Orleans Mardi Gras to little-known annual events like Troy, Ohio's Strawberry Festival.

**4. Nature hikes.** These educational outings are offered by most  national, state and local parks.

**5. Museum field trips.**

**6. City walking tours.** Most cities offer them, either providing  guides or brochures for self-guided discovery walks.

**7. Washington, DC.** Not only America's capital and perhaps its  most beautiful and enjoyable city — but a bargain destination for families. All those wonderful monuments and museums are admission free.

**8. Factory tours.** Check with chambers of commerce for factories  that have guided tours, especially any that offer free samples of  their products. Winery tours can be included in this category.

## SMALL-FRY FREEBIES

Family vacations can be fantastic — and fantastically expensive. All those extra tickets, snacks, fares and Happy Meals have forced many to rethink or cancel carefree summer plans. But if you're married with children, you should know that more and more holiday destinations are offering kiddie discounts. Here's a short list:

**1.** Most major hotels don't charge for kids who share your room. Marriott Suites and Embassy Suites both offer adjoining rooms at a discount for kids.

**2.** Free teen-age programs are offered by many hotels and resorts. For instance, teens vacationing with parents at many Hyatt holiday destinations can take part in "Rock Hyatt," a program offering day and evening entertainment for the 13-to-17 set. Amusements include videos, arcade games, rock music, sight-seeing, sports and social activities.

**3.** Amtrak cuts coach fares in half for passengers between the ages of 2 and 15 — that is, if they bring an adult along. Passengers under 2 ride free.

**4.** Some airlines offer fare breaks for college students. Check with your travel agent — or American Express, which has a "Student Privileges Program" for student cardholders who pay for their tickets with the American Express card. Call Amex at 1-800-582-5823.

**5.** To drastically cut costs of family travel accommodations, consider hosteling. We're not talking about bunking in a huge dormitory room full of guitar-playing teens; for about $25 per night, you and your brood can bed down in a special "family" room at any American Youth Hostel. AYH accommodations vary from mansions to lighthouses. To qualify, you need a one-year family membership for $35 — or get an introductory guest card for $3 per night, good for three-nights stay at any hostel. Members also receive discounts on Alamo or National rental cars. Call AYH at 202-783-6161, and ask for the Travel Center. Caution: Hostels don't usually accept kids younger than 5.

## BARGAIN RATES ON REGULAR HOTELS

With hotels seeing a drop in their occupancy rates as businesses cut back on travel, many are offering specials such as reduced room rates, additional nights at no charge and even free meals — items that could save you up to 50 percent on your hotel costs. Staying at a business hotel over the weekend can also save you up to 50 percent, and even in more popular locations. Travel agents frequently get package deals on hotels, so check with them for better quotes that the ones you get directly from the hotel.

Also try the bargain hotels when you go to major cities, such as New York, where normal rates can run as high as $300 to $400 a night. Some of New York's best bargain (under $100 a night) hotels include the Carlton Arms, 160 E. 25th St.; the Excelsior, 45 W. 81st St.; the Gramercy Park 2, Lexington Ave. at E. 21st St.; the Herald Square, 19 W. 31st St.; and the Olcott, 27 W. 72nd St.

Bonus: Once you arrive at your hotel, don't forget to ask for "freebies" — cosmetics, candy, sewing kits, bath robes, etc. If you are a frequent guest, ask about discounted rooms, free breakfasts and complimentary newspapers. You can also request use of hotel blow dryers, fax machines and VCRs.

## CASHING IN ON AIR-FARE WARS

Naturally, most air travelers seek the lowest possible fare, and assume their travel agents will come up with it. But fares change rapidly — sometimes on a daily basis. In fact, a lower fare may be offered after your ticket is booked and before it's issued (a period which can be up to two weeks for vacationers). Make sure your travel agent uses a computerized program that automatically hunts for lower fares up to the time the ticket is booked. Such search software generally discovers a lower rate for one out of four tickets. One software company claims the average savings is 28 percent of the ticket cost, anywhere from $68 to $130. These programs are growing in use, both in big agencies like Thomas Cook and in many small bureaus.

## WAIT TILL THE NEXT FLIGHT — AND FLY FREE

In an effort to ensure that their flights are as full as possible, most airlines today engage in a practice known as overbooking. What this means is that they allow 130 passengers to reserve space on a plane that has only 120 seats, the theory being that lots of people will change their plans and fail to show up for the flight without bothering to cancel their reservations. Of course, if everyone does show up, the airline has a problem — which it deals with by "bumping" passengers from the overbooked plane and placing them on a later flight. As compensation for being bumped, the airlines usually offer the passengers who are delayed vouchers good for full or partial fares on a future flight of their choice.

The secret here is that the process of bumping passengers isn't arbitrary on the part of the airline. Typically, when it becomes apparent a flight will be oversold, the clerk at the check-in counter will make an announcement asking for volunteers willing to take a later flight. Step up quickly, and you'll almost always be chosen — which will enable you to trade a two or three hour delay on this trip for a free ticket on your next flight. In fact, many people traveling for leisure — i.e., those not on a tight business or vacation schedule — actually schedule certain flights in an effort to get bumped. This can be accomplished by booking the busiest flights on the most popular travel days, then seat-ing yourself very near the check-in counter so you'll be first in line when the call for volunteers comes. Tip: When planning a trip on which you think you have a good chance of being bumped, take only carry-on luggage. The bumping process usually begins in the final 10 or 15 minutes before the plane is scheduled to depart, and there probably won't be time to retrieve luggage from the cargo hold if it has already been checked. Thus, your bags will arrive at your destination two or three hours ahead of you — meaning you could have trouble locating them when you finally get there yourself.

## CATCH A FLYING REBATE

If you flew on a major airline between 1988 and June 30, 1992, somebody owes you money — namely, the airlines who were involved in fare-fixing. How to get yours: To obtain claim forms, write to Airlines Antitrust Litigation, P.O. Box 209, Philadelphia, PA 19107. If you spent less than $2,500 of USAir, United, TWA, Northwest, Delta, Continental or American through any of their hubs, you won't need documentation and can file your claim with the "short" or "intermediate" form. To file a bigger claim, you'll need to show receipts, credit card statements, canceled checks or frequent-flier statements to substantiate each flight you took. The likeliest form of rebate will be by interchangeable vouchers good for three to four years.

## BIG DISCOUNTS ON CRUISES

When booking a cruise with a travel agency, ask if your agent gets unofficial overrides. These are extra commissions for booking certain cruise lines. If they do, many agents will rebate part of this fee to you. Cruise lines who offer overrides are Carnival, Princess, Royal Caribbean and Norwegian Cruise Line. A 35 percent discount isn't uncommon on many cruise lines, reducing fares to under

$100 a day. Also, consider booking the worst cabin on the best ship. After all, you won't be spending much time in your room, so why pay  extra. On most ships (except the Queen Elizabeth II), all passengers  get equal access to all the fun, so you won't miss out.

## MAGIC KINGDOM DISCOUNTS

Disney World remains America's number one vacation destination.  But it's also one of the most expensive. Unless you take advantage of  this insider's secret and buy a share of Disney stock. That's right,  just one share, for around $45 — less than two adult admissions to  the theme park. Guess what stockholder perks you pick up with that share: 10 percent to 40 percent off on Disney resort accommodations,  and a 10 percent discount on Disney theme cruises, Delta flights to  Disney resorts and merchandise at Disney stores.

## WHEN YOU NEED TO RENT A CAR

Thanks to recent changes in both the rental-car and credit-card  industries, you may no longer be properly insured when you rent a  car. Rental agencies used to take primary responsibility for whom and  what you hit while driving one of their vehicles, but this may no  longer be the case. Unless you pay the additional $10 for a collision damage waiver, you could be responsible for any damage, theft or loss  of the vehicle. Your personal auto insurance policy could cover you  — 40 percent of the nation's auto insurers cover rental cars for personal use, but you must check in advance to make sure. However, many   also impose limits on how many consecutive days you can rent a car  and how many days you can rent one within a single year. Many personal insurers also don't cover a car rented for business use. (State  Farm, one of the country's largest insurers, began eliminating automatic collision and liability coverage for business rentals in 1992.)

Don't count on your credit card to protect you either — not unless such coverage is specified in the credit agreement. Chase Manhattan Bank dropped its rental-car collision damage protection in June of 1993, although you can still be assured of collision damage protection from American Express, Diners Club, Discover or Visa or MasterCard "gold" cards. However, Diners Club is the only card that offers primary coverage; the others give only secondary coverage — meaning they pay only what your own insurer won't pick up. Most credit-card policies also don't offer coverage for injuries or property damage.

Strategy: Before renting a car for personal use, check with your insurance carrier about coverage. Most large corporations will cover you for both collision and liability when the car is rented for business. If you're unsure, however, ask your employer what kind of coverage they offer. If you are a frequent rental customer, consider purchasing a $1 million dollar liability umbrella from your insurer — or buy the optional $1 million liability coverage when you rent the car. Good deal: If you are an Auto Club member and rent from Hertz, you receive automatic liability insurance of up to $50,000 per accident.

## WHAT IF YOUR RENTAL CAR'S A LEMON?

Although it often isn't clearly spelled out in your rental agreement, you are NOT financially responsible if your rental car breaks down. If you have mechanical problems, contact the rental location immediately and ask for instructions on where to go for repairs — or, better yet, request that they send out a replacement vehicle. If you are in a remote location, you may be asked to go ahead and have the car fixed. If so, be sure to save receipts and ask for immediate reimbursement (or a written acknowledgment that one is due) when you return the car. Exception: If the vehicle breaks down as a result of off-road driving or other prohibited activities, you'll probably be liable for repairs.

## GOOD TIMING CAN CUT YOUR RENTAL COSTS

Traveling business people account for the bulk of auto rentals, and most business people travel Monday through Friday. As a result, rental car companies usually have lots of available cars on Saturday and Sunday, and give substantial discounts to weekend renters. What most people don't know is that many rental companies extend their weekend rates for up to three additional days, just to keep the car from sitting idle two days a week (after all, 5 days at $35 per day brings in more money than 3 days at $50). As a result, you can save 30 to 60 percent, depending on the car class, if you time your vacation trip to include one or more weekend days and ask for the special weekend rate.

Many companies also offer special rates for full-week rentals — rates that are cheaper than three to four days of regular-price rental. Thus, if you are taking a 5 or 6 day trip, you may save money by renting the car for a week and simply turning it in early. Four other rental savings tips:

**1.** Many rental companies offer corporate discounts; if you're traveling on business, ask for one.

**2.** Many airlines have special fly/drive packages that can cut your rental cost if you book the car through the airline reservations system.

**3.** Reserve your car through the rental company's national reservation system and ask for the best rate available. Rental rates vary widely from city to city — even within the same company — and you could get stuck with a higher rate than expected if you go through the local agency.

**4.** Reserve a smaller car than you really want. It's likely one won't be available and the local clerk will give you a larger model at the same price.

## TIME-SHARE TRAPS

Many who rushed to join the annual time-share migrations to the  ski slopes or seashores have been dissatisfied. Either they got tired of the same-time, same-place vacation restriction — or they started  checking out competing condo rental ads and discovered they'd overpaid. For those who are just looking into buying into a time-share, here are some common-sense guidelines:

* Deal with developers who have a proven track record on maintenance and management problems.

* Never pay more than 10 times the going rate for a hotel or  apartment rental in the same area at the same time of year.

* Buy in early on a new complex. The first few apartments usually  sell for less.

* Singles or three or four room time-shares are harder to sell or swap. Stick to one or two room units.

* Time slots in a peak vacation season are more negotiable, and  thus better deals.

* Your property will be worth more if it's in an area with zoning  against continuing time-share developments. Certain vacation areas, such as Vail, Colorado, have established such moratoriums.

* Try to find an area not too far off the beaten track. If nobody  has ever heard of it, you'll have a hard time selling, renting or  swapping it.

## HEY DUDES, HERE ARE YOUR GUIDES

For big-city folk, a week or two on the wild prairie can be a great change of pace, and such excursions don't have to cost as much as the reward figures on a wanted poster, but only if you know where to look for bargains. Two sources of information on bargains in the dude ranch corral are:

* The Colorado Dude & Guest Ranch Association Directory includes data — including prices, year-round activities, special features and locations — for more than 40 ranches. To get a free copy, write the association at P.O. Box 200, Tabernash, CO 80478; 303-724-3653.

* "Dude Rancher" magazine describes 110 ranches in 11 states and Canada and includes "The Dude's Guide to Picking the Perfect Ranch." It's available for $5 from the Dude Ranchers' Association, P.O. Box 471, LaPorte, CO 80535; 303-223-8840.

Tip: For best selection and rate bargains, book as early as you can. Most ranches begin taking reservations a full year in advance.

## SEE EUROPE BY TRAIN AND SAVE

Want to see Europe at a bargain price without having to go the hiking-and-hostel route? Europe Through the Back Door, a travel-resource center that specializes in independent touring, can help. The agency publishes a special "Annual Guide to European Railpasses," which describes the basic features of most European package rail tickets, how to use them and how their prices compare with other travel options. To obtain a copy, write the agency at P.O. Box 2009, Edmonds, WA 98020; call at 206-771-8303, or fax your request to 206-771-0833.

## COMBINE EDUCATION AND TRAVEL

Feel like learning as well as looking when you travel. An outfit called International Study Tours offers just such opportunities — within America and overseas — including co-sponsoring the Elderhostel educational tour program. For information on rates, schedules and subject areas, call IST at 1-800-833-2111.

## A GUIDE TO LOW-FARE AIRLINES

Spurred by the success of Southwest Airlines in offering cheap short-hop service that gets you there fast but without any frills, a number of other low-fare airlines have sprung up around the country in recent years. These airlines mostly serve specific regions, but they provide an economical alternative to the major carriers for many trips. Following is a listing of some of the leaders in this group:

* Carnival Air Lines is owned by Micky Arison, chairman of Carnival Cruise Lines. Routes are primarily between the Northeast and Florida, although a few Boston-to-Los Angeles flights are available. The company, which began operations in 1988 and is based in Dania, Florida, has 40 daily flights, owns 22 planes and employs 1,200 people.

* Frontier Airlines is a reincarnation of the former Frontier Air that folded in the mid-1980s. Based in Denver, the carrier began operations in 1994 with the intent of filling the service gap left when Continental dropped flights to many small Western cities. Frontier has five planes, 28 daily flights and 330 employees.

* Kiwi International is an employee-owned operation serving the East Coast. Based in Newark, N.J., it was started primarily by ex-employees of Pan American World Airways and Eastern Airlines. The company, which began operations in 1992, has 13 planes, 53 daily flights and 1,000 employees.

\* Leisure Air is primarily a charter service but also has 10 scheduled flights between major eastern cities. Based in Winston— Salem, N.C., the company began operating in 1993, has seven planes  and 650 employees. As a cost-containment measure, every meal served  by the airline is a turkey sandwich.

\* Reno Air is a Reno, Nevada-based operation that is trying to  fill the gap left by American Airlines' withdrawal from short-distance West Coast routes. Started in 1992, the company has 20 planes, 135 daily flights and 1,500 employees.

\* Sun Jet International offers limited service to secondary airports in major cities. Started in 1993 in Large, Florida, the company  has five planes, 10 daily flights, 150 employees — and fresh cookies  actually baked and served on each flight.

\* ValuJet Airlines is one of the most successful of the new bargain carriers, focusing primarily on southern cities served at higher  prices by Delta. Based in Atlanta, the company began flying in 1993  and now has 22 planes, 134 daily flights and 1,700 employees.

For information on specific routes and fares for particular destinations, call "800" directory assistance — 1-800-555-1212 — and  get the toll-free number for the airline in which you're interested.

## LET UNCLE SAM HELP PAY YOUR WAY

As explained earlier, most rental car companies offer package  deals or full-week rates that are actually cheaper than three or four  normal daily charges. By taking advantage of such deals on business  trips, you can actually lower your business expense, which is fully deductible — and get a few free days of personal rental car use in the process. If you're on an expense account, you can use the same strategy to let your boss pay for your use of the car when you extend a business trip for a weekend of fun.

## DEALING WITH A SPEEDING TICKET

If you like auto vacations, one of the biggest items of extra expense could be a speeding ticket. There are no magic words guaranteed to get you out of a speeding ticket. However, there are some words that will improve your odds of getting off with a warning starting with: "I'm sorry, Officer. I know I was going too fast but..." At that point, if you hope to arouse any sympathy at all, you'd better have a reasonable and believable excuse — preferably something that demonstrates your concern for someone other than yourself. Then close with these: "I promise I will be more careful in the future." Added tip: Whatever you do, treat the police officer with the utmost respect — even if he or she is half your age. A belligerent attitude is the quickest way to ensure that you'll get written up, whereas a well-placed, "Yes sir," can go a long way toward keeping the ticket pad closed.

## TRADE HOUSES — AND SEE THE WORLD

A great way to see a different area of the country and experience its attractions in depth — without spending a fortune — is to swap houses for a few weeks with someone who lives there and wants to see the area where you live. The most desirable areas for home swaps are California, Florida, the Northeast and the Northwest. However, you can't wait until the last minute and expect to find a swap mate. The best time to schedule summer exchanges is in February or March. If this sounds like something that would appeal to you, there are two national organizations that help with swaps and match exchange partners. Intervac can be reached by calling 415-435-3497, or you can contact the Vacation Exchange Club at 1-800-638-3841.

## CAMPING CLUES

Late spring is prime time for making reservations for summer camping excursions in the nation's most popular national parks. Wait much later and you'll face a whole string of "Campground Full" signs. To book a campsite at the 13 most popular National Park Service locations (up to two months in advance), call 1-800-365-2267. To get general information about any or all of America's national parks, call 202-208-4747.

## NEWSLETTERS CAN HELP SAVE TRAVEL DOLLARS

Just about everybody likes to travel, and we all have specific needs, requirements and favorite spots — special places we return to and repeatedly recommend to friends. With that in mind, entrepreneurs across the country provide an abundance of specialized newsletters to make your travels more enjoyable. According to the 1994 edition of the Oxbridge Directory of Newsletters, 192 travel-related newsletters are currently up and running. These can generally be broken down into two categories:

* In-house or promotional publications for bed-and-breakfasts, inns, resorts, airlines, hotels, etc.
* General-circulation letters relying on subscriptions.

Both types offer invaluable information and travel tips that are much more current than the local guidebooks. And, since most don't carry advertising, they aren't influenced by outside forces. Hence, they can be more impartial. Many of the general circulation letters are born as a result of a need for specific information, and thus customize their content for a particular readership. The most successful newsletters find a narrow market focus and write to it. One example of finding a niche, is "DogGone" — a travel newsletter for dog owners. Its editor, Wendy Ballard, a dog owner herself, became frustrated by the lack of information on dog-friendly vacation spots. She started writing a bimonthly newsletter after finding out that there are more dogs per household in America than children. (DogGone boasts 2,500 human subscribers.)

Thus, if you have travel on your mind — and have either special needs or just want the latest information on bargain prices — consider looking into a newsletter. Most will provide a sample copy, either free or for a nominal fee. Here are some leading letters:

* Andrew Harper's Hideaway Report, P.O. Box 50, Sun Valley, ID 83353; yearly cost $100. This well known and undisputed king of upscale travel letters started in 1979 with the goal of providing "a connoisseur's worldwide guide to peaceful and unspoiled places." Up-to-date info, phone numbers, addresses and prices on out-of-the-way destinations. Privately published. Subscription is limited, but according to a recent issue, 50 subscriptions are available.

* DogGone, P.O. Box 651155, Vero Beach, FL 32965-1155; six issues per year for $30. If you can't bring yourself to kennel your pup, DogGone will provide you with every range of accommodations — from five-star resorts to motel chains. Presumably not the dog house.

* Out & About, 542 Chapel St., New Haven, CN 06511; 10 issues per year for $49. Specifically targets gay and lesbian travelers. Frank, honest and thorough. Recently featured destinations in Cuba and Morocco, and the 10 best gay ski resorts in the U.S.

\* Consumer Reports Travel Letter, Subscription Department, P.O. Box, 51366, Boulder, CO 80321-1366; yearly $39. If you are looking for travel bargains, this could be the newsletter for you. Put out by the Consumer Reports family, it is a practical, reliable and well-presented rating of hotels, airlines, car rental companies, motels, travel agencies, and more.

\* Las Vegas Advisor, 5280 S. Valley View Blvd. Ste. B, Las Vegas, NV 89118; yearly $45. Everything you ever wanted to know about Las Vegas — best coupon usage, giveaways and comps. Show and tournament dates for hotels. Lots of restaurant and entertainment material.

\* Travelin' Woman, 855 Moraga Drive, No. 14, Los Angeles, CA 90049; Twelve issues for $48. More focus given to anecdotes than info. Includes interviews with travel world luminaries, a book review, a horoscope and exotic recipes.

If you are looking for a newsletter with a foreign focus, try:

\* La Belle France, P.O. Box 3485, Charlottesville, VA 22903-0485; monthly for $67 a year.

\* British Travel Letter, 361-4 Post Road, W., Ste. 194, Westport, CN 06880; 10 issues for $65. For a FREE copy call 1-800-966-0701.

\* Inside Ireland, P.O. Box 271369, Escondido, CA 92027-9935; four issues for $35.

Other speciality newsletters:

\* Traveling Healthy Newsletter, 108-48 70th Road, Forest Hills, NY 11375; bi-monthly for $29.

\* Bicycle Travel Review, P.O. Box 3220, Manhattan Beach, CA 90266; six issues for $44. Focus is on bike trips and routes in California and the West.

\* The Road Best Traveled, P.O. Box 336, Dana Point, CA 92629; monthly for $48. Focus is on hotel, cruise and car rental bargains.

\* Gold Travel, P.O. Box 3485, Charlottesville, VA 22903; monthly for $67. Features golf resorts of the world.

---

---
SECTION SEVENTEEN
## PLAYING TO WIN
---

For many Americans, the gaming life makes up a big part of their regular life — and many of them pay dearly for the diversion. We can't do anything about the built-in house advantage featured in most games of chance, but this section does offer some tips to make sure you keep the odds as much on your side as they're supposed to be.

## TIPS FOR BETTERING SWEEPSTAKES ODDS — AND PROTECTING YOURSELF

Everyone enjoys playing the sweepstakes game, but winning is no easy matter. However, there are some things you can do to improve your chances — and protect against fraud.

* Print your entry clearly in dark ink. Avoid handwriting, calligraphy and peculiar shades of ink. Addresses written with felt-tip pens can smear in the rain. If the entry is a post card, fill out the mailing address in black ink — which post office machines can read — then fill out your entry in red

---

ink — which post office machines can't read. This will insure your post card gets delivered, not sent back to you by the post office.

* Don't accept COD prizes. Legitimate sweepstakes don't require winners to pay any money to collect prices. Swindlers often ask for money to cover "taxes" or "shipping and handling charges." If they do, just say no.

* Beware of phony sweepstakes with entry fees. It's against the law for a sponsor to demand a fee to enter a sweepstakes contest. If you get one, notify your postal inspector.

* Most companies notify winners by mail. Be wary of phone calls informing you that you've won a sweepstakes prize.

* Never give your credit card number as "proof of eligibility."

* Follow all sweepstakes instructions and rules. For instance, you may be disqualified if you don't copy the address exactly as shown.

* Always contact the company conducting the sweepstakes. A list of winners is available on request.

The Federal Trade Commission says sweepstakes fraud costs Americans more than a quarter of a billion dollars a year. If you think someone's a con artist, notify your state attorney general, the Better Business Bureau or call the National Fraud Information Center at 1-800-876-7060.

## WINNING LOTTERY STRATEGIES

The odds against winning a state lottery are almost astronomical, right? Maybe so, but here's one way of improving them dramatically in your favor. In a number lottery, all eligible numbers have an equal probability of being selected in any given drawing. Interestingly enough, however, the payoff on any given lottery drawing reflects not just the numbers that are drawn, but also how many participants selected those winning numbers. Thus, if you select unpopular numbers and they wind up being drawn, you will receive a proportionally larger payoff than you would had you selected popular numbers. (Remember, they all have an equal probability of being drawn.)

Actuaries call these unpopular choices "ugly" and "non-focal" numbers. The theory is that "ugly" numbers are the prime numbers (those that can be divided only by themselves and by 1), and that "non-focal" numbers are those that aren't associated with specific events, such as birthdays or anniversaries. Combining the two categories suggests you can improve your chances of collecting a poten- tially large lottery payoff by selecting prime numbers above 31. In a 53-number lottery, the combined "ugly" and "non-focal" numbers are 37, 41, 43, 47 and 53.

## QUADRUPLE YOUR LOTTERY CHANCES AT NO EXTRA COST

If you want to dramatically improve your chances of winning the lottery at no extra cost, here's a great strategy: If you spend $10 a week on the lottery and know four other people who do the same, you can increase your chances of winning by 400 percent by forming a pool with those other players. Sign a contract (this is important as most states won't split payoffs without one) agreeing to split all winnings equally among the five of you, then go ahead with your normal playing. You'll each have 50 chances a week to win rather than just 10 — and you won't be spending any more money.

## DON'T BE A VICTIM OF THE LOTTERY ANNUITY BLUES

The thrill of winning a state lottery is the stuff that dreams are made of. But many lottery winners end up big losers. Most states spread the payments out over 20 years, pay no interest on the winnings, then stop the payments after 20 years. That means if you win, say, $3 million in the New York, California or Florida state lotteries, after Uncle Sam gouges you, you'd get about $100,000 a year for 20 years. That's nothing to sneeze at, but it leaves you a million short! Alternate choice: The Northwest German State Lottery. This lottery gives you a check for the full amount when you win. Plus, it offers better odds. In a state lottery, your chances of winning are about 15 million to one. The Northwest German State lottery has odds of 750,000 to one. That improves your chances of winning by 20 percent. The lottery also guarantees that more than one-third of all tickets are prize winners. Best of all, after taxes you'll get roughly the same $2 million payout, but it's yours right then — to keep, reinvest or spend.

## CASINO SURVIVAL GUIDE

Those luxury hotel-casinos in Vegas and Atlantic City were built on one simple rule: The house always has the edge. You accept that when you walk in the door. The idea is to use intelligent betting and money-management strategies to cut their advantage down to the minimum. If you know what you're doing, you can get it to around 2 percent, and occasionally a little less. One proven approach to money management:

* For each day of your stay, set aside a gambling stake equal to about 40 times your usual minimum bet. Anything less will cramp your play and enjoyment. Divide that daily stake into two parts, but you'll need at least $100 per gambling session, the bare minimum to keep in the game at a $5 table. (If you find $2 or $3 tables, you can have a smaller stake.)

* Never borrow from the next session's stake. If you lose the whole $100, walk away from the table (and out of the casino, unless you're staying there). If you're barely holding your own or losing slowly, quit after a half-hour or so.

* If you're on a tight budget, stop playing if you lose half your stake.

* As soon as you double your original stake, take half your chips off the table and put them in your pocket. You'll be playing with the casino's money from that point on. Continue removing chips each time you reach another predetermined winning plateau. That way you'll keep the same amount of money on the table at all times. If your luck turns bad, walk away when you've lost half what you're playing with.

* If you're like most people, walking away a winner is just about the hardest thing in the world — another aspect of human nature that casino owners bank on. The best advice is to try it, if only for the novelty. You might like it!

## VIDEO POKER — A HOT MACHINE HELPS

There's a big debate still going on over whether success at video poker — quickly becoming one of the most popular "machine" gambling games — is dependent on finding a hot machine or whether strategy can help improve your odds of winning. Until a firm resolution of that conflict is reached, the best we can do is recommend some additional reading. "Expert Video Poker for Las Vegas" was written by Len Frome, currently recognized as the foremost authority on the game. The book explains how the machines work, outlines his theories on winning and details some strategies he has developed. It's available at most book stores for around $9.95. Another choice is "Video Poker Mania," by Dwight and Louise Crevelt (he's an engineer in the slot manufacturing industry). It costs $5.99, but you'll have to find it at a bookstore as the publisher accepts direct orders only in quantity.

## THE BASICS OF BLACKJACK

For many skillful gamblers (and card counters), black-jack is the casino game of choice. While luck plays a part, skill is also rewarded. And, by simply knowing the best mathematical plays, skillful gamblers can cut the house advantage down to just above 1 percent for certain situations. A short course in hitting-or-standing:

* When the dealer shows a 2, 3 or 4, hit if you have 12 or less, and stand with 13 or more.
* When the dealer shows a 5 or 6, hit if you have 11 or less, and stand with 12 or more.
* When the dealer shows a 7, 8, 9, 10 or ace, hit if you have 16 or less, and stand with 17 or more.

Splitting pairs to make two hands (and thereby doubling your bet) can also increase your advantage. When to split pairs:

* Always split aces, although most casinos allow you take only one additional card on each ace.
* Split 2's and 3's only if the dealer shows a 2, 3, 4, 5, 6 or 7.
* Split 7's only when the dealer's up card is 4, 5, 6 or 7.
* Always split 8's unless the dealer shows a 9, 10 or ace.
* Always split 9's unless the dealer has a 10 or an ace up.
* Never split 4's, 5's, 6's or 10's.

## BLACKJACK MONEY MANAGEMENT

Since wins and losses at 21 tend to come in clusters, you need to bet high when the deck is hot and less when it's cold. A simple way to do this is to increase your bet steadily while winning. But never keep doubling your bets on a losing string, hoping to recover all your losses on an eventual win. This is the oldest wagering system around and one doomed to failure. After a relatively short series of sequential losses (which can happen anytime), you'll either lose your entire gambling stake or reach the table limit.

There are, however, some more sophisticated progressive betting techniques. Here's one for winning progressions starting with a $2 bet: $2, $4, $4, $6, $10, $10, $15, $25, $40, $40, $60, $100. Notice that you bet the same amount on the second and third hands. This returns your original bet, plus a one-bet profit, and lets you play with the house's money for the rest of the progression. When you lose a hand at any point in the progression, go back to your starting bet and stay with that amount till you win again. (Also stay with the same amount after a push or tie.) You should leave the table any time you lose an amount equal to half your starting stake, regardless of your total session profit. It's not easy, but exercising will-power and sticking to a game plan are what often separate winners from losers.

## STAY AWAY FROM ROULETTE AND KENO

If you want to be a consistent winner, avoid the roulette wheels and keno rooms. There's really no way to improve your style of play since the outcome of each spin or draw is pure luck — and, even if you could figure out a way to play better, the odds on these two are still the worst of all the games in the house. In roulette, for example, the best payoffs are on single numbers — 35 to 1 — still well below the true wheel odds of 38 to 1.

## BETTING ON BACCARAT

This is the game of the upper class — you probably won't feel comfortable playing unless you're wearing a tux or evening gown. However, if you do, the safest bet is with the bank. This leaves the house with a 1.19 percent edge, while betting on the player yields a 1.34 percent advantage to the house.

## BABY NEEDS A NEW PAIR OF SHOES — ROLLING THE DICE

This is one of the most popular casino games and the source of most of the yelling you'll hear as you walk around the place. The game is definitely exciting, and you can narrow the odds quite a bit if you know how to play. The house advantage is around 1.40 percent to 1.41 percent on "pass," "come," "don't pass" and "don't come" bets. For better odds, lay "odds" bets after the shooter has established a point. This is the only "pure" play in the casino — meaning you get paid off at exactly the same odds you have of rolling the designated number. The only way to make big money at craps is to capitalize on a "hot" roll (craps is basically a "hot and cold" game).

What you want to catch is a series when a shooter establishes a "point" (4, 5, 6, 8, 9 or 10) and then throws the dice a dozen or more times before making the point or rolling a 7. That way you make lots of money on the "come" bets, or bets placed directly on the numbers. When the dice are running hot, you should also "press" your bets — increasing them in size as the run keeps progressing and you keep winning. The dice will often stay hot for 25 or 30 minutes, with three or four different shooters — and then go completely cold. If three consecutive shooters "crap out" on only two or three rolls, it's time to move on — the table has turned cold.

## NOTES

_____

_____

_____

_____

_____

_____

_____

_____

_____

_____

_____

_____

_____

_____